LUXURY HOTELS

TOP OF THE WORLD

edited by Martin Nicholas Kunz and Patricia Massó

teNeues

Luxury Hotels
TOP OF THE WORLD

Jackson Hole

Chicago

Miami

New York

San Francisco

Big Sur
Beverly Hills
Laguna Niguel

St. Barthélemy

Mustique

Los Cabos

Costalegre

Riviera Maya

Puerto Vallarta

São Paulo

Buenos Aires

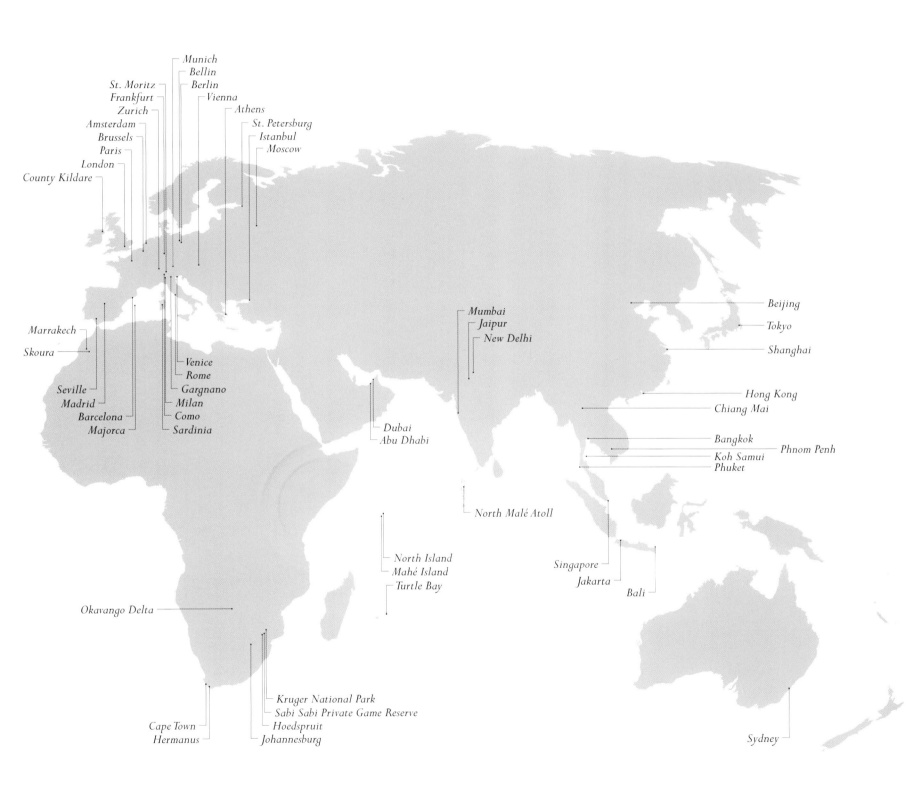

Munich
Bellin
Berlin
St. Moritz
Vienna
Frankfurt
Zurich
Athens
Amsterdam
St. Petersburg
Brussels
Istanbul
Paris
Moscow
London
County Kildare

Marrakech
Skoura

Venice
Rome
Seville
Gargnano
Madrid
Milan
Barcelona
Como
Majorca
Sardinia

Dubai
Abu Dhabi

Mumbai
Jaipur
New Delhi

Beijing
Tokyo
Shanghai

Hong Kong
Chiang Mai

Bangkok
Phnom Penh
Koh Samui
Phuket

North Malé Atoll

North Island
Mahé Island
Turtle Bay

Singapore
Jakarta
Bali

Okavango Delta

Kruger National Park
Sabi Sabi Private Game Reserve
Cape Town
Hoedspruit
Hermanus
Johannesburg

Sydney

Masterpiece Lodging

Top of the World Hotels featured in this book beautifully illustrate the new trend of high-end retreats that perceive ultra-luxury as an art form. These resorts go above and beyond the conventional description of luxury hotels. Here art and travel coincide, not just in architecture and overall aesthetics, but in the fine art of pampering the guest in unique ways. This selection of luxury hotels have evolved to include ultra-personalized service to keep up with the competition, requiring their guests to choose in advance the type of experience they will enjoy. Where once the hotel's style and service determined that experience, today it is the customer that makes that decision.

Whether skiing the stunning, jagged peaks of the snowcapped Alps of St. Moritz, or lounging at the perfect setting in a boutique-sized property that is every bit as fashionable as its city dwelling address in London or New York, the demanding traveler today wants something fresh and different, and out of the ordinary. Many resorts are trying to differentiate their properties by including a marina for large yachts, a shopping and dining complex, award-winning golf course, exotic garden, or magnificent sports and spa facilities.

Top of the World Hotels creatively convert historic buildings, stables, and palaces into graceful living quarters with extraordinary suites, offering the discerning luxury traveler the new ultimate amenity: the art of atmosphere. The Aleenta Resort and Spa Phuket - Phangnga fuses hyper-modern architecture with a gorgeous natural backdrop, as well as commissioning works and indigenous textiles from local artists. The One&Only Royal Mirage in Dubai, for instance, creates an atmosphere of quiet luxury with its exquisite pool that reflects enormous clay vases along the backdrop of the sea. Many resorts offer a twist to what is normally expected, and fuse together exotic cultures at unique settings, such as the Asian influence at the rocky retreat of Amangani in Wyoming, where the East meets West in the wild country. Each room at the Casa Casuarina in South Beach Miami is designed as inhabitable magical art spaces, where original murals are painted over the walls of the lobby, columns shimmer in gold leaf and elaborate mosaics, and exquisite craftsmanship is evident at every turn.

High-end leisure travelers now gravitate towards fashionable establishments that offer original art, personalized music, themed parties and personal panache. From chic boutique hotels to charming inns, hoteliers who treat their spaces and service as art have garnered a high-end, loyal clientele who are looking for that unique experience. In these ultra-luxurious resorts, people come in and fall in love. Guests know that someone was paying attention to details. The interiors, colors, shapes and forms are the masterpieces, and the hotel space is the canvas. And like artistic masterpieces, furnishings and interiors in these upscale resorts carry a particular story or emit an emotional connection, such as in the Faena Hotel + Universe in Buenos Aires, where the art-designed furnishings appear more sculptural than functional.

Many hotels geared for the business traveler have guest rooms that are in itself a model of intelligent planning combined with luxury. Lavishly high-tech, the downtown Peninsula Hotel in Chicago features a rooftop lap pool with skyline views, a lavish spa adjacent, with a leather-walled and art-filled bar is the Gold Coast's top spot to see and be seen. And the Grand Hyatt Shanghai in China, the highest hotel in the world that resides on 53rd to the 87th floor of a modern skyscraper, is best known for its sleek interior design that achieves a cosmopolitan intimacy while being both eye-catching and understated, with an aerie-like indoor Skypool with panoramic city views.

This exquisitely illustrated book proves that even inhabitable spaces can be higher works of sculptural art, where a guest takes center stage and exceptional service is offered with a creative twist, catering to every whim, regardless of its apparent impossibility. For Top of the World Hotels, everything is possible.

Patrice Farameh

Meisterhafte Unterbringung

Die in diesem Buch vorgestellten Weltklassehotels illustrieren wunderbar den neuen Trend der Nobelherbergen, die Ultraluxus als eine Kunstform verstehen. Diese Resorts gehen weit über die konventionelle Vorstellung von Luxushotels hinaus. Hier treffen sich Kunst und Reise, nicht nur in der Architektur und Gesamtästhetik, sondern auch in der Kunst, die Gäste auf einzigartige Weise zu verwöhnen. Diese Luxushotels wurden entwickelt, um einen sehr persönlichen Service zu bieten, durch den sie im Wettbewerb Schritt halten können und der voraussetzt, dass sich ihre Gäste bereits vorher das Erlebnis aussuchen, das sie genießen möchten. Wo einstmals der Stil und der Service des Hotels dieses Erlebnis bestimmten, ist es heute der Kunde, der darüber die Entscheidung trifft.

Ob es nun Skifahren in den atemberaubenden, schroffen Gipfeln der schneebedeckten Alpen von St. Moritz ist oder Faulenzen im perfekten Rahmen einer boutiquegroßen Eigentumswohnung ist, die in jedem Detail genauso elegant ist wie die Stadtwohnung mit Adresse in London oder New York – der anspruchsvolle Reisende von heute möchte etwas Frisches, Anderes und Außergewöhnliches. Viele Resorts versuchen daher sich voneinander zu unterscheiden, indem sie einen Yachthafen für große Yachten, einen Shopping- und Restaurantkomplex, preisgekrönte Golfplätze, exotische Gärten oder herrliche Sport- und Wellnessbereiche in ihre Anlagen einbeziehen.

Top of the World Hotels verwandeln historische Gebäude, Ställe und Paläste auf kreative Weise in anmutige Unterkünfte mit außergewöhnlichen Suiten, um dem anspruchsvollen Luxusreisenden den neuesten, ultimativen Komfort zu bieten: die Kunst der Atmosphäre. Das Aleenta Resort and Spa Phuket - Phangnga vereint hypermoderne Architektur mit einer großartigen Naturkulisse und erwirbt auch Arbeiten und einheimische Textilien lokaler Künstler. Das One&Only Royal Mirage in Dubai beispielsweise schafft eine Atmosphäre des stillen Luxus mit seinem exquisiten Pool, der die enormen, entlang der Meereskulisse aufgestellten Tonvasen reflektiert. Viele Resorts bieten etwas von dem, was normalerweise erwartet wird, und vereinigen exotische Kulturen mit einzigartigen Umgebungen, wie etwa das Amangani in Wyoming, wo asiatischer Einfluss mit felsigem Erholungsort verbunden wird und somit in der Wildnis der Osten auf den Westen trifft. Alle Zimmer in der Casa Casuarina in South Beach Miami sind als bewohnbare magische Kunsträume gestaltet, wo Originalbilder auf die Wände der Lobby gemalt wurden, auf Säulen Blattgold und kunstvolle Mosaiken schimmern und sich überall exquisite Kunstfertigkeit zeigt.

Luxusverwöhnte Vergnügungsreisende fühlen sich zu eleganten Hotelanlagen, die Originalkunst, personalisierte Musik, Themenpartys und einen persönlichen Stil bieten, hingezogen. Von schicken Boutiquehotels bis zu reizvollen Gasthäusern – Hoteliers, die ihre Räume und den Service als Kunst behandeln, haben sich eine noble, loyale Klientel aufgebaut, die nach diesem einzigartigen Erlebnis Ausschau hält. In diese ultraluxuriösen Resorts kommen die Leute herein und verlieben sich sofort. Die Gäste wissen, dass jemand genau auf die Details geachtet hat. Innenausstattung, Farben, Gestaltung und Formen sind die Meisterwerke, und der Hotelraum ist die Leinwand. Und wie Meisterwerke der Kunst haben die Möbel und die Innenausstattung in diesen gehobenen Resorts eine eigene Geschichte oder stellen eine emotionale Verbindung her, wie das Faena Hotel + Universe in Buenos Aires, wo die künstlerisch gestalteten Möbel eher skulptural als funktional sind.

Viele auf Geschäftsreisende ausgerichtete Hotels haben Zimmer, die in sich selbst wie ein Modell intelligenter Planung wirken – kombiniert mit Luxus. Das verschwenderisch mit Hightech ausgestattete Peninsula Hotel in der Innenstadt von Chicago hat auf dem Dach einen Wettkampfpool mit Blick über die Skyline, ein großzügiges Wellness-Center nebenan, und eine Bar mit Lederwänden und Kunstgegenständen ist die Top-Location der Goldküste, wo man sieht und gesehen wird. Und das Grand Hyatt Shanghai in China, das höchste Hotel der Welt, das sich in der 53. bis 87. Etage eines modernen Wolkenkratzers befindet, ist berühmt für seine elegante Innenausstattung, die eine kosmopolite Intimität ausstrahlt und zugleich sowohl auffällig als auch zurückhaltend wirkt. Darüber hinaus hat es einen Indoor-Skypool mit einem Panoramablick auf die Stadt.

Dieses exquisit illustrierte Buch zeigt, dass sogar bewohnbare Räume höhere Werke skulpturaler Kunst sein können, in denen der Gast im Mittelpunkt steht und ein außergewöhnlicher Service mit einem kreativen Kick sowie eine Gastronomie für jeden Geschmack, ungeachtet ihrer scheinbaren Unmöglichkeit, geboten wird. Für die Hotels von Weltklasse ist alles möglich.

Patrice Farameh

Chefs d'oeuvres de logement

Les meilleurs hôtels du monde présentés dans ce livre illustrent en beauté la nouvelle tendance de retraites haut de gamme qui considèrent le luxe ultime comme une forme d'art. Ici, l'art et le voyage coïncident, non seulement dans l'architecture et dans l'esthétisme global, mais aussi dans l'art délicat de choyer les hôtes d'une façon unique. Cette sélection d'hôtels de luxe a évolué pour inclure un service ultra personnalisé afin de faire face à la concurrence, encourageant leur hôtes à choisir d'avance de quel type d'expérience ils souhaitent profiter. Tandis qu'à l'époque, le style et le service déterminaient cette expérience, c'est aujourd'hui le client qui prend cette décision.

Que ce soit le ski dans les pics époustouflants et découpés des sommets enneigés des Alpes de St. Moritz, ou le repos dans l'ambiance parfaite d'une propriété intime qui est tout aussi à la mode que son adresse à Londres ou à New York, le voyageur exigeant souhaite aujourd'hui quelque chose d'innovant et de différent, sortant de l'ordinaire. De nombreux lieux de villégiature essayent de différencier leurs propriétés en y ajoutant une marina ou un complexe de repas, un terrain de golf primé, un jardin exotique ou des installations de sport et de balnéo magnifiques.

Les meilleurs hôtels du monde convertissent des bâtiments historiques, des écuries et des palaces en logements élégants avec des suites extraordinaires, qui offrent au voyageur de luxe distingué le nouveau charme absolu : l'art de l'ambiance. Le Aleenta Resort and Spa Phuket - Phangnga marie une architecture hyper moderne avec un arrière-plan naturel splendide, et expose des œuvres et des tissus indigènes des artistes locaux. Le One&Only Royal Mirage à Dubai, par exemple, crée une ambiance de luxe calme avec sa piscine exquise qui reflète des vases en terre cuite énormes devant l'arrière-plan de la mer. De nombreux lieux de villégiature offrent un plus par rapport à ce qui est escompté normalement et marient les cultures exotiques à des emplacements uniques, tels que l'influence asiatique dans la retraite rocheuse de Amangani dans le Wyoming, où l'Est rencontre l'Ouest dans un paysage sauvage. Chaque chambre de la Casa Casuarina à South Beach Miami est créée comme un espace d'art magique habitable, dans lequel des originaux sont peints sur les murs du lobby, les colonnes brillent de feuilles d'or et de mosaïques élaborées, et l'artisanat exquis est évident partout.

Les voyageurs de la jet-set gravitent maintenant vers les établissements à la mode qui offrent des œuvres originales, une musique personnalisée, des événements à thèmes et un panache personnel. Des hôtels intimes chics aux auberges charmantes, les hôteliers qui considèrent leurs espaces et leurs services comme un art ont acquis une clientèle haut de gamme fidèle qui recherche cette expérience unique. Dans ces lieux de villégiature ultra-luxueux, les gens entrent et tombent amoureux. Les hôtes savent d'expérience si quelqu'un a soigné les détails. Les intérieurs, les couleurs et les formes sont des chefs d'œuvres, et l'espace de l'hôtel en est le support. Et comme les chefs d'œuvres artistiques, les meubles et les intérieurs de ces lieux de villégiature haut de gamme disposent d'une histoire spécifique ou font appel à des liens émotionnels, comme le Faena Hotel + Universe à Buenos Aires, dans lequel les meubles à design artistique paraissent plus sculpturaux que fonctionnels.

De nombreux hôtels adaptés aux voyageurs d'affaires ont des chambres qui constituent en elles-mêmes des modèles de la planification intelligente combinée au luxe. Le Peninsula Hotel dans la downtown de Chicago, très high-tech, dispose d'une piscine sur le toit avec vue sur la silhouette de la ville, d'un spa luxueux adjacent, et d'un bar comportant une profusion d'objets d'art et dont les murs sont habillés de cuir, et est le meilleur endroit de la Gold Coast pour voir et être vu. Et le Grand Hyatt Shanghai en Chine, l'hôtel le plus haut du monde situé entre le 53ème et le 87ème étage d'une tour moderne, est connu surtout pour son design intérieur brillant qui crée un intimité cosmopolitaine tout en étant accrocheur et minimaliste, et est équipé d'une piscine intérieure aérienne avec une vue panoramique sur le ville.

Ce livre illustré d'une manière exquise prouve que même les espaces non habitables peuvent être des grandes œuvres d'arts sculptural, où l'hôte occupe le milieu de la scène et un service exceptionnel est offert avec un plus en créativité, satisfaisant chaque souhait, indépendamment de son apparente irréalisibilité. Pour les meilleurs hôtels du monde, tout est possible.

Patrice Farameh

Hoteles magistrales

Los hoteles de clase mundial que se presentan en este libro ilustran maravillosamente la nueva tendencia de los alojamientos de primera clase, los cuales ven el lujo más absoluto como una forma de expresión artística. Estos resorts superan notablemente las descripciones convencionales de los hoteles de lujo. En ellos coinciden el arte y los viajes, no sólo en la arquitectura y la estética del conjunto, sino también en el arte de atender al huésped de una manera extraordinaria. Estos hoteles de lujo se han ido eligiendo a lo largo del tiempo de acuerdo a un criterio principal, y este es la oferta de un servicio muy personalizado que les permite competir y que da por supuesto que los huéspedes eligen y determinan de antemano el tipo de experiencia que quieren disfrutar. Si antes era el estilo y el servicio del hotel los que determinaban esta experiencia, ahora es el huésped el que decide.

Ya sea, por ejemplo, esquiar en las impresionantes cumbres escarpadas y cubiertas de nieve de los Alpes en St. Moritz u holgazanear en el entorno perfecto de una vivienda particular del tamaño de una boutique, que tenga la misma elegancia de una vivienda londinense o neoyorquina, hoy en día, el viajero exigente quiere algo nuevo y diferente, algo extraordinario. Muchos resorts intentan diferenciarse incluyendo un puerto para yates grandes, un centro comercial con restaurante, un campo de golf galardonado, un jardín exótico o unas instalaciones deportivas y de wellness magníficas.

Top of the World Hotels convierten creativamente edificios históricos, establos y palacios en alojamientos encantadores con suites extraordinarias para ofrecerle al viajero exigente todas las comodidades a la última: el arte de crear ambiente. El Aleenta Resort and Spa Phuket - Phangnga combina la arquitectura ultramoderna con un escenario natural y vende también obras y tejidos regionales de artistas locales. Por ejemplo, el One&Only Royal Mirage, en Dubai, crea un ambiente de lujo sereno con su exquisita piscina, que refleja enormes jarrones de arcilla a lo largo de su escenario marítimo. Muchos resorts ofrecen algo de lo que se espera normalmente y combinan culturas exóticas y entornos extraordinarios como, por ejemplo, la influencia asiática en un lugar de descanso rocoso como Amangani, en Wyoming, donde se encuentran oriente y occidente inmersos en una naturaleza salvaje. Todas las habitaciones de la Casa Casuarina, en South Beach Miami, están diseñadas como espacios habitables artísticos y mágicos. Sobre las paredes del lobby se pintaron frescos originales, sobre sus columnas resplandecen láminas de oro y mosaicos artísticos. El conjunto muestra una exquisita habilidad artística por donde quiera que se mire.

Los huéspedes de primera clase que viajan por placer se sienten atraídos por las elegantes instalaciones del hotel, el arte original, la música personalizada, las fiestas temáticas y el estilo peculiar. Ya se trate de los elegantes hoteles boutique o de las excitantes tabernas, los hosteleros que ven sus espacios y su servicio como una forma de arte han conseguido una fiel clientela de primera clase en busca de una experiencia extraordinaria. El viajero que entra en estos resorts de absoluto lujo se enamora inmediatamente de ellos. Los huéspedes saben que se tiene en cuenta hasta el más mínimo detalle. La decoración interior, los colores, el diseño y las formas son obras maestras y el hotel es su lienzo. Como toda obra maestra, en estos exquisitos resorts tanto los muebles como la decoración interior tienen su propia historia o crean una relación emocional, como el Hotel Faena + Universe en Buenos Aires, donde los muebles, artísticamente dispuestos, son más esculturales que funcionales.

Muchos de los hoteles pensados para los viajeros de negocios tienen habitaciones que son un modelo de planificación inteligente combinada con el lujo. El Peninsula Hotel, que se encuentra en el centro de Chicago, está generosamente equipado con alta tecnología y tiene una piscina con calles sobre el tejado, con vistas al horizonte y un amplio centro de wellness al lado. Su bar con paredes de cuero y objetos artísticos es el lugar perfecto para ver y dejarse ver. El Grand Hyatt Shanghai, en China, es el hotel más alto del mundo. Se encuentra entre los pisos 53 y 87 de un moderno rascacielos y se le conoce por su brillante decoración interior, la cual ha alcanzado un ambiente de intimidad cosmopolita que es tan sobresaliente como modesto. Además, tiene una piscina interior con una vista panorámica de la ciudad.

Este libro ilustrado exquisitamente le muestra que incluso los espacios habitables pueden ser una gran obra de arte escultural en la que el huésped es lo más importante y en la que se ofrece un servicio creativo y una gastronomía para todos los gustos que no conoce límites. Todo es posible para los hoteles de clase mundial.

Patrice Farameh

Residenze Capolavoro

Top of the World Hotels presenta, in questo volume splendidamente illustrato, il nuovo trend dei rifugi di lusso, in cui il lusso sfrenato è visto come una forma d'arte. Questi resort superano la tipicità degli hotel di lusso. Qui l'arte e il viaggio coincidono, non solo nella totalità dell'architettura e dell'estetica, bensì nell'arte raffinata di viziare l'ospite, in maniera unica. Questa selezione di hotel di lusso è stata creata per includere un servizio extra-personalizzato allo scopo di mantenere la competitività, chiedendo agli ospiti di scegliere, in anticipo, il tipo di vacanza che desiderano vivere. In passato questa esperienza è sempre dipesa dallo stile e dai servizi dell'hotel oggi, invece, è il cliente stesso a decidere.

Sia che si tratti di sciare sulle cime fantastiche e innevate delle Alpi di San Moritz, o di alloggiare nell'ambiente perfetto di un centro residenziale esclusivo che ricorda, in ogni angolo, Londra o New York, il viaggiatore pretenzioso desidera qualcosa di nuovo, diverso, e fuori dal comune. Molti resort cercano di differenziare le loro proprietà dotandosi di porti per grandi yacht, di centri per lo shopping e la ristorazione, organizzando tornei di golf a premi, creando giardini esotici, a cui si aggiungono magnifiche strutture per il benessere e lo sport.

Top of the World Hotels trasforma, in maniera creativa, edifici, stabili e palazzi storici in graziosi quartieri residenziali: tutti dotati di suite straordinarie. Ciò permette di offrire al viaggiatore più esigente e raffinato una delle ultime amenità: l'arte dell'atmosfera. L'Aleenta Resort and Spa Phuket - Phangnga mischia la sua architettura ipermoderna ad un favoloso fondale naturale. Inoltre, commissiona opere e tessuti indigeni agli artisti locali. Il One&Only Royal Mirage di Dubai, ad esempio, crea un'atmosfera di tranquilla lussuosità grazie alla sua fantastica piscina che riflette enormi vasi di terracotta, dove il mare è lo sfondo. Molti resort offrono altro rispetto a quanto ci si aspetta normalmente, e fondono culture esotiche in ambienti unici, come l'influenza asiatica nel rifugio roccioso Amangani, nel Wyoming, dove l'oriente incontra l'occidente, in un paesaggio selvaggio. Ogni camera di Casa Casuarina a South Beach, a Miami, è progettata come uno spazio artistico magico e abitabile, dove originali murales sono dipinti sulle pareti dell'atrio, le cui colonne risplendono in fogli dorati ed elaborati mosaici: da ogni angolo emerge uno straordinario lavoro d'artigianato.

I viaggiatori rilassati e di classe sono attirati da aree moderne che offrono originalità artistica, musica personalizzata, party a tema e uno stile personale. Dagli eleganti centri residenziali fino ai graziosi alberghetti, i proprietari, che hanno acquistato i loro spazi e il loro servizi come pezzi d'arte, hanno guadagnato una clientela fedele e di classe, sempre alla ricerca di un'esperienza unica. Le persone entrano e si innamorano di questi resort ultra lussuosi. Gli ospiti sanno che qualcuno ha dato particolare importanza ai dettagli. Gli interni, i colori, le ombre e le forme sono i capolavori, e lo spazio dell'hotel è la tela. E come delle opere d'arte, anche gli arredi e gli interni di questi resort di alta classe sono testimoni di una storia particolare, o rievocano un'emozione, come ad esempio al Faena Hotel + Universe a Buenos Aires, dove gli arredi, concepiti in maniera artistica, sembrano essere più delle sculture che avere un'utilità funzionale.

Molti hotel adattati al cliente che viaggia per lavoro, hanno ideato stanze che sono in sè un modello di intelligenza e lusso. Altamente hi-tech, il Peninsula Hotel, nel centro di Chicago, offre una piscina in cima al tetto con vista sull'orizzonte, un lussuoso centro benessere, con il suo bar dalle pareti rivestite in pelle e ricco d'arte, è la località della Gold Coast da cui guardare e farsi guardare. Ed il Grand Hyatt Shanghai in Cina, il più alto hotel al mondo che si trova tra il 53esimo e l'87esimo piano di un grattacielo moderno, è il più famoso per il suo stile interno sinuoso che permette un'intimità cosmopolita, attraente ma contemporaneamente discreta, grazie ad una piscina coperta con una vista panoramica sulla città.

Questo libro squisitamente illustrato dimostra che persino spazi abitabili possono rappresentare delle grandi opere d'arte scultorea, di cui l'ospite è il protagonista. Come tale riceve un servizio creativo, capace di soddisfare ogni desiderio anche il più impensabile. Per Top of the World Hotels, infatti, tutto è possibile.

Patrice Farameh

Amangani

Jackson Hole, Wyoming

Wyoming's wild landscape is home to Asia-based Aman Group's first luxury hotel in the U.S. The grounds are centered around an elongated building whose hip roof mimics the contours of the rocky scenery. Covered with cedar wood slates, it could almost be a mountain ledge. The exquisitely decorated interior nods to the simpler life associated with log cabins—polished wooden slats conceal soft lighting, while perfectly sculpted tree stumps serve as tables.

In der wilden Landschaft Wyomings hat die asiatische Aman-Gruppe ihr erstes Haus in den USA platziert. Das lang gestreckte Gebäude fügt sich in das Gelände ein, sein Walmdach nimmt die Umrisse der charakteristischen Felsenlandschaft auf. Eingedeckt mit Zedernholzschindeln wirkt es fast wie ein Felsvorsprung. Die Interieurs sind edel und doch erlauben sie die Assoziation eines einfachen Lebens in einer Blockhütte: Indirektes Licht verbirgt sich hinter plan geschliffenen Brettern, als Tisch fungiert ein perfekt bearbeiteter Baumstumpf.

C'est dans le paysage sauvage du Wyoming que le groupe asiatique Aman a installé son premier hôtel aux États-Unis. Le bâtiment allongé se fond dans le terrain, son toit en croupe épouse les contours du paysage rocheux caractéristique. Couvert de bardeaux en cèdre, il ressemble presque à une saillie rocheuse. Les intérieurs sont élégants, mais ils permettent cependant d'y associer un mode de vie simple dans une cabane en rondins : la lumière indirecte est cachée derrière des planches surfacées, et une souche d'arbre parfaitement travaillée sert de table.

El grupo asiático Aman ha elegido este paisaje salvaje de Wyoming para ubicar su primer hotel en los Estados Unidos. El largo edificio se integra en el paisaje y su tejado a cuatro aguas toma la silueta del característico paisaje rocoso. El techo cubierto con ripia de madera de cedro simula un saliente de roca. El interior, aunque elegante, transmite la sencillez de una cabaña de madera: La luz indirecta se oculta detrás de tablones de madera, un tronco de árbol de perfecto acabado hace de mesa.

È nel paesaggio selvaggio dello Wyoming che il gruppo asiatico Aman ha collocato il suo primo resort costruito negli Stati Uniti. La struttura oblunga, come incastonata nel paesaggio roccioso e sovrastata da un tetto a padiglione, si armonizza perfettamente con l'ambiente circostante: rivestito di scandole di cedro, sembra scaturire dalla montagna come uno sperone roccioso. Gli arredamenti interni sono ricercati e nel contempo consoni all'ideale di una vita semplice ispirato dalla struttura in legno. La luce indiretta si nasconde dietro assi levigate, dove dei ceppi perfettamente lavorati fungono da tavolo.

Oklahoma sandstone and lovingly finished wood conjure up an atmosphere of elegant simplicity.

Sandstein aus Oklahoma und sorgfältig bearbeitetes Holz kreieren einen Stil edler Schlichtheit.

Le grès d'Oklahoma et le bois travaillé avec soin créent un style simple et élégant.

La arenisca de Oklahoma y las maderas perfectamente trabajadas crean un estilo de elegante sencillez.

Pietra arenaria dell'Oklahoma e legno lavorato con cura contribuiscono a creare uno stile di raffinata semplicità.

From the pool there is a grandiose view of the peaks of the Rocky Mountains and the Snake River.

Vom Pool aus eröffnet sich ein grandioser Blick auf die Gipfel der Rocky Mountains und den Snake River.

La piscine offre une vue grandiose sur les sommets des Montagnes Rocheuses et la Snake River.

Desde la piscina se disfruta de una vista sublime de la cumbre de las montañas rocosas y del río Snake.

Dalla piscina si apre un panorama grandioso sulla punta delle Rocky Mountains e del fiume Snake.

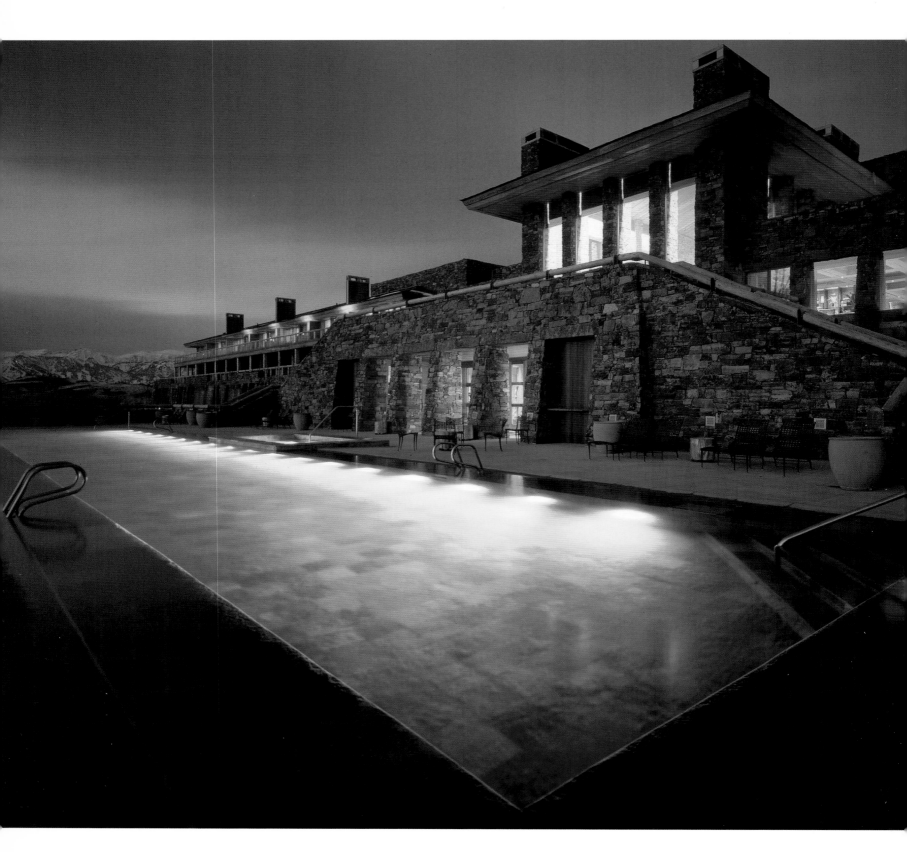

The Ritz-Carlton, Laguna Niguel

Laguna Niguel, California

Old World meets the Pacific Rim. This regal 4-story Mediterranean-style refuge is legendary for its luxury and magnificent setting in front of a 2-mile-long beach with ocean panoramas. A gorgeous marble fireplace stands in the silk-lined lobby, and the arched, wood-paneled Lobby Lounge is a former library that was transformed into a cozy bar perfect for sipping a cocktail while watching the sunset.

Alte Welt trifft auf pazifische Randgebiete. Diese fürstliche vierstöckige Unterkunft im mediterranen Stil ist legendär für ihren Luxus und die wunderbare Lage an einem 3 km langen Strand mit Meerespanorama. Ein prächtiger Marmorkamin steht in der mit Seide ausgekleideten Lobby, und die bogenförmige, mit Holzpaneelen versehene Lobby Lounge ist eine ehemalige Bibliothek, die in eine gemütliche Bar verwandelt wurde und in der man wunderbar an einem Cocktail nippen kann, während man den Sonnenuntergang genießt.

L'ancien monde rencontre le bord du Pacifique. Ce refuge royal de 4 étages dans le style méditerranéen est légendaire pour son luxe et sa situation magnifique face à une côte de 3 km de panoramas océaniques. Le lobby dispose de murs couverts de soie et d'une opulente cheminée ouverte en marbre, le Lobby-Lounge avec ses murs habillés de bois est une ancienne bibliothèque transformée en un bar confortable, invitant à y déguster un cocktail en regardant le coucher du soleil.

El viejo mundo se encuentra con las costas del pacífico. Este majestuoso hotel de 4 plantas de estilo mediterráneo es legendario por su lujo y su entorno maravilloso de 3 kilómetros de playa con vistas al mar. Su magnífica chimenea de mármol se encuentra en un lobby revestido de seda. El lobby, arqueado y adornado con paneles de madera, era antiguamente una biblioteca que fue convertida en un bar agradable en el que se puede disfrutar maravillosamente de un cóctel mientras se observa la puesta de sol.

Il vecchio mondo si incontra con le terre che si affacciano sul Pacifico. Questo rifugio regale in stile mediterraneo si distribuisce su 4 piani. È famoso per la sua magnifica posizione di fronte ad una spiaggia lunga quasi 3 km, che offre una vista stupenda sull'oceano. Nell'atrio rivestito in seta, si trova un bellissimo camino in marmo, e la lobby-lounge ad archi, con i suoi pannelli in legno è un'ex biblioteca trasformata in un bar accogliente e perfetto dove gustare un cocktail al tramonto.

Elegant European ambience and unobstructed views of the Pacific. There are lush terraces with colorful flower gardens throughout the well-tended property.

Ein elegantes europäisches Ambiente und ungehinderte Ausblicke auf den Pazifik. Mit bunten Gartenblumen üppig bewachsene Terrassen zeichnen das gesamte gut gepflegte Grundstück aus.

Une ambiance européenne élégante et une vue panoramique sur l'Océan Pacifique. L'ensemble de la propriété comprend des terrasses dissimulées et des jardins de fleurs multicolores.

Un elegante ambiente europeo y unas claras vistas al Pacífico. Las terrazas están cubiertas de césped y las exuberantes flores de colores de un jardín bien cuidado.

Atmosfera europea ed elegante con vista diretta sul Pacifico. Ci sono delle terrazze straboccanti di fiori colorati nell'intera proprietà particolarmente curata.

393 rooms have interiors in sand tones, supplemented by cool palettes of blue and silver with magenta accents, and triple-layered glass panels that suggest an undersea world.

Die Einrichtung der 393 Zimmer ist in Sandtönen gehalten und wird durch kühle Blau- und Silbertöne mit Magentaakzenten sowie dreischichtige Glasscheiben ergänzt, die die Vorstellung einer Unterwasserwelt erwecken.

L'intérieur des 393 chambres est tenu en des tons sable, complémenté par des palettes de teintes fraîches bleus et argents avec des accents de magenta, et des panneaux en verre triple suggérant un monde subaquatique.

En el diseño de las 393 habitaciones se han mantenido los tonos de playa, a los que complementan el azul frío y tonos plateados con matices magenta y ventanas con triple acristalamiento que dan la sensación de estar en un mundo submarino.

Gli interni delle 393 camere sono nei toni del sabbia, cui si aggiungono tonalità fredde di blu e argento con accenni di magenta, ci sono poi pannelli con triplo vetro che danno l'idea di un mondo sottomarino.

The Beverly Hills Hotel
Beverly Hills, California

Ever since its opening in 1912, the famed pink stucco Spanish-style mansion known as the "Pink Palace" remains a magnet for the Hollywood movie colony. Known for its mythic garden bungalows and the Polo Lounge, the hotel still remains one of the most secluded and luxurious residences by retaining its over-the-top glory. Legendary stars such as Marilyn Monroe, Howard Hughes, and Greta Garbo lived in the fabled private bungalows that are nestled within 12 acres of tropical-like grounds.

Seit seiner Eröffnung im Jahre 1912 ist die berühmte, mit rosa Stuck verzierte Villa im spanischen Stil, die auch als „Rosa Palast" bekannt ist, ein Magnet für die Filmkolonie Hollywoods gewesen. Das für seine märchenhaften Gartenbungalows und die Polo Lounge bekannte Hotel ist immer noch eine der abgeschiedensten und luxuriösesten Residenzen und hat ihre überaus große Pracht bewahrt. Legendäre Stars wie Marilyn Monroe, Howard Hughes und Greta Garbo lebten in den herrlichen Privatbungalows, die sich in die knapp 5 Hektar große, tropisch anmutende Anlage einfügen.

Depuis sont inauguration en 1912, la fameuse bâtisse de stuc rose du style espagnol connue sous le nom de « Pink Palace » attire toujours autant la colonie des cinéastes hollywoodiens. Connue pour ses bungalows de jardin mystiques et son Polo Lounge, l'hôtel est toujours une des résidences les plus fermées et les plus luxueuses, et cultive cette gloire. Des stars légendaires tels que Marilyn Monroe, Howard Hughes et Greta Garbo ont vécu dans les fameux bungalows privés qui sont nichés dans le parc tropical de 5 hectares.

Esta villa de estilo español con sus estucos rosas, también conocida como el palacio rosa, ha sido un imán para la colonia cinematográfica de Hollywood desde que se inauguró en 1912. El hotel, conocido por sus míticos bungalows con jardín y por su Polo Lounge, sigue siendo una de las residencias más retiradas y lujosas, como demuestra su gran suntuosidad. Estrellas legendarias como Marilyn Monroe, Howard Hughes y Greta Garbo vivieron en los fabulosos bungalows privados, que se encuentran en este terreno de 5 hectáreas que recuerda a los grandes trópicos.

Da sempre, sin dal momento della sua apertura nel 1912, la famosa villa con stucchi in stile spagnolo, conosciuta come il "Pink Palace", attira la comunità cinematografica di Hollywood. Famoso per i suoi garden bungalow e per la Polo Lounge, l'hotel è una delle residenze più tranquille e lussuose e continua a guadagnarsi l'ammirazione di tutti. Star leggendarie come Marilyn Monroe, Howard Hughes e Greta Garbo hanno soggiornato in bungalow fiabeschi, circondati da terreni tropicali di circa 5 ettari.

Its 204 rooms are all lavishly outfitted with state-of-the-art luxury, each uniquely decorated in a subdued palette of pinks, greens, apricots, and yellows.

Seine 204 Zimmer sind alle großzügig mit modernstem Luxus ausgestattet, und jedes ist auf einzigartige Weise in gedämpften Rosa-, Grün-, Apricot- und Gelbtönen gestaltet.

Les 204 chambres sont toutes équipées abondamment du luxe le plus exquis, décorées chacune individuellement dans des teintes douces de rose, vert, abricot et jaune.

Sus 204 habitaciones están diseñadas con todo el lujo moderno y cada una de ellas está decorada con suaves tonos rosas, verdes, albaricoques y amarillos.

Le sue 204 camere sono dotate di ogni lusso, e decorate in maniera unica in tonalità tenui di rosa, verde, albibocca, e giallo.

Behind the famous facade, the Beverly Hills Hotel remains the star-studded haven it was in Hollywood's golden days.

Hinter der berühmten Fassade ist das Beverly Hills Hotel immer noch die Oase der Stars, die sie in den goldenen Tagen Hollywoods war.

Derrière sa fameuse façade, le Beverly Hills Hotel reste le havre étoilé qu'il a été durant l'époque de gloire de Hollywood.

Detrás de su famosa fachada, el hotel Beverly Hills sigue siendo el oasis de las estrellas que siempre fue durante los días dorados de Hollywood.

Dietro la sua famosa facciata, il Beverly Hills Hotel rimane anche oggi un porto sicuro per le star così come lo era durante gli anni d'oro di Hollywood.

Four Seasons San Francisco

San Francisco, California

Luxurious hotel towers over the Financial District of San Francisco, sandwiched between multimillion-dollar condos and elite shops, and a premier sports-and-fitness complex. Spacious rooms are decorated in soothing hues of green, beige, and taupe, with custom-made bedding, original contemporary artwork, and huge luxury marble bathrooms. The 277 guest rooms include 46 suites with floor-to-ceiling windows overlooking the bay, or stunning views of the city.

Luxuriöse Hoteltürme über dem Finanzbezirk von San Francisco, zwischen mehrere Millionen teuren Eigentumswohnungen, erlesenen Geschäften und einem erstklassigen Sport- und Fitnesskomplex gelegen. Die geräumigen Zimmer sind in beruhigenden Farbnuancen von Grün-, Beige- und Taupetönen gestaltet und verfügen über maßgefertigte Betten, zeitgenössische Originalkunstwerke und weiträumige, luxuriöse Marmorbadezimmer. Zu den 277 Gästezimmern gehören 46 Suiten mit raumhohen Fenstern, aus denen man die Bucht überblicken kann oder einen atemberaubenden Ausblick über die Stadt hat.

Tours d'hôtel luxueuses au-dessus du quartier financier de San Francisco, prises entre les appartements des multimillionnaires et les boutiques de luxe, disposant de l'un des complexes de remise en forme et de sport les plus luxueux. Des chambres spacieuses décorées dans des teintes douces vertes, beiges et taupe, équipées de lits faits sur mesure, d'oeuvres d'art originales contemporaines et de grandes salles de bains en marbre luxueuses. Les 277 chambres comprennent 46 suites disposant de façades entièrement vitrées avec vue sur la baie ou sur la ville.

Estas lujosas torres se encuentran encima del distrito financiero de San Francisco, entre viviendas particulares tasadas en varios millones, comercios selectos y un complejo polideportivo de primera clase. Sus habitaciones amplias están decoradas con matices verdes, beiges y marrones. Tienen camas hechas a medida, obras de arte contemporáneas originales y lujosos cuartos de baño de mármol. 46 de las 277 habitaciones son suites con ventanas que van del suelo al techo, desde las cuales se puede ver la bahía o disfrutar de unas vistas impresionantes de la ciudad.

Le lussuose torri dell'hotel, emergono nel Financial District di San Francisco, schiacchiate tra condomini super costosi e boutique, e tra uno dei complessi più importanti per lo sport e il fitness. Le camere spaziose sono decorate nei toni leggeri del verde, del beige, e del grigio, con biancheria personalizzata, originali opere d'arte contemporanea, e bagni in marmo incredibilmente lussuosi. Le 277 camere per gli ospiti includono 46 suite con vetrate che vanno dal pavimento al soffitto offrendo una vista della baia, e bellissime panoramiche della città.

*42 **stories** towering over the heart of downtown; a perfect combination of elegance and modern luxury with a vibe that combines sophistication with trendy.*

*42 **Stockwerke** erheben sich über dem Stadtzentrum — eine perfekte Kombination aus Eleganz und modernem Luxus mit einer Atmosphäre, die Finesse mit Schick verbindet.*

*42 **étages** s'élevant au-dessus du cœur de la ville : une combinaison parfaite d'élégance et de luxe moderne, mariant une ambiance de sophistication et de tendance.*

*Esta **torre** de 42 plantas, que está situada sobre el centro de la ciudad, es una perfecta combinación de elegancia y lujo moderno, con un ambiente que combina el refinamiento y el buen gusto.*

*42 **piani** sovrastano il centro cittadino: una combinazione perfetta tra eleganza e modernità lussuosità in un'atmosfera che unisce il sofisticato al trendy.*

160,000–square feet flexible indoor/outdoor space is available for special events and business meetings, offering views of the city skyline.

Es steht ein 15.000 m² großer Indoor/Outdoor-Bereich für besondere Events und Geschäftstreffen zurVerfügung, der flexibel den jeweiligen Bedürfnissen angepasst werden kann und einen wunderbaren Ausblick auf die Skyline der Stadt bietet.

15 000 m² d'espaces souples intérieurs / extérieurs sont disponibles pour des événements et des réunions professionnelles, en offrant une vue sur la silhouette de la ville.

El hotel pone a su disposición un espacio interior y exterior de 15.000 m² para celebrar eventos especiales o para los meetings de negocios, desde los cuales se disfruta de una vista maravillosa del horizonte de la ciudad.

15.000 m² di spazi esterni/interni sono disponibili per eventi speciali ed incontri di business, regalando splendide vedute del profilo urbano.

Post Ranch Inn

Big Sur, California

Set 1,200 feet above the sea is California's secret laid-back luxury resort that is both modern and rustic, as well as environmentally aware. The stylish accommodations consist mainly of separate houses perched up on the cliff, with a cozy fireplace, marble Jacuzzi spa tub, and a private deck with wide-angle mountain and ocean views. Amenities include in-room spa treatments, meditative yoga in a circular canvas yurt, as well as lectures on stargazing.

365 Meter über dem Meer liegt Kaliforniens abgeschiedenes Luxusresort, dass sich sowohl modern als auch rustikal und umweltbewusst gibt. Die eleganten Unterkünfte bestehen hauptsächlich aus separaten, an die Klippen gebauten Häusern mit einem gemütlichen Kamin, einer Marmor-Whirlpoolwanne und einer privaten Dachterrasse mit Panoramablick über die Berge und das Meer. Zu den Annehmlichkeiten zählen Heilkurbehandlungen im Zimmer, meditatives Yoga in einer Jurte sowie Vorträge zur Sternbeobachtung.

Situé à 365 mètres au-dessus du niveau de la mer se trouve le lieu de villégiature secret californien, moderne ainsi que rustique, tout en tenant compte des enjeux environnementaux. Cet ensemble de style se compose essentiellement de maisons individuelles perchées sur les falaises, disposant d'une cheminée ouverte confortable, d'une baignoire jacuzzi balnéo et d'une terrasse privée avec une vue imprenable sur la mer et la montagne. Les services comprennent des soins balnéaires à domicile, des séances de yoga dans des yourtes circulaires en feutre, ainsi que des conférences sur l'observation des étoiles.

A 365 metros sobre el nivel del mar se encuentra el resort de lujo secreto de California, un lugar para relajarse, moderno y rústico al mismo tiempo y que tiene conciencia medioambiental. Sus modernos espacios son principalmente casas separadas, construidas sobre el acantilado, que tienen una acogedora chimenea, una bañera de burbujas de mármol y una terraza privada en el techo, con vistas panorámicas a las montañas y al mar. Entre los servicios disponibles hay tratamientos de cura en la habitación, yoga meditativo en una tienda de campaña, así como conferencias sobre la observación de las estrellas.

Sito a 365 metri sopra il livello del mare, il resort dal lusso rilassato è il segreto della California, moderno ma rustico, e rispettoso dell'ambiente. Le residenze di stile consistono principalmente in case separate a picco sugli scogli, con un camino intimo, vasche idromassaggio in marmo, ed una terrazza privata ad angolo con vista sulle montagne e sull'oceano. Le comodità includono trattamenti benessere in camera, yoga in uno yurt, e seminari di astronomia.

Splurge on one of the luxurious grass-roofed suites tucked away into the landscape, with stunning ocean views and majestic treescapes.

Gönnen Sie sich eine der luxuriösen Grasdach-Suiten, die versteckt in der Landschaft liegen und atemberaubende Blicke auf das Meer und die majestätischen Silhouetten der Wälder bieten.

Démonstration bruyante sur l'une des suites luxueuses à toits enherbés dissimulées dans le paysage, avec une vue époustouflante sur la mer et les silhouettes majestueuses des arbres.

Permítase el placer de disfrutar de una lujosa Suite con césped en el techo, que se confunden con el paisaje y que tienen vistas impresionantes al mar y a los árboles majestuosos.

Immergetevi in una delle suite con il tetto d'erba mimetizzati col paesaggio, godendo di incredibili viste sul mare e di maestosi paesaggi alberati.

The Setai

Miami, Florida

This meticulously replicated Art Deco landmark from the 1930s is now the hippest hotel to hit Miami's glitziest neighborhood. The original low-rise Art Deco building is accompanied by a soaring 40-story, blue-glass-clad tower, part hotel, part luxury condominiums. Set amid tropical gardens and sparkling pools this hotel introduces Asian traditions of simplicity and elegance to South Beach.

Dieses auf das Genauste nachempfundene Art déco-Wahrzeichen aus den 1930er Jahren ist jetzt das angesagteste Hotel in Miamis glamouröser Umgebung. Der ursprünglich niedrige Art déco Bau wird von einem hoch emporragenden 40-stöckigen, mit blauem Glas verkleideten Turm – teilweise Hotel, teilweise Eigentumswohnungen – begleitet. Dieses inmitten tropischer Gärten und sprudelnden Pools gelegene Hotel führt die asiatischen Traditionen der Einfachheit und Eleganz in South Beach ein.

Cet emblème Art Déco des années 1930 méticuleusement reconstitué est aujourd'hui l'hôtel le plus tendance du voisinage très extravagant de Miami. La bâtisse Art Déco d'origine, de faible hauteur, est accompagnée d'une tour haute de 40 étages et couverte de verre bleuté, occupée en partie par l'hôtel et en partie par des appartements de luxe. Logé dans des jardins tropicaux et entre des piscines scintillantes, cet hôtel apporte les traditions asiatiques de la simplicité et de l'élégance à South Beach.

Esta minuciosa reconstrucción del símbolo del Art Déco de los años treinta es ahora uno de los hoteles más de moda de la zona glamourosa de Miami. A la construcción de baja altura original le acompaña una torre de 40 plantas, revestida de cristal azul, que en parte es un hotel y en parte viviendas particulares. Este hotel, situado en medio del jardín tropical y entre piscinas de burbujas, sigue las tradiciones asiáticas de la sencillez y la elegancia en South Beach.

Questo angolo di terra degli anni '30, che si rifà in maniera meticolosa all'art deco, è ora l'hotel più hippy tale da superare la sfavillante e vicina Miami. L'edificio in art deco, originariamente non molto alto, è affiancato da una torre in vetro blu che raggiunge i 40 piani, in parte usata come hotel, e in parte destinata a lussuosi appartamenti. Sito tra giardini tropicali e idromassaggi, questo hotel porta a South Beach le semplici ed eleganti tradizioni asiatiche.

For the quintessential Miami Beach experience, guests lounge beside any of the three pools and order drinks from the 90-foot bar, or hide away in teak cabanas.

Für das vollkommene Miami-Beach-Erlebnis entspannen sich die Gäste an einem der drei Pools und bestellen Getränke an der 30 Meter langen Bar oder ziehen sich in die Teakhütten zurück.

Pour vivre l'ambiance typique de Miami Beach, les hôtes se reposent à côté de l'une des trois piscines et commandent des boissons au bar long de 30 mètres, ou se retirent dans les cabanes en tek.

Para vivir completamente la experiencia al estilo de Miami Beach, los huéspedes se relajan en una de las tres piscinas y piden sus bebidas en una barra que mide 30 metros o se retiran a una de las cabañas de madera.

Per godere appieno del Miami Beach, gli ospiti si rilassano vicino ad una delle tre piscine ordinando drink dal bancone lungo 30 metri, o appartandosi nelle casette di teck.

The 125 spacious suites have Oriental decor, with Thai silk headboards and Indonesian ebony furniture.

Die 125 geräumigen Suiten haben ein orientalisches Dekor mit thailändischen seidenbespannten Kopfteilen an den Betten und indonesischen Ebenholzmöbeln.

Les 125 suites spacieuses disposent d'un décor oriental, avec des têtes de lit couvertes de soie thaï et des meubles indonésiens en ébène.

Las 125 habitaciones espaciosas están decoradas al estilo oriental, con almohadas de seda tailandesas y muebles indonesios de ébano.

Le 125 spaziose suite presentano decori orientali, con soffitti in seta tailandese ed un arredo indonesiano in legno d'ebano.

Ancient Beijing paving stones top tables, glinting mother-of-pearl make up the mile-long bar counter, and door handles are covered with stingray skin.

Alte Pekinger Pflastersteinplatten bedecken die Tische, glänzendes Perlmutt dekoriert den sehr langen Tresen der Bar und die Türgriffe sind mit Stachelrochenhaut überzogen.

Les plateaux des tables sont constitués d'anciens pavés de Beijing, toute la longueur du bar est habillée en nacre, et les poignées des portes sont couvertes de peau de pastenague.

La larguísima barra del bar está compuesta de antiguas placas de adoquines pequineses y de madreperla resplandeciente y los pomos de las puertas están cubiertos con piel de pastinaca.

Tavoli rivestiti da antiche pietre cinesi, madreperla luccicante sul lunghissimo bancone del bar, e le maniglie delle porte rivestite da pelle di pastinache.

Casa Casuarina

Miami Beach, Florida

This Italianate villa incongruously tucked in the middle of the Art Deco historic district in Miami remains a monument to glamour, sophistication and celebrity. Each of its 10 suites has its own unique decor, capturing a different element of the house's colorful, cosmopolitan spirit, with elaborate wall paintings, fanciful frescoes, stained-glass French doors and windows, and elaborate marble floors.

Diese italienisch anmutende Villa, die unvereinbar mit der Umgebung mitten im historischen Art-déco-Viertel Miamis liegt, ist ein verbliebenes Monument des Glamours, von Kultiviertheit und Ruhm. Jede ihrer 10 Suiten hat ein eigenes, einzigartiges Dekor, das mit kunstvollen Wandmalereien, fantasiereichen Fresken, Türen und Fenstern aus französischem Buntglas sowie kunstvoll gestalteten Marmorfluren ein anderes Element des vielseitigen, weltoffenen Geistes des Hauses erfasst.

Cette villa de style italien implantée de façon incongrue dans le quartier historique art déco de Miami reste un monument au faste, à la sophistication et à la célébrité. Chacune de ses 10 suites dispose d'un aménagement unique, saisissant un élément différent de l'esprit coloré et cosmopolite de la bâtisse, de ses peintures murales complexes, ses fresques fantaisistes, ses fenêtres et portes à la française en verre teinté et ses sols en marbre élaborés.

Esta Villa, que evoca el estilo italiano, discordante con su entorno en medio del histórico barrio de estilo art déco en Miami, constituye un monumento al glamour, la distinción y la fama. Cada una de sus 10 suites tiene su propia decoración única, que refleja los diferentes elementos del espíritu colorido y cosmopolita de la casa a través de paredes pintadas artísticamente, frescos fantásticos, puertas francesas de cristal policromado y pasillos artísticosde mármol.

Questa villa italiana, gelosamente custodita nel centro del quartiere art déco di Miami, è un monumento attraente,sofisticato e celebre. Ognuna delle 10 suite è decorata in modo unico riprendendo lo spirito ricco di colori e cosmopolita dell'abitazione, con pareti dipinte in modo puntiglioso, affreschi fantasiosi, porte in vetro colorato, infissi alla francese, e elaborati pavimenti in marmo.

Originally built in 1930, Casa Casuarina was once Gianni Versace's personal palace and has now reopened.

Die ursprünglich 1930 erbaute Casa Casuarina, einmal der persönliche Palast von Gianni Versace, ist jetzt wiedereröffnet worden.

Construite en 1930, la Casa Casuarina était à l'époque le palais personnel de Gianni Versace, et est maintenant devenu.

La Casa Casuarina, construida en 1930, fue en otro tiempo el palacio privado de Gianni Versace y ahora ha reabierto sus puertas.

Originariamente costruita nel 1930, Casa Casuarina una tempo era la residenza privata di Gianni Versace. Ora è stata riaperta.

The exuberant pool with mosaics offers a magical setting in which guests can unwind and socialize.

Der üppige Pool mit seinen Mosaiken bietet einen magischen Rahmen, in dem sich Gäste entspannen und Kontakte knüpfen können.

La piscine exubérante avec ses mosaïques offre un cadre magique dans lequel les hôtes peuvent se détendre et se rencontrer.

La exuberante piscina, con sus mosaicos, ofrece un espacio mágico en el que los huéspedes se pueden relajar y hacer nuevos amigos o amigas.

La lussuosa piscina con i suoi mosaici offre un ambiente magico, nel quale gli ospiti possono rilassarsi e socializzare.

For those simply seeking a day of decadent indulgence, they need look no further then the luxury boutique spa, housed in the rooms overlooking the pool and tropical garden area.

Diejenigen, denen einfach an einem Tag mit dekadentem Genuss liegt, müssen nicht weiter als bis zum luxuriösen Wellness-Center schauen, das in den Räumen untergebracht ist, von denen aus man den Pool und den tropischen Garten überblicken kann.

Pour ceux qui souhaitent seulement profiter d'une journée décadente, il leur suffit de se rendre dans l'espace balnéaire luxueux, logé dans des pièces surplombant la piscine et le jardin tropical.

Aquellos que simplemente busquen un día de deleite decadente no tienen más que ir al lujoso centro de wellness, que se encuentra en un área desde la cual se ve la piscina y el jardín tropical.

Per coloro che semplicemente cercano una giornata di dolce far niente, non è necessario andare molto lontano: nelle sale del centro benessere, che si affacciano sulla piscina e sul giardino tropicale, si può trovare quanto desiderato.

The Ritz-Carlton, South Beach

Miami Beach, Florida

Morris Lapidus, representative of the design style Miami Modern (MiMo), wrote architectural history with the DiLido Hotel, which was opened in 1953 in a perfect beach location. During the elaborate and exorbitantly expensive renovation by The Ritz-Carlton Hotel Company, emphasis was placed on maintaining as much as possible of the historical substance of the building: the concave interior and exterior walls, the typical pastel colors, the amoeba-shaped sections on the ceilings and walls. The interior of the 376 rooms is modeled after the design of luxury yachts.

Mit dem DiLido Hotel, das 1953 in bester Strandlage eröffnet wurde, schrieb Morris Lapidus, Vertreter des Designstils Miami Modern (MiMo), Architekturgeschichte. Bei der aufwändigen und exorbitant teuren Renovierung durch die The Ritz-Carlton Hotel Company wurde darauf geachtet, möglichst viel von der historischen Bausubstanz zu erhalten: die konkaven Innen- und Außenwände, die typischen Pastellfarben, die amöbenförmigen Ausschnitte an Decken und Wänden. Das Interieur der 376 Zimmer ist der Gestaltung von Luxusyachten entlehnt.

Avec l'hôtel DiLido, inauguré en 1953 sur un site balnéaire exceptionnel, Morris Lapidus, le fameux représentant du style de design Miami Modern (MiMo), a écrit une page de l'histoire de l'architecture. Lors de sa restauration très complexe et extrêmement coûteuse par la The Ritz-Carlton Hotel Company, une attention particulière a été accordée à la préservation d'un maximum de l'ancienne bâtisse : les murs intérieurs et extérieurs concaves, les couleurs pastelle typiques, les découpes en forme d'amibes sur les plafonds et les murs. L'aménagement intérieur des 376 chambres ressemble à celui des yachts de luxe.

Morris Lapidus, representante del estilo Miami Modern (MiMo), entraba en la historia de la arquitectura con el hotel DiLido, que se inauguró en 1953 en el mejor lugar de la playa. Durante la renovación minuciosa y desorbitantemente cara realizada por la The Ritz-Carlton Hotel Company, se procuró conservar la esencia histórica de la construcción en la mayor medida posible: las paredes cóncavas interiores y exteriores, los típicos colores pastel, los detalles con forma de ameba de los techos y paredes. El interior de las 376 habitaciones reproduce el diseño de los yates de lujo.

Con l'hotel DiLido, aperto nel 1953, nella migliore zona di spiaggia, Morris Lapidus, rappresentante dello stile di Design Miami Modern (MiMo), ha scritto la storia dell'architettura. Durante il restauro, molto accurato ed incredibilmente costoso, da parte della The Ritz-Carlton Hotel Company si è posta particolare attenzione perché restasse intatta una gran parte della sostanza storica della costruzione: le mura interne ed esterne di forma concava, i tipici colori pastello, i tagli a forma di ameba su soffitti e pareti. Gli interni delle 376 camere sono stati riprodotti come quelli degli yacht di lusso.

The formal expressions by Morris Lapidus are unmistakable and the high-gloss cherry wood wall with the 72 cupola-formed wall lights is legendary.

Unverkennbar ist die Formensprache von Morris Lapidus, legendär die auf Hochglanz polierte Kirschholzwand in der Hotelhalle mit den 72 kuppelförmigen Wandleuchten.

Les lignes imaginées par Morris Lapidus sont flagrantes, la cloison polie en bois de merisier du hall avec ses 72 appliques murales en forme de coupoles est légendaire.

El lenguaje de las formas de Morris Lapidus es inconfundible y es legendaria la pared de madera de cerezo pulida situada en el vestíbulo del hotel y que tiene 72 lámparas abovedadas.

Chiaramente riconoscibile è il linguaggio delle forme di Morris Lapidus: leggendaria la parete lucidissima in legno di ciliegio nella halle dell'hotel con 72 lampadari a forma di cupola.

Contemporary luxury, *which combines stylistic elements of modern art, is concealed behind the façade from the 1950s, which is protected as a historic monument.*

Hinter der denkmalgeschützten Fassade *aus den 50er Jahren verbirgt sich zeitgemäßer Luxus, der Stilelemente der Art Modern aufgreift.*

Derrière la façade classée *des années 1950 se dissimule un luxe contemporain qui reprend des éléments de style de l'Art Moderne.*

Detrás de esta fachada *de los años 50, declarada monumento protegido, se esconden el lujo contemporáneo, que adopta elementos estilísticos del arte moderno.*

Dietro alla facciata *degli Anni '50, che si trova sotto tutela monumentale, si nasconde un lusso contemporaneo che riprende elementi dello stile dell' arte moderna.*

The Peninsula Chicago

Chicago, Illinois

This luxury hotel owned by the Peninsula hotels is located right next to Chicago's iconic Tribune Tower along the "Magnificent Mile". The design was inspired by the Art Deco style so popular in the city during the 1920s and 1930s. Murano glass lights and hand-polished stone tiles conjure up an elegant ambience, while the culinary highlight is the Shanghai Terrace in an oriental theme—a contemporary interpretation of an exclusive dining club from the Shanghai of the 1930s.

An der „Magnificent Mile", in direkter Nachbarschaft zum Chicagoer Wahrzeichen, dem Tribune Tower, liegt das zur den Peninsula Hotels gehörende Luxus-Hotel. Das Design orientiert sich am Stil des Art déco, der in den 20er und 30er Jahren das Stadtbild Chicagos prägte. Leuchten aus Murano-Glas und handpolierte Steinfliesen kreieren ein edles Ambiente. Highlight des Restaurants ist die asiatische Shanghai-Terrasse, die zeitgenössische Version eines exklusiven Dinnerclubs aus dem Shanghai der 30er Jahre.

C'est sur la « Magnificent Mile », à proximité directe de l'emblème de Chicago, la Tribune Tower, que se trouve l'hôtel de luxe appartenant aux Peninsula hôtels. Le design s'inspire du style art déco qui caractérisait l'image de la ville dans les années 1920 et les années 1930. Les lampes en verre Murano et le carrelage en pierre poli à la main créent une ambiance recherchée. L'attraction du restaurant est la terrasse asiatique Shanghai, version contemporaine d'un club-restaurant exclusif du Shanghai des années 1930.

En la "Magnificent Mile", muy cerca del monumento característico de Chicago, la Tribune Tower, se encuentra este hotel de lujo, propiedad del grupo Peninsula. Su diseño es de tendencia art déco, característico del Chicago de los años 20 y 30. Las lámparas de murano y baldosas de piedra pulidas a mano crean un ambiente exclusivo. Lo más llamativo del restaurante es su terraza asiática Shanghai, una versión moderna de los "dinnerclubs" del Shanghai de los años 30.

Affacciato sul "Magnificent Mile", nelle dirette vicinanze della Tribune Tower, simbolo della città di Chicago: questa l'ubicazione d'eccezione dell'hotel di lusso della catena Peninsula. Il design trae ispirazione dallo stile art déco che negli anni 1920 e 1930 ha dato un'impronta inconfondibile alla città di Chicago. Le lampade in vetro di Murano e le mattonelle di pietra levigate a mano danno all'ambiente un tocco ricercato. L'highlight del ristorante è il terrazzo asiatico Shanghai, la versione contemporanea di un Dinnerclub esclusivo nello stile di Shanghai degli Anni 30.

As well as a huge indoor pool, the two-story hotel spa boasts floor-to-ceiling windows that offer stunning views of North Michigan Avenue.

Die über zwei Stockwerke reichende Fensterfront des Spas mit seinem großzügigen Indoor-Pool gibt einen fantastischen Blick auf die North Michigan Avenue frei.

Les fenêtres en façade hautes de deux étages du spa, doté d'une piscine intérieure généreuse, offrent une vue sensationnelle sur la North Michigan Avenue.

La fachada de vidrio del spa, que ocupa dos pisos, con su amplia piscina interior, ofrece una vista fantástica sobre la North Michigan Avenue.

Il centro benessere con la sua facciata a vetro alta oltre due piani, ospita un'ampia piscina interna, e permette di spaziare con lo sguardo sulla North Michigan Avenue.

All 339 rooms and suites feature luxurious, spacious marble bathtubs. A glass installation by the artist Paul Housberg sets a distinctive tone in the hotel lobby.

Sämtliche 339 Zimmer und Suiten verfügen über komfortable, großzügige Marmorbäder. Die Glasinstallation des Künstlers Paul Housberg setzt im Eingangsbereich des Hotels einen markanten Akzent.

Les 339 chambres et suites disposent de salles de bain en marbre confortables et généreuses. L'installation en verre de l'artiste Paul Housberg donne un accent particulier au hall d'entrée de l'hôtel.

Las 339 habitaciones y suites cuentan con amplios y confortables cuartos de baño en mármol. Las instalaciones de vidrio del artista Paul Housberg aportan un toque especial a la entrada del hotel.

Tutte le 339 stanze e suite dispongono di bagni in marmo spaziosi e confortevoli. Di grande impatto l'installazione in vetro dell'artista Paul Housberg all'ingresso.

Four Seasons Hotel New York

New York, New York

A grandiose skyscraper and a unique cosmopolitan hang-out between Park and Madison Avenue. The design by IM Pei and Frank Williams reinterprets the style of New York's legendary grand hotels from the 1920s. In the bar and restaurant, the clientele is about as exclusive as it gets—Hollywood stars mingle with Wall Street bankers and Park Avenue princesses. The hotel's 368 rooms cover 52 floors, with the upper levels enjoying unrivalled views of Central Park.

Ein grandioser Wolkenkratzer und ein einzigartiger kosmopolitischer Treffpunkt. Zwischen Park und Madison Avenue haben IM Pei und Frank Williams ein Hotel geschaffen, das den Stil der legendären New Yorker Grand-Hotels der 20er Jahre neu interpretiert. Die Zusammensetzung des Publikums in Bar und Restaurant ist an Exklusivität kaum zu übertreffen, Westküsten-Celebrities treffen hier auf Wallstreet-Banker und Park-Avenue-Prinzessinnen. Auf 52 Etagen verteilen sich 368 Zimmer, die oberen haben einen unvergleichlichen Blick auf den Central Park.

Un gratte-ciel grandiose et un rendez-vous cosmopolite unique. IM Pei et Frank Williams ont créé un hôtel entre Park et Madison Avenue qui offre une nouvelle interprétation du style des grands hôtels légendaires des années 1920. Le rapprochement du public dans le bar et le restaurant ne manque pas d'exclusivité, les célébrités de la côte ouest rencontrent ici les banquiers de Wallstreet et les princesses de Park Avenue. 368 chambres sont réparties sur 52 étages, les chambres du dernier étage offrent une vue imprenable sur Central Park.

Un grandioso rascacielos y un punto de encuentro único y cosmopolita. IM Pei y Frank Williams crearon entre Park y Madison Avenue un hotel que interpreta de forma novedosa el estilo legendario de los grandes hoteles neoyorquinos de los años 20. Reunirse en el bar y el restaurante es algo exclusivo para el público, difícil de encontrar, es un lugar de encuentro de celebridades de la costa oeste, banqueros de Wallstreet y princesas de la Park Avenue. Las 368 habitaciones del hotel se distribuyen en 52 pisos; las de la parte superior ofrecen inolvidables vistas al Central Park.

Un maestoso grattacielo nonché un luogo d'incontro singolare e cosmopolita. Con il Four Seasons Hotel, di New York, situato fra Park e Madison Avenue, IM Pei e Frank Williams hanno dato vita ad un'interpretazione, in chiave contemporanea, dello stile dei leggendari Grand Hotel di New York degli anni '20. Ineguagliabile per esclusività la composizione variegata degli assidui frequentatori del locale notturno e del ristorante: dalle celebrità della West Coast ai banchieri di Wall Street o ancora alle debuttanti dell'alta società. 368 stanze sono disposte su 52 piani, e ai piani superiori si gode di una vista incomparabile su Central Park.

The interior design is dominated by honey-colored sandstone, which IM Pei also used for the Louvre extension in Paris.

Im Inneren dominiert der honigfarbene Sandstein, den IM Pei auch für den Louvre-Anbau in Paris verwendete.

À l'intérieur, c'est le grès couleur miel, également utilisé par IM Pei pour l'agrandissement du Louvre à Paris, qui domine.

En el interior domina la arenisca de color miel, la misma que IM Pei utilizó para la ampliación del Louvre en París.

All'interno, predomina la pietra arenaria color miele utilizzata da IM Pei anche per l'ampliamento del Louvre di Parigi.

Relax and unwind next to the busy lobby in the lounge or the seating areas in front of the huge fireplace. The Art deco accents are clear for all to see.

Neben dem belebten Foyer bieten die Lounge sowie Plätze vor dem überdimensionierten Kamin die Möglichkeit zum Rückzug. Die Anklänge an die Formen des Art déco sind unübersehbar.

Parallèlement au foyer animé, la lounge et l'espace disponible devant la cheminée surdimensionnée permettent de se retirer. Les réminiscences des formes du style Art déco sont évidentes.

Junto al animado vestíbulo, el lounge y el entorno a la gran chimenea invitan al recogimiento. Las semejanzas con las formas del art déco saltan a la vista.

Oltre che nell'animato foyer è possibile ritirarsi in un angolo più tranquillo prendendo posto nella lounge o davanti al grande camino. Numerosissime le reminiscenze estetiche dell'art déco.

The oversized windows in the rooms and suites provide stunning unobscured views of Central Park and the New York skyline.

Die übergroßen Fenster in den Zimmern und Suiten gewährleisten einen ungestörten, fantastischen Blick auf den Central Park oder die Skyline der Stadt.

Les fenêtres surdimensionnées des chambres et des suites garantissent une vue tranquille et fantastique sur Central Park ou la silhouette caractéristique de la ville.

Los grandes ventanales en las habitaciones y suites garantizan fantásticas claras vistas al Central Park o al conjunto de la ciudad.

Dalle enormi finestre delle stanze e delle suite è possibile godere di una fantastica ed indisturbata vista su Central Park o sull'intera città.

Mandarin Oriental New York

New York, New York

The exclusive development on the top floors of the Time Warner Center is a prestigious address in the heart of Manhattan, with floor-to-ceiling windows that offer paramount views. This luxury hotel with 248 rooms and suites provides a stunning blend of modern interiors with 1940s-style furnishings and elegant Asian-influenced design. Ornate kimonos and contemporary art decorate the walls, notably two modern sculptures by Dale Chihuly graces the public spaces.

Diese exklusive Einrichtung in den oberen Stockwerken des Time Warner Centers ist eine angesehene Adresse im Herzen Manhattans mit raumhohen Fenstern, die einen Blick über die Stadt bieten. Dieses Luxushotel mit 248 Zimmern und Suiten bietet eine atemberaubende Mischung aus modernem Interieur mit Möbeln im Stil der 1940er Jahre und elegantem, asiatisch beeinflussten Design. Kunstvolle Kimonos und zeitgenössische Kunst zieren die Wände, insbesondere zwei moderne Skulpturen von Dale Chihuly schmücken die allgemeinen Bereiche.

L'aménagement exclusif des étages supérieurs du Time Warner Center est une adresse prestigieuse au cœur de Manhattan, disposant de baies vitrées qui offrent des vues formidables. Cet hôtel de luxe de 248 chambres et suites offre un mariage surprenant d'intérieurs modernes avec des meubles du style des années 1940 et d'un design élégant influencé par le style asiatique. Des kimonos brodés et de l'art contemporain décorent les murs, notamment deux sculptures modernes de Dale Chihuly disposées dans les espaces publics.

El exclusivo Time Warner Center, construido sobre la azotea, es uno de los lugares más prestigiosos del corazón de Manhattan. Desde sus ventanas, que van dell techo al suelo, se disfruta de una bonita vista panorámica. Este hotel de lujo de 248 habitaciones y suites ofrece una mezcla impresionante de estilos, por una parte con su moderna decoración interior compuesta de muebles al estilo de los años cuarenta y por otra por su elegante diseño con influencias asiáticas. Las paredes están adornadas con kimonos artísticos y arte contemporáneo. Especialmente dos esculturas modernas de Dale Chihuly adornan los espacios públicos.

L'incredibile sviluppo nei piani superiori del Time Warner Center rappresenta un punto prestigioso nel cuore di Manhattan, con vetrate che permettono delle viste panoramiche meravigliose. Questo hotel di lusso, con 248 camere e suite, offre un incredibile miscuglio tra modernità e stile anni '40 ed un elegante design dalle influenze asiatiche. Kimono ornati e arte contemporanea decorano le pareti, in particolare due sculture moderne di Dale Chihuly abbelliscono gli spazi comuni.

The guest rooms are larger than some New York apartments, and have stunning views over Midtown Manhattan, Central Park, and the Hudson River.

Die Gästezimmer sind größer als einige New Yorker Appartements und bieten atemberaubende Blicke über Midtown Manhattan, den Central Park und den Hudson River.

Les chambres sont plus spacieuses que certains appartements new-yorkais et disposent de vues panoramiques époustouflantes sur le centre de Manhattan, le Central Park et l'Hudson River.

Las habitaciones son más grandes que algunos de los apartamentos neoyorquinos y ofrecen vistas impresionantes de la Midtown Manhattan, el Central Park y el río Hudson.

Le camere degli ospiti sono più spaziose di alcuni appartamenti di New York, ed offrono delle vedute incredibili sopra Midtown Manhattan, il Central Park, ed il fiume Hudson.

Hotel (The Mercer)

New York, New York

An engaging, glamorous SoHo hangout with a hint of Bohemia housed in a splendid Romanesque revival building. All 75 guest rooms have the minimalist design of a New York City loft, with exposed brickwork, bare wooden floors, industry size windows, and floor-to-ceiling iron support columns. The serene lobby has an unmarked reception desk and a wood-paneled library full of books for guests. Furnishings are spare, since the beauty of a place lays in its empty spaces.

Ein einnehmender, glamouröser SoHo-Treffpunkt mit einer Prise Boheme-Stil in einem glanzvollen Gebäude im neoromanischen Stil. Alle 75 Gästezimmer haben das minimalistische Design eines New York City-Lofts mit sichtbarem Mauerwerk, blanken Holzfußböden, Fenstern gemäß Industrienorm und raumhohen Eisenstützen. Die heiter gestaltete Lobby hat eine nicht gekennzeichnete Rezeption und eine mit Holz verkleidete, gut bestückte Bibliothek für die Gäste. Die Einrichtung ist spärlich, da die Schönheit des Ortes durch die freien Räume betont wird.

Une adresse attrayante et glamoureuse de Soho avec un soupçon de bohème, logé dans un superbe bâtiment romanesque. Les 75 chambres disposent toutes du design minimaliste d'un loft de New York City, avec des murs en briques apparentes, des sols en parquet nu, des fenêtres de tailles industrielles et des poutrelles de support non encastrées. Le lobby très serein est pourvu d'un accueil discret et d'une bibliothèque à habillage en bois pleine de livres destinés aux hôtes. Les meubles sont rares, puisque la beauté de l'endroit vient de ses espaces vides.

Un punto de encuentro agradable y glamouroso en el SoHo, con un toque bohemio en un edificio resplandeciente de estilo neorromántico. Las 75 habitaciones tienen el diseño minimalista de un loft neoyorquino. Los ladrillos de los muros están al descubierto, los suelos son de madera pulida y las ventanas están construidas siguiendo los estándares. Las columnas de acero que soportan el edificio van del techo al suelo. El lobby es tranquilo y su recepción no está señalizada. Tiene una biblioteca sólo para los huéspedes, que está revestida con paneles de madera y que posee muchos fondos. La decoración no es abundante, debido a que la belleza del lugar se basa en los espacios vacíos.

Un posto ricco di glamour, nel quartiere di SoHo, con un tocco bohémien, si trova in uno splendido edificio del revival romanico. Tutte le 75 camere degli ospiti hanno il design minimalistico di un loft di New York, con mattoni a vista, pavimenti in parquet, serramenti industriali, e colonne portanti di ferro. L'atrio tranquillo ha un receptiondesk aperto ed una biblioteca rivestita in legno piena di libri per gli ospiti. Gli arredi sono ridotti, poiché la bellezza di un luogo è nei suoi spazi vuoti.

*The **almost** decadent two-person marble tubs, some surrounded by mirrors, open up to the rustic decor of the minimalistic bedroom.*

***Die fast** dekadenten Marmorwannen für zwei Personen, von denen einige von Spiegeln umgeben sind, öffnen das schlichte Dekor des minimalistischen Schlafzimmers.*

***Les baignoires** pour deux personnes presque décadentes, dont certaines sont entourées de miroirs, s'ouvrent sur le décor rustique des chambres à coucher minimalistes.*

***Las bañeras** de mármol casi decadentes son para dos personas. Algunas están rodeadas de espejos y es el único elemento que rompe con el diseño minimalista del dormitorio.*

***Le vasche,** in marmo, per due persone, alcune circondate da specchi, si aprono alla decorazione rustica della camera da letto minimalista.*

Interiors are designed with pale leather screens and banquettes, low oval coffee tables on antique Turkish carpets, dark African woods and custom-designed Christian Liaigre furniture upholstered in natural fibers.

Das Interieur *ist mit blassen Schirmen und gepolsterten Sitzbänken aus Leder, niedrigen ovalen Kaffeetischen auf alten türkischen Teppichen, dunklen afrikanischen Hölzern und maßgefertigten Möbeln von Christian Liaigre ausgestattet, die mit Naturfasern aufgepolstert wurden.*

Les intérieurs *sont aménagés avec des écrans et des banquettes en cuir pâle, des tables de thé ovales sur des tapis turcs antiques, des bois foncés africains et du mobilier tapissé en fibres naturelles créé sur mesure par Christian Liaigre.*

El interior *está decorado con mesillas y fundas de cuero pálido, mesitas de café ovales y bajas colocadas sobre una antigua alfombra turca, maderas africanas oscuras y muebles de Christian Liaigre, hechos a medida y tapizados con tejidos naturales.*

Gli interni *sono divisi da separé in pelle delicata, e vi si trovano panche, tavolini bassi e ovali che poggiano su antichi tappeti turchi, scuri legni africani e arredi Christian Liaigre rivestiti in fibre naturali e fatti su misura.*

The Lowell New York

New York, New York

Located on a quiet, tree-lined residential street, the Lowell epitomizes "Old New York" luxury. The suites have an understated European style and elegance but with all of the civilized comforts of home, replete with stocked bookshelves, gilt-framed paintings and plush armchairs and sofas. All 70 deluxe rooms and suites are individually decorated with lush carpets, fine antiques, and such ornamental accents as Chinese porcelain bowls, bronze figurines and botanical prints.

Das Lowell, an einer ruhigen, mit Bäumen gesäumten Wohnstraße gelegen, verkörpert den „alten New Yorker" Luxus. Die Suiten sind in zurückhaltendem europäischen Stil und entsprechender Eleganz gehalten, aber mit dem kultivierten Komfort eines Heims, voll gestopft mit bestückten Bücherregalen, Gemälden mit Goldrahmen und Sesseln und Sofas aus Plüsch. Alle 70 Deluxe-Zimmer und -suiten sind mit dicken Teppichen, feinen Antiquitäten und zierenden Akzenten wie chinesischen Porzellanschalen, Bronzefigürchen und botanischen Drucken individuell eingerichtet.

Situé dans une rue résidentielle calme et bordée d'arbres, le Lowell illustre un luxe « new-yorkais ancien ». Les suites sont d'un style européen discret et élégant, mais disposent de tout le confort civilisé d'un domicile, sont remplies d'étagères à livres pleines, de tableaux en cadres dorés et de fauteuils et de canapés douillets. L'ensemble des 70 chambres et suites de luxe sont aménagées individuellement avec des tapis épais, de belles antiquités et des objets de décoration tels que des bols en porcelaine chinoise, des figurines en bronze et des estampes botaniques.

El Lowell representa el tradicional lujo neoyorquino. El hotel se encuentra situado en una calle tranquila de viviendas, flanqueada por una fila de árboles. Las suites tienen un toque del estilo y la elegancia europeos, pero con la comodidad refinada de una residencia. Abundan las estanterías repletas de libros, pinturas en marcos de oro, sillones y sofás de felpa. Las 70 habitaciones y suites de lujo están decoradas individualmente con alfombras gruesas, antigüedades finas y otros detalles decorativos como cuencos de porcelana china, figuritas de bronce e impresiones con motivos botánicos.

Situato in una via residenziale tranquilla con file di alberi, il Lowell rappresenta il lusso della "vecchia New York". Le suite sono arredate in uno stile ed un'eleganza europei molto modesti, ma con tutti i comfort di casa nostra, ricca di mensole ben fornite di libri, dipinti dalle cornici dorate e poltrone e sofà con rivestimenti in tessuto felpato. Le 70 camere e suite di lusso sono singolarmente arredate con ricchi tappeti, fine antiquariato, e decorazioni come vasi in porcellana cinese, statuine di bronzo e stampe botaniche.

Wood-burning fireplaces, a rarity for New York City hotels, are lined with bookshelves, and almost all of the 47 individually decorated suites have fully equipped kitchens.

In den von Bücherregalen umrahmten Kaminen brennen echte Holzscheite, eine Seltenheit in New Yorker Hotels. Fast jede der 47 individuell dekorierten Suiten hat eine voll ausgestattete Küche.

Dans les cheminées flanquées de rayonnages brûlent de vraies bûches, une rareté dans les hôtels new-yorkais. Presque toutes les suites sur les 47 décorées différemment possèdent une cuisine entièrement équipée.

En las chimeneas rodeadas de libros arden auténticos haces de leña, algo inusual en los hoteles neoyorquinos. De las 47 suites, casi todas están decoradas individualmente y poseen una cocina completamente equipada.

Nei camini posti tra gli scaffali pieni di libri bruciano veri ciocchi di legno, una rarità in un hotel newyorkese. Quasi tutte le 47 suite arredate con gusto individuale dispongono di una cucina modernamente attrezzata.

Guest rooms are adorned with beautiful antique furniture and prints, rich chintzes, satins, and other rich floral fabrics. Large desks and engulfing comforters make you feel at home.

Die Gästezimmer sind mit wunderschönen Antiquitäten und Drucken, feinem Chintz, Satin und anderen reichen Stoffen mit Blumenmuster verziert. Große Tische und üppige Bettdecken lassen Sie sich wie zu Hause fühlen.

Les chambres sont décorées de superbes meubles, de gravures anciennes, de chintz luxueux, et de tissus floraux exubérants. De grands bureaux et des couettes douillettes vous donnent l'impression d'être chez vous.

Las habitaciones están decoradas con maravillosos muebles antiguos e impresiones, indiana fina, satén y otros tejidos finos. Las mesas grandes y la enorme ropa de cama harán que se sienta como en casa.

Le camere per gli ospiti sono arredate da fantastici pezzi d'antiquariato e decorate da stampe d'epoca, ricchi tessuti calancà, sete, ed altre preziose stoffe floreali. Grandi tavoli e ogni sorta di lusso vi faranno sentire come a casa.

Cotton House

Mustique, Caribbean

Mustique is a remarkable and exclusive island in the Grenadines. It is privately owned by a company which presides over a portfolio of 60 luxury villas, an intimate holiday lodge and Cotton House, its one and only hotel. Guests are welcomed in a distinctly British style. Indeed the elegant suites were modeled on designs by celebrated stage architect Oliver Messel. The island's beaches are almost exclusively the domain of the world's rich, powerful and beautiful.

Das zu den Grenadinen zählende Mustique ist ungewöhnlich und exklusiv zugleich. Die Insel ist im Besitz einer Firma, die neben 60 Luxusvillen und einem kleinen Gästehaus auch das Cotton House als einziges Hotel im Portfolio hat. Dort empfängt man die Gäste ausgesprochen britisch. Die exklusiven Suiten entstammen den Entwürfen des Designers und Bühnenbildners Oliver Messel. An den Stränden sind die Schönen, Reichen und Prominenten aus aller Welt fast unter sich.

Appartenant aux Grenadines, l'Île Moustique est à la fois insolite et exclusive. L'île est administrée par une société qui possède également, outre 60 villas de luxe et un petit hôtel, un complexe hôtelier unique, le Cotton House. On y accueille les visiteurs de manière très britannique. Les suites exclusives ont été conçues à partir des créations du designer et scénographe Oliver Messel. Sur les plages, les beaux, riches et célèbres du monde entier se retrouvent quasiment entre eux.

La isla Mustique, parte del archipielago de las Granadinas, es extraordinaria y exclusiva a la vez. Ésta es propiedad de una empresa, que junto a 60 villas de lujo y un pequeño hotel, posee también el Cotton House, el único hotel entre sus inversiones. Aquí se recibe a los huéspedes con un marcado estilo británico. Las exclusivas suites son obras originales del escenógrafo y diseñador Oliver Messel. Por sus playas pasean los más guapos y guapas, ricos y personalidades de todo el mundo.

Fra le isole Grenadine, di cui fa parte Mustique, è la proprietà più insolita ed allo stesso tempo esclusiva: di proprietà di un gruppo che annovera nel suo portafoglio come unico hotel, oltre a 60 ville di lusso e ad una piccola foresteria, il Cotton House. Qui agli ospiti viene riservato un trattamento consono alla migliore tradizione britannica. Le suite esclusive sono opera del designer e scenografo Oliver Messel. Le spiagge sono animate quasi esclusivamente dai ricchi, belli e famosi di tutto il mondo.

Tradition meets the modern age—the Veranda made of wood and open stone walls teams up with contemporary design and inviting pool facilities.

Tradition trifft auf Moderne — zur Veranda aus Holz und offenen Steinmauern gesellen sich zeitgenössisches Design und einladende Poolanlagen.

La tradition croise le moderne — à la véranda en bois et aux murs en pierres apparentes viennent se joindre un design contemporain et des piscines attrayants.

La tradición se combina con la modernidad. Al mirador de madera y los muros de piedra abiertos se le unen el diseño contemporáneo y las atractivas instalaciones de la piscina.

La tradizione incontra la modernità — con la veranda in legno e le mura aperte in pietra — si combina un design comtemporaneo ad una piscina molto invitante.

Pure colonial style and canopy beds—19 suites and rooms are scattered in six buildings and cottages across the park-like premises.

Purer Kolonialstil und Himmelbetten – 19 Suiten und Zimmer sind in sechs Gebäuden und Cottages über das parkartige Gelände verstreut.

Un style colonial typique et des lits à baldaquin – 19 suites et chambres sont réparties dans six bâtiments et cottages disséminés sur le terrain aménagé en parc.

Al puro estilo colonial y con camas con dosel, las 19 suites y habitaciones se reparten en seis edificios y casas rurales sobre el terreno ajardinado.

Puro stile coloniale e letti a baldacchino – 19 suite e camere distribuite in sei edifici e cottage in un terreno simile ad un parco.

Le Sereno

St. Barthélemy, Caribbean

An intimate, elegant beachfront sanctuary with only 37 exquisitely furnished suites that are placed directly on the 600 feet of beach that overlooks the picturesque turquoise cove called Grand Cul-de Sac. The famed Parisian interior designer Christian Liaigre created sleek villas with stylishly minimal taupe and cream furnishings with straight lines, white fabrics, and dark warm woods that evoke a relaxed St. Barths feel.

Ein intimer, eleganter Ruheort am Meer mit nur 37 exquisit eingerichteten Suiten, die direkt auf dem 183 Meter breiten Strand liegen, von dem aus die malerische türkise Bucht namens Grand Cul-de Sac überblickt werden kann. Der berühmte Pariser Innenarchitekt Christian Liaigre entwarf schicke Villen mit stilvoller minimalistischer, gradliniger Einrichtung in Taupe und Cremefarbe, mit weißen Stoffen und dunklen warmen Hölzern, die ein entspanntes St.-Barths-Gefühl hervorrufen.

Un sanctuaire intime et élégant sur la côte, ne disposant que de 37 suites aménagées de façon exquises et situées directement au-dessus des 183 mètres de plage de la baie turquoise picturale appelée Grand Cul-de-Sac. Le fameux designer d'intérieur parisien Christian Liaigre a créé des villas avec un mobilier d'un style minimaliste taupe et crème à lignes pures, des tissus blancs et des bois foncés qui évoquent un feeling détendu de St. Barths.

Un lugar de descanso elegante e íntimo que sólo posee 37 suites decoradas exquisitamente que están situadas directamente en la playa de 183 metros, desde la que se ve la pintoresca bahía color turquesa llamada Grand Cul-de Sac. El famoso arquitecto de interiores Christian Liaigre diseñó estas villas de paredes lisas y su decoración reposada y minimalista que se basa en colores marrones y crema, líneas rectas, tejido blanco y maderas de colores oscuros y cálidos que emanan la sensación de calma de St. Barths.

Un rifugio intimo ed elegante con 37 suite arredate in maniera squisita e situato sui 183 metri di spiaggia che si affacciano sulla costa turchese e pittoresca chiamata Grand Cul-de Sac. Il famoso designer d'interni parigino, Christian Liaigre, ha ideato delle ville geometriche con arredi lineari in stile minimalista nei toni del grigio e della crema, con tessuti bianchi e legni scuri e caldi che rimandano al relax di San Bartolomeo.

Le Sereno is like St. Barths itself, a forever fashionable, magical contradiction of simplicity and luxury, and an incredible blend of both modern style and serenity.

Le Sereno ist, wie St. Barths selbst, ein ewiger eleganter, magischer Widerspruch von Einfachheit und Luxus, und eine unglaubliche Mischung von sowohl modernem Stil als auch Ruhe.

Le Sereno est comme St. Barths : une contradiction toujours à la mode et magique de simplicité et de luxe, et un mariage incroyable d'un style moderne et de sérénité.

Al igual que el mismo St. Barths, Le Sereno es una contradicción elegante, mágica y eterna entre la sencillez y el lujo, así como una mezcla increíble de tranquilidad y estilo moderno.

Il Le Sereno rispecchia San Bartolomeo nella magicità di una continua contraddizione tra la semplicità e il lusso, e nell'incredibile equilibrio tra la frenesia moderna e la tranquillità.

Luxurious, spacious suites feature a generously sized living area with a sofa bed, a large wooden coffee table, a four poster bed, and a wooden deck.

Luxuriöse, geräumige Suiten bieten einen großzügigen Wohnraum mit Bettsofa, einem großen hölzernen Kaffeetisch, einem Himmelbett und einer Dachterrasse aus Holz.

Les suites spacieuses et luxueuses disposent d'un grand séjour avec un canapé, une grande table de thé en bois, un lit à baldaquin et une terrasse en bois.

Sus suites lujosas y amplias ofrecen un generoso espacio habitable compuesto por un sofá cama, una gran mesa de café de madera, una cama con dosel y una terraza de madera en el techo.

Le suite lussuose e spaziose offrono un soggiorno dalle dimensioni generose, con il pavimento in legno, dotate di un divano-letto, un amplio tavolino in legno e un letto a baldacchino.

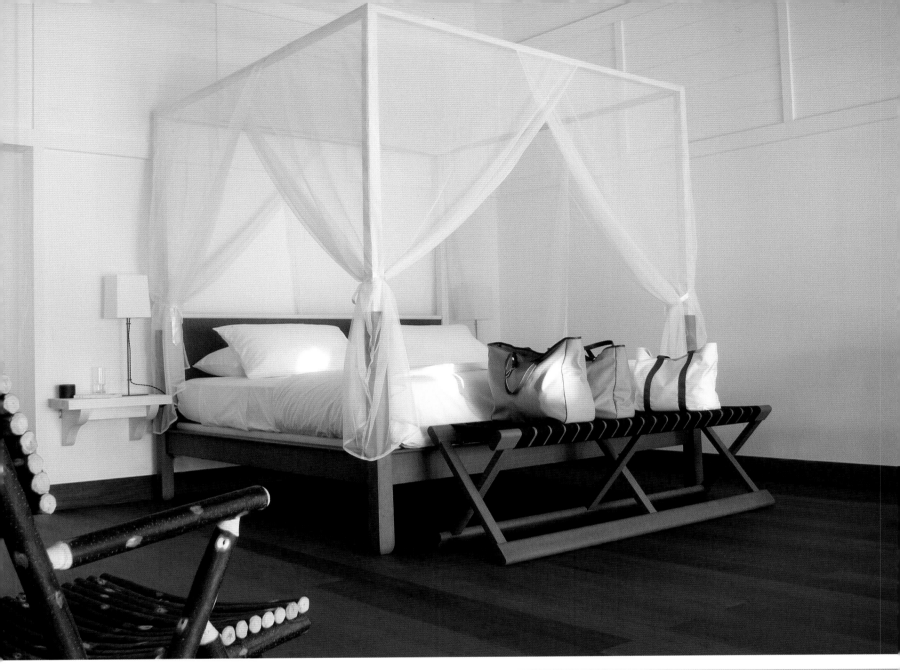

Las Ventanas al Paraíso
A Rosewood Resort

Los Cabos, Mexico

This authentic hacienda-style hotel is a flower-filled oasis of meandering waterways that spill through a series of ponds. Architectural features of rough stone, thatched roofs, and wrought-iron touches meets high-end indulgence. 71 spacious beachfront suites have handcrafted platform beds, terracotta fireplaces, and a large whirlpool with ocean views.

Dieses authentische Hotel im Hazienda-Stil ist eine Oase voller Blumen mit sich mäandernden Wasserwegen, die sich in einer Reihe von Teichen ergießen. Architektonische Merkmale wie Ziegelstein, Reetdächer und schmiedeeiserne Teile treffen auf High-End-Luxus. 71 geräumige zum Strand hin gelegene Suiten sind mit handgefertigten Betten auf Podesten, Terrakotta-Kaminen und einem großen Whirlpool mit Meeresblick ausgestattet.

Cet hôtel dans le style d'une authentique hacienda est un oasis fleuri de petits ruisseaux coulant à travers une série de bassins. Une architecture de pierre brute, de toits couverts de chaume, et d'éléments en fer forgé rencontre ici une indulgence de première catégorie. Les 71 suites face à la mer sont équipées de lits à plateformes fabriqués à la main, de cheminées en terre cuite et d'une grande piscine balnéo avec une vue sur la mer.

Este hotel auténtico, que evoca un estilo tipo hacienda, es un oasis repleto de flores y meandros que desembocan en una serie de lagunas. Algunas de sus características arquitectónicas como el ladrillo, los tejados de caña y piezas de acero forjado contrastan con el lujo absoluto. Sus 71 suites, que dan a la playa, son amplias y están diseñadas con plataformas de madera hechas a mano y chimeneas de terracota y una gran piscina de burbujas tiene vistas al mar.

Questo hotel, in autentico stile hacienda, è un'oasi piena di fiori in cui i corsi d'acqua serpeggiano da uno stagno ad un altro. L'architettura caratterizzata da pietre grezze, paglia, e lavorazioni in ferro battuto soddisfa la clientela più raffinata. Le 71 spaziose suites per gli ospiti, di fronte alla spiaggia, hanno letti fatti a mano, camini in cotto rustico, ed un grande idromassaggio con vista sull'oceano.

An open-air lounge affords vistas of stone terraces descending into the boulder-laden shoreline of miles of deserted beach.

Eine Freiluftlounge bietet einen Blick auf Steinterrassen, die auf die felsige Küste mit vielen Meilen verlassenem Strand hinabführen.

Un lounge à ciel ouvert offre une vue sur les terrasses en pierre qui descendent vers la côte couverte de rochers et des kilomètres de plages désertes.

El lounge al aire libre ofrece vistas a las terrazas de piedra que cuelgan sobre la costa rocosa de varias millas de playa abandonada.

Una lounge all'aperto offre una magnifica vista sulle terrazze rocciose che scendono fino agli scogli lungo chilometri di spiaggia deserta.

This jewel resort is a secluded desert setting with a serpentine network of infinity edge pools that disappear into the horizon.

Dieses schmucke Resort ist ein abgelegener Ort in Wüstenumgebung mit einem serpentinenartigen Netz von unendlich erscheinenden randlosen Überlaufpools, die sich am Horizont verlieren.

Ce joyau est situé dans un environnement désertique isolé et dispose d'un réseau de petits bassins qui s'étirent jusqu'à l'horizon.

Este bello resort es un lugar retirado en el entorno del desierto, con una red serpenteante de infinitas piscinas sin bordes que se pierden en el horizonte.

Questo resort gioiello, isolato e tranquillo, ha una fitta rete di piscine dal bordo sfioratore che sembrano sparire nell'orizzonte.

One&Only Palmilla

Los Cabos, Mexico

As the name suggests, this lushly landscaped property is overflowing with towering palms on a rocky promontory overlooking the Sea of Cortez. This oceanfront hacienda style resort reflects Old World architectural design with its red-tiled roofs, mosaic tile, and whitewashed stucco. Low-slung buildings are scattered throughout the exquisite gardens and vanishing ponds. The Spa is a 25,000-square-foot haven where consultants provide each guest with a personalized program.

Wie der Name schon vermuten lässt, wachsen auf diesem mit vielen Pflanzen verschönerten Grundstück haushohe Palmen auf einem Felsvorsprung, von dem aus man die Cortez-See überblicken kann. Dieses direkt am Meer gelegene Resort im Hazienda-Stil spiegelt die architektonische Bauweise der Alten Welt mit den mit roten Ziegeln gedeckten Dächern, Mosaikkacheln und weiß getünchtem Stuck wider. Niedrige Gebäude sind in die exquisiten Gärten und zwischen die sich in der Ferne verlierenden Teiche eingebettet. Das Wellness-Center ist eine 2320 m² große Oase, in der Betreuer jedem Gast ein persönliches Programm bieten.

Comme le nom l'indique, cette propriété luxueuse dispose d'une palmeraie aménagée sur un promontoire rocheux au-dessus de la Mer de Cortez. Ce lieu de villégiature en bord de mer tenu dans le style d'une hacienda reflète une architecture de l'ancien monde avec ses toits à tuiles rouges, ses mosaïques de terres cuites et ses stucs blanchis à la chaux. Des bâtiments bas sont éparpillés parmi les jardins exquis et les bassins cachés. L'espace balnéo est un havre de 2320 m² dans lequel des spécialistes préparent pour chaque hôte un programme personnalisé.

Como su propio nombre indica, en este terreno, embellecido por muchas plantas, crecen enormes palmeras sobre un saliente rocoso desde el que se ve el Mar de Cortez. Este resort tipo hacienda, que situado frente al mar, refleja el estilo arquitectónico del viejo mundo con sus tejados de teja roja, sus mosaicos de loseta y su estuco enlucido. Los edificios bajos están dispersos entre jardines exquisitos y estanques que desaparecen. El Wellness Center es un oasis de 2320 m², en el que los especialistas ofrecen a cada huésped un programa personalizado.

Come suggerisce il nome, questa proprietà, dalla natura rigogliosa è ricoperta da palme alte come torri che si estendono su di un promontorio roccioso sul Mare di Cortez. Questo resort di fronte all'oceano, in stile hacienda, riflette il design architettonico del Vecchio Mondo con i suoi tetti di mattoncini rossi, mattonelle a mosaico, e gesso. Edifici bassi si estendono lungo deliziosi giardini e stagni. Il centro benessere è un paradiso di 2320 m² dove degli esperti propongono programmi personalizzati per ciascun ospite.

A personal butler is part of the service in the 172 casually elegant rooms and suites and, depending on the time of year, a telescope for whale watching.

Zum Service der 172 leger-eleganten Zimmer und Suiten gehört ein persönlicher Butler und je nach Jahreszeit ein Teleskop zum Beobachten von Walen.

Chacune des 172 chambres et suites, à l'élégance légère, dispose d'un majordome personnel et, selon la saison, d'un télescope pour l'observation des baleines.

Las 172 habitaciones y suites de toque elegante y fresco, incluyen en el servicio un mayordomo y, dependiendo de la estación, un telescopio para observar las ballenas.

Del servizio delle 172 camere e suite, arredate in stile semplice ed elegante, fa parte un maggiordomo personale e, a seconda della stagione, un telescopio per osservare le balene.

Each of the 172 guest rooms completes the gracious style of Old Mexico with its travertine floors, hand-crafted furniture, and marble bathtubs.

Jedes der 172 Gästezimmer komplettiert den anmutigen Stil des Alten Mexiko mit Travertinböden, handgefertigten Möbeln und Marmorbadewannen.

Chacune des 172 chambres ajoute au style gracieux de l'ancienne Mexique par ses sols en travertin, ses meubles fabriqués à la main et ses baignoires en marbre.

Cada una de las 172 habitaciones completa el diseño, que recuerda al viejo México por sus suelos de mármol travertino, sus muebles hechos a mano y sus bañeras de mármol.

Ognuna delle 172 camere per gli ospiti completa lo stile grazioso del vecchio Messico con i suoi pavimenti in travertino, gli arredamenti fatti a mano e le vasche da bagno in marmo.

A private beach stretches below the infinity-edge pool, with lounge chairs laid out for those perfect afternoon siestas in the sun.

Ein privater Strand, auf dem sich Clubstühle für ein perfektes Nachmittagsschläfchen in der Sonne befinden, erstreckt sich unter dem Überlaufpool.

Une plage privée s'étire sous la piscine apparemment sans limites, dont les fauteuils sont à la disposition des hôtes désireux de profiter d'une siesta parfaite au soleil.

Una playa privada se extiende bajo la piscina sin bordes. Las sillas del club son ideales para echarse una siesta al sol.

Una spiaggia privata si estende sotto la piscina dal bordo sfioratore ed offre sdraio – perfette per la siesta sotto il sole.

Las Alamandas

Puerto Vallarta, Mexico

The actual luxury of this hotel is the complete silence and seclusion awaiting the guest. A mere 15 suites are spread across grounds of over 1500 acres. A tropical park with lagoons and exotic birds tempt one to enjoy long walks, a white beach to bathe in the pacific, and for those wanting to travel with a private airplane will even find a hotel-own landing strip. The restaurant offers local specialties, whereby much of the fruit and vegetables are grown on the hotel premises.

Der eigentliche Luxus dieses Hotels ist die völlige Ruhe und Abgeschiedenheit, die den Gast erwartet. Nur 15 Suiten verteilen sich auf einem Gelände von über 600 Hektar. Eine tropische Parkanlage mit Lagunen und exotischen Vögeln lädt zu ausführlichen Spaziergängen ein, ein weißer Strand zum Baden im Pazifik, und wer mit dem Privatflugzeug anreisen möchte, findet sogar eine hoteleigene Landepiste vor. Das Restaurant bietet lokale Spezialitäten, wobei ein großer Teil des Obstes und Gemüses auf dem Hotelgelände angebaut wird.

Le vrai luxe de cet hôtel, c'est la tranquillité et l'isolement total qui attendent l'hôte. 15 suites seulement se partagent un terrain de plus de 600 hectares. Un parc tropical avec des lagunes et des oiseaux exotiques invitent à de longues promenades, une plage de sable fin à se baigner dans le Pacifique et celui qui souhaiterait voyager avec son avion privé trouvera même une piste d'atterrissage appartenant à l'hôtel. Le restaurant propose des spécialités locales, la plupart des fruits et des légumes étant cultivés sur le terrain de l'hôtel.

El verdadero lujo de este hotel es la total tranquilidad y el aislamiento que esperan al huésped. Tan sólo 15 suites se encuentran repartidas en un área de más de 600 hectáreas. Un recinto tropical con lagunas y aves exóticas invita a hacer largos paseos; una playa blanca, a bañarse, y, el que quiere viajar con su avión particular, puede incluso aterrizar en la pista de aterrizaje del hotel. El restaurante ofrece especialidades de la región, entre las que se cuentan frutas y verduras que en gran parte se cultivan en el terreno del hotel.

Il vero lusso di questo hotel sta nell'assoluta tranquillità e solitudine che aspettano l'ospite. Solo 15 suite si distribuiscono su un terreno di 600 ettari. Il parco tropicale, con lagune ed uccelli esotici, invita a fare lunghe passeggiate, la spiaggia bianca a fare il bagno nel Pacifico e per chi volesse arrivare con l'areo privato si trova persino una pista di atterraggio nell'albergo. Il ristorante offre specialità locali e una gran parte di frutta e verdura è coltivata nei campi di proprietà dell'hotel.

The terraces offer ideal conditions for undisturbed recreation.

Die Terrassen bieten ein Maximum an ungestörter Erholung.

Les terrasses permettent de se détendre sans être dérangé.

Las terrazas ofrecen la posibilidad de descansar al máximo y sin molestias.

Le terrazze offrono il massimo del riposo indisturbato.

*The **powerful** fresh colors are a hallmark of the hotel.*

*Die **kräftigen** frischen Farben sind ein Markenzeichen des Hotels.*

*Les **peintures** vives et récentes sont la marque de fabrique de l'hôtel.*

*Los **colores** fuertes y vivaces son una característica distintiva del hotel.*

*I **colori** forti e freschi rappresentano la caratteristica dell'hotel.*

El Tamarindo

Costalegre, Mexico

A rainforest resort on the Costalegre's southern fringe set on a 8,25-square kilometer ecological preserve. This exclusive Mexican hideaway hotel has 29 thatched-roof bungalows that blend with the untamed beauty of the seaside tropical forest. Each serene villa has a crocheted white hammock next to its own private serpentine pool to achieve the perfect relaxing environment.

Ein Regenwaldresort am südlichen Rand der Costalegre auf einem 8,25 km² großen Naturschutzgebiet. Dieses exklusive mexikanische Hotelrefugium hat 29 reetgedeckte Bungalows, die sich mit der wilden Schönheit des Tropenwaldes an der Küste mischen. Jede der ruhigen Villen hat eine grobmaschige weiße Hängematte am eigenen, privaten Serpentinenpool, um eine perfekt entspannende Umgebung zu schaffen.

Un lieu de villégiature tropical sur le bord Sud de la Costalegre, situé dans une réserve écologique de 8,25 kilomètre carré. Cet hôtel mexicain exclusif et dissimulé dispose de 29 bungalows à toits de chaume qui s'intègrent parfaitement dans la beauté sauvage de la forêt tropicale du bord de mer. Chacune de ces villas sereines est équipée d'un hamac blanc à proximité de sa piscine privée en méandres afin de parfaire un environnement d'un relaxant exquis.

Un resort en el bosque lluvioso en la franja sureña de Costalegre, situada en una reserva integral de 8,25 km². Este exclusivo refugio mexicano tiene 29 bungalows cubiertos con teja, que se mezclan con la belleza indómita de la selva tropical costera. Cada una de las tranquilas villas tiene una hamaca de malla blanca en su propia piscina privada para conseguir el efecto de un entorno tranquilo.

Un resort nella foresta pluviale, lungo la punta sud di Costalegre, sito in una riserva ecologica di circa 8,25 chilometro quadrato. Questo hotel messicano esclusivo e riservato conta 29 bungalow dal tetto di paglia che si fondono nella bellezza incontaminata della foresta tropicale all'interno del contesto marittimo. In ogni villa si trova un'amaca bianca e intrecciata ad uncinetto, vicino alla propria piscina per godere della massima tranquillità.

A special treatment under the palms at the jungle spa, or in one of their beachfront cabañas, will transport you to another world.

Eine spezielle Behandlung unter Palmen im Dschungel-Wellness-Center oder in einer der Strandhütten entführt Sie in eine andere Welt.

Un traitement spécial sous les palmiers du Jungle Spa ou dans l'une des cabañas du bord de mer vous transporte dans un autre monde.

Un tratamiento especial bajo las palmeras en el centro de wellness de la jungla o en una de las cabañas de la playa le transportará a otro mundo.

Un trattamento speciale sotto le palme del centro benessere dentro la giungla, oppure in una delle cabaña di fronte alla spiaggia, vi trasporterà su un altro pianeta.

The spa's signature treatment is the cleaning ritual Temascal. Guests apply an herbal healing mud wrap while resting in an igloo constructed of clay bricks.

Die Behandlung, für die das Wellness-Center bekannt ist, ist das Reinigungsritual Temascal. Den Gästen wird eine Fangopackung aus Heilkräutern aufgelegt, während sie in einem Lehmziegeliglu sitzen.

L'élément emblématique du traitement balnéaire est le rituel de nettoyage Temascal. Les hôtes appliquent un bain de boue à plantes médicinales sur leur peau tandis qu'ils se reposent dans un igloo construit en briques d'argile.

El tratamiento característico del centro de wellness es el Temascal, un ritual de purificación, mediante el cual se impregna a los huéspedes fango hecho de hierbas curativas, mientras están sentados en una cabaña de adobe.

Il trattamento esclusivo del centro benessere è rappresentato dal rituale di pulizia Temascal. Gli ospiti vengono avvolti in un impacco di fanghi di alghe curative mentre si rilassano in un igloo costruito con dei mattoni di argilla.

Ikal del Mar

Riviera Maya, Mexico

"Respect nature" represents the motto of this boutique resort north of Playa del Carmen. Its 30 villas are intended to visually melt into the surrounding jungle; the paths were laid out so that no older tree had to give way. They wind in a meandering form through the estate. At night, the outdoor facilities are not illuminated with artificial light that could disturb the view of the starry sky, but with torches. All the villas were erected with wood and stone from the region.

Respekt vor der Natur ist das Motto dieses Boutique-Resorts nördlich von Playa del Carmen. Seine 30 Villen sollen optisch mit dem umgebenden Dschungel verschmelzen; die Wege wurden so angelegt, dass kein alter Baum weichen musste. Sie winden sich mäanderförmig durch das Anwesen. Bei Nacht werden die Außenanlagen nicht mit Kunstlicht beleuchtet, das den Blick auf den Sternenhimmel stören könnte, sondern mit Fackeln. Alle Villen wurden mit Holz und Stein aus der Region errichtet.

Le respect de la nature est le thème de cet hôtel-boutique, au Nord de Playa del Carmen. Ses 30 villas se fondent visuellement dans la jungle environnante ; les chemins ont été tracés de façon à préserver les vieux arbres. Ils dessinent un méandre à travers la propriété. Le soir, les espaces extérieurs ne sont pas éclairés artificiellement mais par des flambeaux afin de ne pas gêner l'oeil perdu dans la contemplation des étoiles. Toutes les villas ont été construites à partir du bois et des pierres de la région.

El lema de este resort tipo boutique al norte de Playa del Carmen es el respeto por la naturaleza. Sus 30 chalés se funden visualmente con la selva que los rodea. Los senderos que serpentean a través del recinto, están diseñados de tal manera que no hubo necesidad de quitar ningún árbol antiguo. Por la noche las zonas exteriores se iluminan con antorchas y no con luz artificial, ya que ésta podría perturbar la vista del cielo lleno de estrellas. Todos los chalés han sido construidos en madera y piedra de la región.

Il rispetto per la natura è il motto per questo centro residenziale esclusivo a nord di Playa del Carmen. Le sue 30 ville si confondono con la giungla circostante; i sentieri sono stati tracciati in modo da non dover sradicare vecchi alberi. S'intrecciano a meandri attraverso la tenuta. Di notte gli impianti esterni non sono illuminati con la luce artificiale che potrebbe disturbare lo sguardo nel cielo stellato, ma con le fiaccole. Tutte le ville sono state costruite con legno e pietre locali.

In complete seclusion amidst nature, such elementary things as sun, wind, and shade can be consciously experienced.

In völliger Zurückgezogenheit, mitten in der Natur, lassen sich so elementare Dinge wie Sonne, Wind und Schatten bewusst erleben.

Dans cet isolement total, au milieu de la nature, des éléments aussi simples que le soleil, le vent et l'ombre deviennent perceptibles.

En el total aislamiento en medio de la naturaleza se viven a conciencia las cosas más elementales: El sol, el viento y la sombra.

In assoluta solitudine, in mezzo alla natura, gli elementi naturali come il sole, il vento e l'ombra si possono godere con tutti i sensi.

"Ikal del Mar" translated means *"Poetry of the Sea".* Each luxurious hut is dedicated to a different poet.

"Ikal del Mar" bedeutet übersetzt *"Poesie des Meeres".* Jede Luxushütte des Resorts ist einem anderen Dichter gewidmet.

« Ikal del Mar » signifie *« poésie de la mer ».* Chacune des luxueuses cabanes du domaine est dédiée à un poète.

"Ikal del Mar" significa *"poesía del mar".* Todas las cabañas de lujo del resort están dedicadas a un poeta diferente.

"Ikal del Mar" significa *"poesie del mare".* Ogni capanna di lusso del resort è dedicata ad un poeta.

Faena Hotel + Universe

Buenos Aires, Argentina

The entrance already bears resemblance to a cathedral. Alan Faena, founder of the fashion label Via Vai, created a previously unparalleled lifestyle universe for Buenos Aires from an old silo. A hint of Belle Époque blends in with the design by Philippe Starck—recognizable in the white-gold pomp of the bistro and the furniture. The hotel provides a complete area for exquisite lifestyle: a stage, spa, boutique, pool bar, and noble rooms for special events.

Bereits das Entree wirkt wie eine Kathedrale. Alan Faena, Gründer des Modelabels Via Vai, erschuf aus einem alten Getreidespeicher ein für Buenos Aires bisher einmaliges Lifestyle-Universum. In das Design von Philippe Starck mischt sich ein Hauch von Belle Époque – sichtbar am weiß-goldenen Pomp des Bistros und dem Mobiliar. Das Hotel stellt ein komplettes Areal für ein Leben der Extraklasse dar: mit Bühne, Spa, Boutique, Poolbar und edel anmutenden Räumen für besondere Events.

L'entrée fait déjà l'effet d'une cathédrale. Alan Faena, fondateur du label de mode Via Vai, a transformé un ancien dépôt de céréales en un univers Lifestyle jusqu'à présent unique à Buenos Aires. Au design de Philippe Starck s'ajoute un soupçon de Belle Epoque, décelable dans le faste blanc et or du bistro et du mobilier. L'hôtel est un espace complet dédié à une vie de première classe : il dispose d'un théâtre, d'un spa, d'une boutique, d'un bar à proximité de la piscine et de salles élégantes destinées à des événements spéciaux.

La entrada misma parece una catedral. Alan Faena, fundador de la marca Via Vai, creó, desde un viejo almacén de grano, un universo que ha marcado un estilo de vida hasta ahora único para Buenos Aires. En el diseño de Philippe Starck se mezcla un matiz de la Belle Époque que se aprecia en la pompa blanca y dorada del pequeño restaurante y del mobiliario. El hotel representa un área completa para una vida de clase extra: escenario, spa, boutique, bar en la piscina y espacios nobles y elegantes para los eventos especiales.

Entrando sembra di arrivare in una cattedrale. Alan Faena, fondatore del marchio Via Vai, ha ricavato da un vecchio granaio un universo del lifestyle unico per Buenos Aires. Nel design di Philippe Starck si fonde un soffio di Belle Époque – visibile dalla pompa bianco-dorata del bistrò e dalla mobilia. L'hotel rappresenta un areale completo per una vita di prima classe: con palcoscenico, centro benessere, boutique, bar sulla piscina e stanze con un tocco di nobiltà per avvenimenti speciali.

Royal red-white is predominant in the more than 100 rooms and suites.

Königliches Rot-Weiß dominiert die über 100 Zimmer und Suiten.

Les couleurs royales, le rouge et le blanc, sont prédominantes dans la centaine de chambres et de suites.

Dominan el blanco y el rojo royal en las más de 100 habitaciones y suites.

Un rosso-bianco reale domina nelle più di 100 camere e suite.

*A **regal** reception—the central aisle of the brick-built structure extends to a height of ten meters.*

*Ein **großer** Empfang – das zehn Meter hohe Mittelschiff des Backsteingebäudes.*

*Un **hall** d'accueil grandiose qui affiche dix mètres de hauteur constitue la nef centrale du bâtiment en briques.*

*Una **gran** entrada –la nave central de diez metros de altura del edificio de ladrillo.*

*Una **grande** reception si trova nella "navata centrale" e alta dieci metri dell'edificio in mattoni a vista.*

Alvear Palace

Buenos Aires, Argentina

When it comes to awards from the world's big magazines, this palace hotel is at the very top. Nonetheless, the hotel is among the most pompous that Latin America has to offer. The opulence of the décor spans from the marble bathrooms to the gold mirrors. The European elegance is cultivated in the spirit of the empire. The restaurant La Bourgogne delights with its excellent cuisine and the chic spa complex offers "balsam" for the soul.

Geht es nach den Auszeichnungen durch die großen Magazine der Welt, dann nimmt dieses Palasthotel einen absoluten Spitzenrang ein. Doch ungeachtet dessen gehört das Haus auch so mit zum Prunkvollsten, was Lateinamerika zu bieten hat. Die Opulenz in der Ausstattung reicht von Marmorbädern bis hin zu Goldspiegeln. Gepflegt wird europäische Eleganz im Geiste des Empire. Das Restaurant La Bourgogne verwöhnt mit einer exzellenten Küche und der schicke Spa-Komplex bietet Balsam für die Seele.

Si l'on considère les prix attribués par les grands magazines du monde entier, ce palace occupe une place de tout premier choix. Mais même sans cela, cet hôtel compte parmi ce que l'Amérique Latine à de plus fastueux à offrir. L'opulence des équipements s'étend des salles de bains en marbre jusqu'aux miroirs en or. L'élégance à l'européenne particulièrement soignée s'inspire du style Empire. Le Restaurant La Bourgogne offre à ses hôtes une cuisine excellente et les installations balnéaires leur promettent une détente absolue.

Si se tienen en cuenta los reconocimientos de las grandes revistas internacionales, este hotel tiene el rango absoluto de hotel de primera clase. Si no se tienen en cuenta, este hotel pertenece igualmente a los más suntuosos de los que se encuentran en América Latina. La opulencia de la decoración abarca desde las bañeras de mármol hasta los espejos de oro. Se promueve la elegancia europea inmersa en el espíritu del imperio. El restaurante La Bourgogne colma al huésped con una cocina excelente y las elegantes instalaciones del spa le ofrecen una cura para el alma.

Se si considerano le critiche da parte delle grandi riviste del mondo, allora questo hotel-palazzo ricopre una posizione di assoluto prestigio. Ma oltre a ciò l'edificio è anche tra i più sfarzosi di quelli che l'America Latina può offrire. L'opulenza nell'arredamento va dai bagni in marmo fino agli specchi dorati. Si coltiva un'eleganza europea, in spirito imperiale. Il ristorante La Bourgogne vi vizierà con una cucina eccellente e un complesso elegante per il benessere: entrambi un vero piacere per l'anima.

The entrance is second to no other palace entrance. The elegance is lodged in the detail.

Das Entree steht einem Palasteingang in nichts nach. Die Eleganz steckt im Detail.

L'entrée n'a rien à envier à l'entrée d'un palais. L'élégance se manifeste dans tous les détails.

La entrada no tiene nada que envidiar a la entrada de un palacio. La elegancia se esconde en cada detalle.

L'entrata non ha nulla da invidiare all'entrata di un palazzo. L'eleganza risiede nel dettaglio.

The palace hotel combines the manorial style of the empire with baroque elements.

Das Palasthotel vereint den herrschaftlichen Stil des Empires mit Elementen des Barock.

Le palace concilie le style noble de l'Empire avec des éléments baroques.

Este hotel palacio aúna el estilo majestuoso del imperio con elementos del barroco.

Il hotel-palazzo unisce lo stile signorile imperiale con elementi barocchi.

Emiliano

São Paulo, Brazil

This narrow, architecturally impressive building towers high in the São Paulo skyline. Located in the heart of the city's most fashionable district alongside designer-label boutiques and international banks, it features 38 spacious rooms and 19 even larger suites in the building's upper levels. Highlights include the classical modern restaurant that serves exquisite Italian cuisine and the striking hotel bar. A top-floor spa offers relaxing indulgences and stunning views of the city below.

Das schmale, architektonisch eindrucksvolle Gebäude ragt wie ein Fingerzeig auf. Es liegt mitten im besten Viertel von São Paulo – dort, wo sich die Designläden und Banken der Welt präsentieren. Im oberen Teil des Gebäudes ist das Hotel mit 38 großen Zimmern und 19 noch größeren Suiten untergebracht. Glanzstücke der Adresse sind das klassisch-moderne Restaurant mit feiner italienischer Küche sowie die Bar mit ungewöhnlichem Design. Als einzigartig erweist sich zudem der Ausblick auf São Paulo beim Relaxen in dem Spa in der obersten Etage.

Le bâtiment étroit à l'architecture impressionnante se dresse comme s'il souhaitait indiquer son emplacement. Il se trouve au beau milieu du meilleur quartier de São Paulo, là où les boutiques design et les banques mondiales sont représentés. Dans la partie supérieure du bâtiment, l'hôtel comprend 38 grandes chambres et 19 suites encore plus spacieuses. Les joyaux de cette adresse sont le restaurant de style classique et moderne avec sa délicieuse cuisine italienne, ainsi que le bar affichant un design insolite. En outre, la vue sur São Paulo que nous offre le spa du dernier étage est incomparable.

Este estrecho e impactante edificio se eleva como si fuera un dedo en alto. Está situado en el mejor barrio de São Paulo, donde se encuentran las boutiques de los diseñadores y los bancos más importantes del mundo. En la parte superior del edificio se sitúa el hotel con 38 habitaciones grandes y 19 suites aún más amplias. Las piezas de mayor atractivo de este hotel son el restaurante típicamente moderno de alta cocina italiana y el bar, de extraordinario diseño. Las vistas desde el relajante spa de la planta superior constituyen una experiencia única.

Il piccolo edificio ma architettonicamente imponente, si erige in posizione strategica nel miglior quartiere di São Paulo, là dove negozi di design e banche internazionali si presentano nella loro veste migliore. Situato ai piani superiori, l'hotel dispone di 38 stanze spaziose e 19 suite di ancor più ampia metratura. Fiore all'occhiello dell'Emiliano sono il ristorante classico-moderno con raffinata cucina italiana e il bar dal design insolito. Notevole la vista panoramica sulla città di cui si può godere in pieno relax dalla Spa, all'ultimo piano.

*The **lobby** of the hotel is marked by contemporary design—spacious and "to-the-point" in the selection of the furniture objects.*

*Die **Lobby** des Hotels ist geprägt von zeitgemäßem Design – weitläufig und pointiert in der Auswahl der Einrichtungsgegenstände.*

*Le **hall** de l'hôtel est dominé par le design contemporain – spacieux et ciblé dans le choix des objets de décoration.*

*El **vestíbulo** del hotel está impregnado del diseño contemporáneo, difuso y acentuado en la elección de los objetos decorativos.*

*La **lobby** dell'hotel è caratterizzata da un design contemporaneo – ampia e arguta nella scelta dei complementi d'arredo.*

The suites spanning 84 m² present themselves in warm shades of wood. The bathrooms are furnished with Carrara marble imported from Italy.

Die 84 m² großen Suiten zeigen sich in warmen Holztönen. Die Bäder sind mit aus Italien importiertem Carrara Marmor ausgestattet.

Les suites d'une superficie de 84 m² sont aménagées dans des tons de bois chaleureux. Les salles de bains sont habillées de marbre de Carrare importé d'Italie.

Las suites de 84 m² se muestran en tonos madera cálidos. Los baños son de mármol de Carrara, importado de Italia.

Le suite, grandi 84 m², sono arredate nei caldi toni del legno. I bagni sono realizzati in marmo di Carrara proveniente dall'Italia.

Swissôtel Krasnye Holmy

Moscow, Russia

Opened only in 2005, the Moscow hotel can already boast numerous international awards for service and design. With its 34 floors and impressive architecture, the building ranks among the highest in Moscow. The City Space Bar & Lounge in the uppermost floor offers a panoramic view of the entire city and is a popular hot spot for the hotel guests and the city's young people. The interior is classical-modern and decorated with clear lines and plenty of wood.

Erst 2005 eröffnet, kann das Moskauer Hotel schon etliche internationale Auszeichnungen für Service und Design vorweisen. Mit seinen 34 Stockwerken und einer beeindruckenden Architektur zählt das Gebäude zu den höchsten in Moskau. Die City Space Bar & Lounge in der obersten Etage bietet einen Panoramablick über die ganze Stadt und ist ein beliebter Hotspot für die Hotelgäste und jungen Leute der Stadt. Das Interieur ist klassisch-modern, und mit klaren Linien und viel Holz ausgestattet.

Bien qu'inauguré seulement en 2005, cet hôtel de Moscou a déjà obtenu de nombreux prix internationaux pour le service et le design. Ses 34 étages et son architecture impressionnante font de ce bâtiment l'un des plus hauts de Moscou. Le City Space Bar & Lounge au dernier étage offre une vue panoramique sur toute la ville et est l'un des lieux favoris des hôtes de l'hôtel et des jeunes de la ville. L'intérieur présente un style à la fois classique et moderne, avec des lignes claires et beaucoup de bois.

Aunque se inauguró en 2005, el hotel moscovita cuenta ya con algunas condecoraciones al servicio y al diseño. Con sus 34 plantas y su impresionante arquitectura, el edificio es uno de los más altos de Moscú. El City Space Bar & Lounge, que se encuentra en la última planta, ofrece una vista panorámica de toda la ciudad y es uno de los puntos de encuentro y entretenimiento preferidos por los huéspedes del hotel y los jóvenes de la ciudad. La decoración interior es clásica, pero a la vez moderna, de líneas claras y contiene mucha madera.

Aperto solo nel 2005 l'hotel moscovita può fregiarsi di numerosi premi internazionali per il servizio ed il design. Con i suoi 34 piani ed un'architettura imponente l'edificio è tra quelli più alti di tutta Mosca. Il City Space Bar & Lounge al piano più alto offre una vista panoramica sull'intera città ed è un amato punto d'incontro per gli ospiti dell'hotel e per i giovani della città. Gli interni sono in stile classico-moderno, e arredati con linee chiare e molto legno..

With its architecture and interior design, the hotel follows the international trend towards clear and reserved elegance.

Mit der Architektur und der Inneneinrichtung folgt das Hotel dem internationalen Trend nach klarer und zurückhaltender Eleganz.

De par son architecture et son aménagement intérieur, l'hôtel suit la tendance internationale actuelle en faveur d'une élégance claire et discrète.

Con su arquitectura y decoración de interiores, el hotel sigue la tendencia internacional hacia una elegancia reservada y clara.

Con la sua architettura ed il suo arredamento interno, l'hotel segue il trend internazionale dell'eleganza sobria e contenuta.

Whether in the rooms and suites or in the public areas of the hotel such as its bars, guests will find an abundance of wood everywhere as well as a discreet selection of colors.

Ob in den Zimmern und Suiten oder in den öffentlichen Hotelbereichen wie den Bars, überall findet man viel Holz und eine dezente Farbwahl.

Que ce soit dans les chambres et les suites ou dans les espaces publics de l'hôtel tels que les bars, le bois et les couleurs discrètes sont partout présents.

La madera y los colores discretos están presentes tanto en las habitaciones y suites como en las áreas del hotel abiertas al público, por ejemplo, en los bares.

Nelle camere o nelle suite oppure nelle zone comuni dell'hotel, come ad es. i bar, si trova molto legno ed un' elegante scelta nei colori.

Hotel Astoria

St. Petersburg, Russia

Paying tribute to the surrounding location makes up part of the principle of the luxury hotels of the Rocco Forte Group. Accordingly, the hotel itself gives off the aura inherent to St. Petersburg as the former capital of the Czar's empire. As the finest address on the square, the hotel offers all the extras one might expect. It appears even more remarkable how ancient Russian craftwork comes to life in the many minute details in the more than 200 rooms, while the white-gray marble from Italy endows the bathrooms with a luxurious radiance.

Tribut zu zollen an den Ort, der sie umgibt, gehört zum Prinzip der Luxushotels der Rocco Forte Gruppe. Dementsprechend verströmt das Hotel selbst jene Aura, die St. Petersburg als früherer Hauptstadt des Zarenreiches innewohnt. Als feinste Adresse am Platz offeriert das Hotel all die zu erwartenden Extras. Bemerkenswerter erscheint, wie in vielen kleinen Details in den über 200 Räumen altes russisches Kunsthandwerk zum Vorschein kommt, während der weißgraue Marmor aus Italien den Badezimmern luxuriösen Glanz verleiht.

La prise en compte du lieu qui les entoure fait partie du principe des hôtels de luxe du Groupe Rocco Forte. Ainsi l'hôtel lui-même répand cette aura qui était jadis l'attribut de St. Petersbourg en tant que capitale de l'empire russe. Etant la meilleure adresse de la ville, l'hôtel se doit d'offrir tous les services supplémentaires escomptés. Il convient de remarquer à quel point les nombreux petits détails dans les quelque 200 chambres font apparaître l'ancien artisanat russe, tandis que le marbre blanc et gris d'Italie souligne le luxe des salles de bains.

Integrarse en el lugar que la rodea es el principio de los hoteles de lujo del Grupo Rocco Forte. En consecuencia, el hotel mismo irradia ese aura que posee San Petersburgo como antigua capital del imperio zarino. Como uno de los lugares más finos de la zona, el hotel ofrece todos los extras que son de esperar. Es notable la manera en que se manifiestan muchos de los pequeños detalles, como se puede ver en las más de 200 salas que poseen antiguas obras de arte rusas hechas a mano, mientras el mármol blanco grisáceo de Italia dota a los cuartos de baño de un lujoso brillo.

Fare emergere i luoghi in cui sorgono è un principio degli hotel di lusso del Gruppo Rocco Forte. Di conseguenza, l'hotel trasmette la magia di San Pietroburgo, ex capitale del regno degli zar. Quale migliore sul mercato, l'hotel offre i più diversi extra che ci si possano immaginare. Degno di maggiore nota è il modo in cui in molti piccoli dettagli si evidenzia l'antico lavoro artigianale artistico presente in più di 200 camere, e il marmo bianco-grigio dall'Italia dona uno splendore lussuoso ai bagni.

The direct view of the St. Isaac's Cathedral represents only one attraction offered by the hotel. The beds with their hand-woven linen and imprinted monograms are an additional surprise.

Die direkte Sicht auf die St. Isaak Kathedrale ist nur ein Reiz, den das Hotel bietet. Die Betten überraschen mit handgewebtem Leinen und eingearbeiteten Monogrammen.

La vue directe sur la cathédrale St. Isaak n'est que l'un des attraits de l'hôtel. Les lits surprennent avec des draps tissés à la main et portant des monogrammes.

Las vistas directas a la Catedral de San Isaac es sólo uno de los atractivos que ofrece este hotel. Las camas sorprenden por sus linos confeccionados a mano y sus monogramas grabados.

La vista diretta sulla cattedrale di S. Isacco rappresenta solo una delle attrazioni dell'hotel. I letti sorprendono grazie al lino lavorato a mano ed ai monogrammi inseriti.

Breakfast is served in the hotel's lobby lounge, which traditionally also includes samovar. The rooms flirt with the style of the 1920s.

In der Lobby-Lounge serviert das Hotel das Frühstück als Büffet, zu dem traditionell auch Samoware gehören. Die Räume spielen mit dem Stil der 20er Jahre.

Dans le lobby-lounge, le petit déjeuner est servi sous la forme d'un buffet, dont font aussi partie les traditionnels samovars. Les salles sont de style années 1920.

En el lobby lounge el hotel sirve el desayuno como un buffet, en el que también se sirve el tradicional samowar. Las salas tienen un toque al estilo de los años veinte.

Nella lobby-lounge l'hotel serve la colazione a buffet, di ciò fanno tradizionalmente parte anche i tipici samovar. Le stanze giocano sullo stile degli anni '20.

Brown's Hotel

London, United Kingdom

Luxurious hotel right in the heart of Mayfair, Brown's occupies eleven historic houses just off Berkeley Square. Its most distinguished feature is the Georgian facade, and the sumptuous interior is reminiscent of an English country manor house. All of its 117 guest rooms have been completely renovated to a more sleek, modern look that varies considerably in decor, but still show a restrained style in decoration and appointments; even the wash basins are antiques.

Ein luxuriöses Hotel im Herzen von Mayfair. Das Brown's umfasst elf historische Häuser, die gleich am Berkeley Square gelegen sind. Sein hervorstechendstes Merkmal ist die Fassade aus Georgianischer Zeit und der prächtige Innenbereich, der an ein englisches Herrenhaus erinnert. Alle 117 Gästezimmer wurden komplett renoviert und haben jetzt ein eleganteres, moderneres Aussehen. In ihrer Ausstattung unterscheiden sie sich deutlich voneinander, doch ist ihnen ein zurückhaltender Dekorations- und Einrichtungsstil zueigen; sogar die Waschbecken sind antik.

Hôtel Luxueux dans le centre de Mayfair, Brown's occupe onze bâtisses historiques à proximité de Berkeley Square. Son élément le plus distingué est la façade géorgienne, et son intérieur somptueux rappelle un manoir de campagne anglais. L'ensemble de ses 117 chambres a été rénové dans un style plus moderne dont les décors varient considérablement, mais restent restreints dans le domaine de la décoration et des facilités ; même les lavabos sont des antiquités.

Un hotel de lujo en el corazón de Mayfair. El Brown's ocupa once casas históricas de la Berkeley Square. Su rasgo más sobresaliente es la fachada de estilo georgiano. Su magnífico interior recuerda a un latifundio inglés. Sus 117 habitaciones han sido renovadas totalmente y ahora poseen un diseño más proporcionado y moderno que aunque muestra diferencias notables, sigue teniendo un estilo reservado en lo referente a la decoración y la disposición. Incluso los lavabos son antiguos.

Hotel di lusso direttamente nel cuore di Mayfair, il Brown's occupa undici palazzi storici nei pressi di Berkeley Square. La sua caratteristica principale è la facciata georgiana dove i suntuosi interni ricordano una casa di campagna padronale inglese. Le 117 camere per gli ospiti sono state tutte completamente ristrutturate ottenendo un look più sobrio e moderno, diverso nel decoro ma continuando a dimostrare uno stile pulito anche negli arredi: persino i lavabi sono pezzi d'antiquariato.

Founded in 1837 by James Brown, the hotel consists of eleven Georgian town houses that are patronized by many notable names.

Das 1837 von James Brown gegründete Hotel besteht aus elf Stadthäusern im georgianischen Stil und beherbergt viele berühmte Persönlichkeiten.

Fondé en 1837 par James Brown, l'hôtel se compose de onze hôtels particuliers qui accueillent de nombreux personnages notables.

El hotel, fundado por James Brown en 1837, comprende once casas de estilo georgiano que fueron patrocinadas por muchas personas célebres.

Fondato nel 1837 da James Brown, l'hotel è composto da undici ville a schiera in stile georgiano, tutte possedute da personaggi importanti.

Interiors are contemporary and have a real sense of style, while retaining much of their original English elegance.

Das Interieur ist zeitgenössisch und verrät ein wirkliches Gespür für Stil, während zugleich viel seiner ursprünglichen englischen Eleganz beibehalten wird.

Les aménagements intérieurs sont contemporains et démontrent un réel sens du style, tout en préservant en grande partie leur élégance anglaise d'origine.

El interior sigue la corriente contemporánea y tiene un verdadero sentido del estilo, aunque también ha mantenido mucha de su elegancia inglesa originaria.

Gli interni sono contemporanei e mostrano vero senso dello stile, mantenendo però intatta gran parte dell'eleganza originale inglese.

The Lanesborough

London, United Kingdom

Ideally located in Knightsbridge, the Lanesborough was restored to its white-stucco grandeur under the supervision of experts and artisans from the Georgian Society, The Royal Fine Arts Commission, and English Heritage. 95 rooms, including 46 suites, incorporate handsome 1820s furnishings: armoires, desks, and selected works of art that blend seamlessly with the modern technology of a contemporary hotel.

Das idyllisch in Knightsbridge gelegene Lanesborough erhielt durch eine Renovierung seine alte Pracht und seinen weißen Stuck unter der Aufsicht von Experten und Künstlern der Georgian Society, der Royal Fine Arts Commission und des English Heritage wieder zurück. Die 95 Zimmer, einschließlich der 46 Suiten, sind mit edlem Mobiliar aus den 1820er Jahren eingerichtet: Kleiderschränke, Schreibtische und ausgewählte Kunstwerke passen sich nahtlos in die moderne Technologie eines zeitgemäßen Hotels ein.

Avec sa situation idyllique à Knightsbridge, le Lanesborough a retrouvé sa grandeur et ses stucs blancs suite à une rénovation réalisée sous l'égide d'experts et d'artisans de la Georgian Societé, de la Royal Fine Arts Commission et de l'English Heritage. 95 chambres, dont 46 suites, contiennent de beaux meubles du style des années 1820 : armoires, bureaux et objets d'arts sélectionnés qui intègrent sans le moindre problème la technologie d'un hôtel moderne.

El Lanesborough, que se encuentra en una zona ideal de Knightsbridge, ha sido renovado hace poco y recuperó la grandeza magnífica blancura de los estucos que se restauraron bajo la supervisión de expertos y artistas de la Georgian Society, la Royal Fine Arts Commission y el English Heritage. En sus 95 habitaciones, incluidas sus 46 suites, se encuentra el elegante mobiliario de la década de 1820: armarios, mesas de escritorio y obras de arte selectas que acompañan a la tecnología de un hotel moderno.

Situato in una posizione ideale a Knightsbridge, Il Lanesborough ha riottenuto il suo antico splendore ed i suoi stucchi bianchi grazie ad una ristrutturazione avvenuta sotto l'egida di esperti e artigiani della Georgian Society, della Royal Fine Arts Commission, e dell'English Heritage. 95 camere, tra cui 46 suite, con arredamenti signorili del 1820: armadi, scrivanie e opere d'arte selezionate che si fondono invisibilmente nella tecnologia moderna di un hotel contemporaneo.

Occupying an enviable position on Hyde Park Corner, this is one of London's most traditional hotels, offering the highest international standards of comfort, quality and security.

Das Hotel liegt an einem beneidenswert günstigen Platz am Hyde Park Corner und ist eines der traditionsreichsten Häuser Londons, das höchste internationale Standards in Komfort, Qualität und Sicherheit bietet.

Occupant une situation enviable sur Hyde Park Corner, le Lanesborough est l'un des hôtels les plus traditionnels de Londres, tout en se conformant aux standards internationaux les plus élevés en matière de confort, de qualité et de sécurité.

El hotel está situado en una zona envidiable de la Hyde Park Corner y es uno de los hoteles más tradicionales, que ofrece el más alto estándar internacional de confort, calidad y seguridad.

Con la sua posizione invidiabile all'angolo di Hyde Park, questo è uno degli hotel più tradizionali di Londra. Offre i più alti standard internazionali in termini di comodità, qualità e sicurezza.

The rich interiors are based on a 19th century town house, with moiré silks and fleurs-de-lis in the colors of precious stones, magnificent antiques, oil paintings, and hand-woven carpet.

Das reich ausgestattete Interieur ist einem Landhaus des 19. Jahrhunderts mit Moiréseiden und Lilien in Edelsteinfarben, wunderbaren Antiquitäten, Ölgemälden und handgewebtem Teppich nachempfunden.

Son aménagement intérieur luxueux est intégré à un hôtel particulier du 19ème siècle, et comprend des soies moirées et à décors de lys en des teintes précieuses, des antiquités superbes, des huiles et des tapis fabriqués à la main.

El interior está decorado generosamente, siguiendo el estilo de una casa rural del siglo XIX con sus sedas moiré, lirios del color de piedras preciosas, antigüedades magníficas y alfombras hechas a mano.

I ricchi interni sono ispirati su una casa a schiera del XIX secolo, con sete ad effetto moiré e aranciato nelle tonalità delle pietre preziose, con antiquariato magnifico, dipinti ad olio e tappeti tessuti a mano.

The Berkeley

London, United Kingdom

The Berkeley is housed in a travertine-faced French Regency-inspired building in Knightsbridge near Hyde Park. The dramatic architecture blends the old and the new in a luxurious, modern building with a splendid rooftop swimming pool. All of the 214 rooms are individually designed in soothing, classic contemporary style; some are spectacular penthouse suites with their own conservatory terraces and others with saunas or balconies.

The Berkeley ist in einem von dem Stil der französischen Régence inspiriertem Gebäude mit Travertinfassade in Knightsbridge nahe des Hyde Parks untergebracht. Die spektakuläre Architektur verbindet Altes mit Neuem zu einem luxuriösen, modernen Gebäude mit einem herrlichen Schwimmbad auf dem Dach. Alle 214 Zimmer sind individuell in einem beruhigenden, klassisch-zeitgenössischen Stil gestaltet worden; darunter sind einige eindrucksvolle Penthousesuiten mit eigenen Wintergartenterrassen, andere haben Saunen oder Balkons.

The Berkeley se trouve dans un bâtiment à Knightsbridge à proximité de Hyde Park, dont la façade en travertin est inspirée du style régence français. L'architecture dramatique marie l'ancien et le récent dans un luxueux immeuble moderne avec une superbe piscine sur le toit. Chacune des 214 chambres a été aménagée individuellement dans un style contemporain reposant et classique ; quelques unes sont des suites de toit spectaculaires avec des terrasses privées, tandis que d'autres disposent de saunas ou de balcons.

El Berkeley se encuentra en un edificio con fachada de mármol traventino inspirado por el estilo de la época de la regencia francesa. Este edificio se encuentra situado en Knightsbridge, cerca del Hyde Park. Su tremenda arquitectura mezcla lo antiguo con lo nuevo en un edificio de lujo, moderno, que posee una piscina cubierta majestosa. Cada una de las 214 habitaciones está decorada con un estilo sereno, clásico pero a la vez contemporáneo. Algunas son impresionantes suites tipo penthouse, que tienen sus propias terrazas con jardín de invierno. Otras tienen sauna o balcón.

Berkeley si trova a Knightsbridge, vicino a Hyde Park, in un edificio dalla facciata in travertino, ispirato al palazzo reale francese. La notevole architettura mischia il vecchio ed il nuovo in un edificio lussuoso e moderno, con una splendida piscina sul tetto. Le 214 camere sono caratterizzate da un design rilassante e personalizzato, classicamente contemporaneo; alcune sono delle spettacolari mansarde con i loro giardini d'inverno e altre hanno saune o balconi.

Several rooms have William Morris prints or Art Deco touches with black-and-white checkerboard floors.

In mehreren Räumen hängen Drucke von William Morris oder ihnen ist ein Hauch von Art déco mit schwarzweißen Schachbrettböden zueigen.

De nombreuses pièces contiennent des reproductions de William Morris ou des touches art déco avec des sols en échiquiers noirs et blancs.

Muchas habitaciones están decoradas con impresiones de William Morris o con un toque a lo art déco en sus suelos, los cuales recuerdan a un tablero de ajedrez.

Molte camere hanno alle pareti stampe di William Morris, o tocchi art déco con pavimenti a scacchiera.

Inside the popular David Collins-designed Blue Bar there is an understated ambiance inspired by Art Deco and French classical precedents, all with a contemporary edge.

In der berühmten, von David Collins entworfenen Blue Bar herrscht eine zurückhaltende, vom Art déco und seinen klassischen französischen Vorläufern inspirierte Atmosphäre, alles mit zeitgenössischem Anklang.

L'ambiance dans le Blue Bar conçu par David Collins est minimaliste et inspirée par l'art déco et des précédents classiques Français, toujours avec un soupçon contemporain.

En el famoso Blue Bar, que fue decorado por David Collins, reina un ambiente atenuado, inspirado por el art déco y los precursores clásicos franceses, todo ello unido en un espacio contemporáneo.

All'interno del popolare Blue Bar, ideato da David Collins, si trova un ambiente da urlo ispirato all'art déco e ai precedenti classici francesi, tutto con una punta di contemporaneità.

Claridge's
London, United Kingdom

A true grand dame on the London hotel circuit situated in the fashionable West End, Claridge's underwent a groundbreaking renovation in 2006. While the changes are extensive, the hotel has retained its turn-of-the-century look and continues to feel more like an elegant apartment building than a hotel. Designed with an elegant blend of Art Deco touches mixed in with Edwardian and French influences, the majestic Claridge's is as splendid today as it was when it first opened its doors in 1854.

Als wahre Grand Dame des Londoner Hotelgewerbes im eleganten West End wurde das Claridge's 2006 grundlegend renoviert. Obwohl die Veränderungen sehr weitreichend waren, hat das Hotel sein Aussehen aus der Zeit der Jahrhundertwende bewahrt und vermittelt immer noch eher das Gefühl eines eleganten Appartement-gebäudes als das eines Hotels. Das majestätische Claridge's ist mit seiner eleganten Mischung aus Art déco mit edwardianischen und französischen Einflüssen heute noch genauso glanzvoll wie 1854, als es erstmals seine Türen öffnete.

Une vraie Grande Dame parmi les hôtels londoniens et situé dans le West End chic, le Claridge's a subi en 2006 une rénovation de fond en combles. Bien que les modifications soient nombreuses, l'hôtel a gardé son look de fin de siècle et ressemble d'avantage à un immeuble d'appartements élégants qu'à un hôtel. Conçu avec un mélange élégant d'art déco et d'influences edwardiennes et françaises, le majestueux Claridge's est aujourd'hui aussi splendide qu'il ne l'a été lorsqu'il a ouvert pour la première fois ses portes en 1854.

Esta verdadera gran dama del sector hotelero londinense, el hotel Claridge's, se encuentra en el elegante West End y fue renovado hasta sus cimientos en el 2006. Aunque las modificaciones fueron muy amplias, el hotel ha conservado su apariencia típica de cambio de siglo y sigue dando la sensación de ser más bien un elegante edificio de apartamentos en lugar de un hotel. El majestuoso Claridge's brilla hoy con su elegante mezcla con toques art déco con influencias francesas y del estilo eduardiano, manteniendo su esplendor de 1854, gual que cuando abrió sus puertas por primera vez.

Un vero signore tra gli hotel londinesi, il The Claridge's, situato nel zona trendy del West End, è stato sottoposto ad un rinnovo straordinario nel 2006. Nonostante le numerose modifiche, l'hotel ha mantenuto intatto il suo look e continua a sembrare più simile ad un palazzo elegante che ad un hotel. Il maestoso The Claridge's, concepito con un elegante miscuglio tra art déco, periodo Edwardiano e arte francese, oggi è splendido come quando aprì, per la prima volta, le sue porte nel 1854.

Guest rooms are designed with exceedingly comfortable beds, elegant linens, chandeliers, and exquisite bathrooms with enormous tubs.

Die Gästezimmer sind mit überaus komfortablen Betten, eleganter Bettwäsche, Kronleuchtern und exquisiten Badezimmern mit riesigen Badewannen ausgestattet.

Les chambres sont équipées de lits extrêmement confortables, de draps élégants, de chandeliers et de salles de bains exquises avec des baignoires énormes.

Las habitaciones están dotadas de camas muy cómodas, ropa de cama elegante, arañas y cuartos de baño exquisitos con bañeras enormes.

Le camere per gli ospiti offrono letti esageratamente comodi, con biancheria elegante, candelabri, e bagni deliziosi con vasche enormi.

Many of the features of the communal areas and the diverse 203 rooms date back to the late 1920s.

Viele der charakteristischen Besonderheiten der Gemeinschaftsbereiche und der unterschiedlichen 203 Zimmer gehen zurück auf die späten 1920er Jahre.

Une bonne partie du mobilier des espaces publics et des 203 chambres diverses date de la fin des années 1920.

Muchos de los rasgos de las salas comunes y de las 203 habitaciones se remontan a finales de los años veinte.

Molte delle parti delle zone comuni e delle 203 camere risalgono alla fine degli anni '20.

The Kildare Hotel, Spa & Country Club

County Kildare, Ireland

The approach through the parkland and estate alone promises a grand entry. Once you step inside the hotel building, you're greeted by a hint of aristocratic past that leaves you feeling a little like the owner of a large country estate. In fact, in the year 550, this Irish country estate was home to the ancestors of King John of England and his brother Richard the Lionheart. Nowadays, international club members and hotel guests occupy the rooms furnished with antiques and precious oil paintings in the spirit of "noblesse oblige". The 555 acre park borders directly on the Liffey river, connecting the resort to the two golf courses designed by Arnold Palmer—and the venue for the 2006 Ryder Cup.

Schon die Auffahrt durch die Parkanlage verspricht einen großen Auftritt. Betritt man das Hotelgebäude, weht dem Besucher der Hauch adliger Vergangenheit entgegen und man fühlt sich selbst ein wenig als Großgrundbesitzer. Tatsächlich war der irische Landsitz im Jahr 550 das Heim der Vorfahren König John's von England und seinem Bruder Richard Löwenherz. Heute bewohnen internationale Clubmitglieder und Hotelgäste die Räume, die gemäß des Anspruchs „Noblesse oblige" mit antikem Mobiliar und kostbaren Ölgemälden ausgestattet sind. Der 225 Hektar große Park grenzt direkt an den Fluss Liffey und verbindet das Resort mit zwei von Arnold Palmer entworfenen Golfplätzen.

L'accès à la demeure à travers le parc promet déjà une grande entrée en scène. En pénétrant dans le bâtiment, l'hôte perçoit le souffle d'une noblesse passée et se sent devenir un peu propriétaire terrien. En effet, cette propriété irlandaise était en 550 la demeure des ancêtres du Roi Jean d'Angleterre et de son frère Richard Coeur de Lion. Aujourd'hui, des membres de clubs internationaux et les hôtes de l'hôtel habitent ces pièces qui, conformément à la devise « Noblesse oblige », abritent des meubles anciens et de précieuses peintures à l'huile. Le parc de 225 hectares longe la rivière Liffey et relie les deux terrains de golf dessinés par Arnold Palmer.

Sólo la entrada a través del parque ya promete grandeza. Y efectivamente, nada más acceder al edificio un aire de noble pasado se apodera del ambiente y lleva incluso a imaginarse ser dueño del lugar. De hecho, en el año 550 el castillo era parte de los dominios irlandeses de los antepasados del rey Juan Sin Tierra de Inglaterra y su hermano Ricardo I Corazón de León. Hoy son miembros del club y huéspedes de todo el mundo los que ocupan las suntuosas habitaciones equipadas con antigüedades y exquisitos lienzos, según los cánones de la "Noblesse oblige". El vasto parque de 225 hectáreas limita con el río Liffey y une los dos campos de golf, diseño de Arnold Palmer, que albergarán la Ryder Cup de 2006.

L'entrata dal parco non deluderà le aspettative. Chi entra nell'hotel, viene colto da un'atmosfera dal nobile passato, e l'ospite si sente un po' protagonista di questo ambiente aristocratico. Effettivamente, nel 550 la tenuta irlandese è stata la dimora degli antenati di re Giovanni d'Inghilterra e di suo fratello Riccardo Cuor di Leone. Oggi soci internazionali del club e ospiti dell'hotel occupano le sale che, rispondendo alle esigenze del motto "Noblesse oblige", sono arredate con mobili antichi e preziosi dipinti ad olio. Il parco, che si estende su 225 ettari, è delimitato dal fiume Liffey e collega il resort con due campi da golf – teatro della Ryder Cup 2006 – progettati da Arnold Palmer.

Although the Irish country estate emanates the venerability of times gone by, it's equipped with every modern comfort.

Der irische Landsitz strahlt zwar Altehrwürdigkeit aus, doch ist er mit modernstem Komfort ausgestattet.

La demeure irlandaise a certes un aspect ancien, mais elle est dotée de tout le confort moderne.

Esta propiedad irlandesa irradia toda la dignidad de tiempos pasados sin despreciar el confort actual.

La tenuta irlandese irradia austerità, ma è dotata di oghi comfort moderno.

A club atmosphere prevails in the library, various salons or the private dining rooms. Antique furniture and paintings can be found around every corner.

Clubatmosphäre herrscht in der Bibliothek, diversen Salons oder den privaten Speiseräumen. Überall finden sich alte Möbel und Gemälde.

Il règne une atmosphère de club dans la bibliothèque, les divers salons et les salles à manger privées. Des meubles anciens et des tableaux complètent la décoration.

En la biblioteca, los salones y comedores privados dominan el ambiente del selecto club.

Un'atmosfera da Club regna nella biblioteca, nei diversi saloni e nelle sale da pranzo private.

Hotel Amigo

Brussels, Belgium

The residents of Brussels took a liking to the translation of "friend" assigned by the unpopular Spanish rulers to the hotel, which served as a prison in the 16th century. And thus the name Amigo has remained with the handsome red brick building with its renaissance facade situated only mere steps from Brussels' famous Grand Place. Thanks to renovations carried out in 2002, nothing reminiscent of the previous role of the distinguished luxury hotel remains. The stylish design of Olga Polizzi is unmistakable.

Den Brüsselern gefiel es, dass die ungeliebten spanischen Machthaber den flämischen Namen des Hauses, das im 16. Jahrhundert als Gefängnis diente, mit „Freund" übersetzten. Und so ist der Name Amigo dem stattlichen roten Backsteinbau mit der Renaissance-Fassade, das nur wenige Schritte von Brüssels berühmtem Grand Place entfernt liegt, erhalten geblieben. An seine frühere Bestimmung erinnert in dem distinguierten Luxushotel seit der Renovierung 2002 rein gar nichts mehr. Unübersehbar ist die Handschrift der Designerin Olga Polizzi.

Les bruxellois d'autrefois appréciaient que les souverains espagnols qu'ils détestaient traduisent par « Ami » le nom flamand du bâtiment, qui servait de prison au 16ème siècle. C'est ainsi que le nom Amigo est resté à cette bâtisse impressionnante en briques rouges avec sa façade renaissance, qui est située à proximité de la fameuse Grand Place bruxelloise. Dans cet hôtel de luxe distingué, plus rien ne rappelle son utilisation antérieure depuis sa rénovation en 2002. La main de la créatrice Olga Polizzi est évidente.

A los bruselenses les gustó que los poco queridos gobernantes españoles tradujeran como "Amigo" el nombre flamenco de la casa que en el siglo XVI servía de prisión. Por ese motivo esta espléndida construcción de ladrillo rojo ha conservado el nombre Amigo con fachada renacentista, que se encuentra a tan sólo unos pasos de la famosa Grand Place de Bruselas. Nada recuerda ya a la función que desempeñó anteriormente este distinguido hotel de lujo desde que se le renovó en el 2002. Destaca el toque personal de la diseñadora Olga Polizzi.

Ai cittadini di Bruxelles piacque l'idea che i poco amati spagnoli, al potere, tradussero il nome fiammingo dell'edificio, che nel XVI secolo venne utilizzato come carcere, con la parola "amigo". E così è rimasto il nome Amigo per la costruzione imponente in mattoni rossi con la facciata rinascimentale, che dista solo pochi passi dal famoso Grand Place di Bruxelles. Dal suo restauro nel 2002, niente ricorda più la funzione passata all'interno dell'hotel caratterizzato da un lusso distinto. Non può non saltare all'occhio la firma della designer Olga Polizzi.

A hang-out for Brussels' diplomats: the lobby lounge and the restaurant Bocconi.

Treffpunkt für Brüsseler Diplomaten: die Lobby Lounge und das Restaurant Bocconi.

Rendez-vous des diplomates bruxellois : le Lobby Lounge et le restaurant Bocconi.

El vestíbulo, el lounge y el restaurante Bocconi son puntos de encuentro para los diplomáticos bruselenses.

Punto d'incontro per i diplomatici di Bruxelles: la lobby-lounge ed il ristorante Bocconi.

Soft pastel tones characterize the warm, elegant style of the 192 rooms and suites.

Sanfte Pastelltöne bestimmen den warmen, eleganten Stil der 192 Zimmer und Suiten.

Le style chaleureux et élégant des 192 chambres et suites est caractérisé par de tendres coloris pastel.

El estilo cálido y elegante de las 192 habitaciones y suites está marcado por tonos suaves pastel.

Delicati toni pastello caratterizzano lo stile caldo ed elegante delle 192 camere e suite.

The Dylan Amsterdam

Amsterdam, Netherlands

A legendary name surrounds this design hotel featuring a carefully chosen reminiscent theme for behind the brick facade lies an exceedingly intimate and avant-garde world of rooms. The hotel offers 8 suites with a variety of styles to choose from. Striking color tones or cultural innuendos define the interior, which proves to be selective and tasteful. The same holds true for the hotel's French-contemporary cuisine.

Ein legendärer Name umweht dieses Designhotel. Eine Reminiszenz, die mit Bedacht gewählt wurde. Denn hinter der alten Backsteinfassade öffnet sich eine äußerst intime wie avantgardistische Raumwelt. 8 Suiten in verschiedenen Stilen stehen zur Auswahl. Markante Farbklänge oder kulturelle Anspielungen bestimmen das Interieur, das sich als ausgesucht geschmackvoll erweist. Gleiches gilt für die moderne französische Küche des Hotels.

Un nom légendaire entoure ce hôtel design. Une réminiscence choisie avec soin. Derrière l'ancienne façade en briques se cache un monde d'espaces avant-gardistes et très intimes. 8 suites de style différent s'offrent à vous. Des tons de couleurs affirmés et des allusions culturelles dominent l'intérieur, qui s'avère extrêmement élégant. Ceci s'applique également à la cuisine française moderne de l'hôtel.

Un nombre legendario acompaña a este hotel de diseño, una reminiscencia que se sopesó bien antes de elegirla, pues detrás de la antigua fachada de ladrillo se abre un espacio tan extremadamente íntimo como de vanguardia. Se puede elegir entre 8 suites de diferentes estilos. Los colores marcados o las alusiones culturales caracterizan los interiores que se nota que han sido elegidos con buen gusto. Lo mismo se puede decir de la cocina francesa moderna del hotel.

Un nome leggendario per questo hotel di design. Una reminescenza volontariamente scelta. Infatti dietro alla vecchia facciata in pietra si apre un mondo di spazi incredibilmente intimo ed avanguardistico. Sono a disposizione 8 suite in diversi stili. Toni marcati di colore oppure accenni culturali caratterizzano gli interni che si dimostrano essere ricercati e di gusto. Lo stesso vale per la moderna cucina francese dell'hotel.

In some of the 41 guest rooms and suites modern styles alternate with an ethno-look.

In einigen der 41 Gästezimmer und Suiten stehen moderne Stile im Wechsel mit einem Ethno-Look.

Dans certaines des 41 chambres et suites les styles modernes côtoyent des éléments ethniques.

Algunas de las 41 habitaciones y suites, los estilos modernos se alternan con un estilo etno.

In alcune delle 41 camere per gli ospiti e suite lo stile moderno si alterna ad un look etnico.

At times, the simple purism prevails, while at other times powerful colors define the rooms.

Mal dominiert der schlichte Purismus, mal bestimmen kraftvolle Farben die Räume.

Tantôt, c'est le purisme simple qui domine, tantôt, ce sont les couleurs vives des chambres.

Unas veces, el purismo simple domina los espacios y otras veces los colores fuertes.

A volte domina il semplice purismo, a volte sono i colori forti a caratterizzare le camere.

Adlon Kempinski

Berlin, Germany

The first Hotel Adlon was opened in 1907 on the same square and with the same name. Sponsored by Emperor Wilhelm II, it constituted the German reply to the legendary luxury hotels of London and Paris. The complex, which was reconstructed after the fall of the Berlin Wall, directly taps into this tradition: with magnificent halls, palace-like rooms and exceedingly decorated restaurants. And still today, international VIPs from the political, cultural, and entertainment scene spend the night here.

Am selben Platz und unter gleichem Namen eröffnet 1907 das erste Hotel Adlon. Protegiert von Kaiser Wilhelm II. stellte es die deutsche Antwort auf die legendären Luxushotels von London und Paris dar. Der nach dem Mauerfall wieder errichtete Komplex knüpft nahtlos an diese Tradition an: mit prunkvollen Hallen, palastartigen Räumen und hoch dekorierten Restaurants. Und auch heute übernachten hier wieder die internationalen Größen aus Politik, Kultur und Unterhaltungsbranche.

Le premier hôtel Adlon a ouvert ses portes au même endroit et sous le même nom en 1907. Sous l'égide de l'Empereur Guillaume II, il constituait la réponse allemande aux légendaires hôtels de luxe de Londres et de Paris. Ce complexe reconstruit après la chute du mur poursuit cette tradition sans rupture : des halls fastueux, des chambres dignes d'un palais et des restaurants ayant obtenu bon nombre d'étoiles. De nos jours, il accueille de nouveau les personnages importants de la politique, de l'art et du divertissement.

En 1907 se inauguró, en la misma plaza y con el mismo nombre, el primer hotel Adlon. Protegido por el emperador Guillermo II, este hotel era la respuesta alemana a los legendarios hoteles de lujo de Londres y París. El complejo, que se reconstruyó después de la caída del muro, se mantuvo en esa tradición: vestíbulos suntuosos, espacios al estilo palaciego y restaurantes muy decorados. Hoy en día se alojan aquí de nuevo los grandes del mundo de la política, la cultura y el entretenimiento.

Allo stesso posto e con lo stesso nome nel 1907 apre il primo Hotel Adlon. Con il sostegno dell'Imperatore Guglielmo II ha rappresentato la risposta tedesca ai leggendari hotel di lusso di Londra e Parigi. Il complesso, ricostruito dopo la caduta del muro, si ricollega senza interruzioni a questa tradizione: con sfarzose sale come quelle dei palazzi e dei ristoranti altamente decorati. Ed ancora oggi pernottano qui grandi personalità internazionali della politica, cultura e dell'intrattenimento.

The view from the quadriga falls on a hotel with a turbulent past—a stage for a glamorous world, both then and now.

Der Blick von der Quadriga fällt auf ein Hotel mit bewegter Geschichte – dereinst wie heute Bühne für eine glamouröse Welt.

Le regard du quadrige tombe sur un hôtel à l'histoire mouvementée – par le passé comme aujourd'hui, le haut lieu d'un monde prestigieux.

La mirada de la cuadriga se clava en este hotel lleno de historia y que, tanto hoy como antaño, fue y es la escena de un mundo glamouroso.

Lo sguardo della Quadriga ricade su un hotel con una storia movimentata – oggi come allora palcoscenico del glamour.

Rooms, the way Emperor Wilhelm II admired them—not only because of the then seldom luxury of running warm and cold water.

Gemächer, so wie sie schon Kaiser Wilhelm II. schätzte – nicht nur wegen des damals seltenen Luxus des fließend warmen und kalten Wassers.

Des pièces comme déjà l'Empereur Guillaume II les appréciait – et ce, pas uniquement pour le luxe, rare à l'époque, de l'eau froide et chaude au robinet.

Sus aposentos ya eran apreciados por el emperador Guillermo II y no sólo por el lujo que suponía entonces disponer de agua corriente caliente y fría.

Appartamenti creati come apprezzati dall'Imperatore Guglielmo II – non solamente per via del lusso dell'acqua corrente calda e fredda, rara a quei tempi.

The art nouveau bath in the hotel is but one example of the many historical impressions conveyed by the hotel.

Das Jugendstil-Bad im Haus ist nur ein Beispiel der vielen historischen Anklänge des Hotels.

La piscine de style Art nouveau ne constitue qu'un exemple des nombreux détails historiques de cet hôtel.

El baño de estilo modernista es sólo un ejemplo de las muchas reminiscencias históricas del hotel.

Il bagno in stile Jugendstil è solo un esempio dei molti accenni storici dell'hotel.

Ritz Carlton Berlin

Berlin, Germany

The bellboys and concierge in tails and livery are just one part of the high standards in place at the grand hotel at Potsdamer Platz. Behind the charming facade of the modern construction lies a world of luxury conscious of tradition: marble columns, manorial stairways, classic leather furnishings, fireplaces and gold adornments. The rooms and service correspond to the highest level of comfort. The brasserie in the hotel is very popular, while a visit to the spa club leaves a lasting impression.

Pagen und Concierge in Frack und Livree sind nur ein Zeichen des Anspruchs, den das Grandhotel am Potsdamer Platz an sich selbst stellt. Hinter der anmutigen Fassade des Neubaus öffnet sich eine traditionsbewusste Welt des Luxus: Marmorsäulen, herrschaftliche Aufgänge, klassisches Ledermobiliar, Kamine und goldene Dekorationen. Die Zimmer und der Service bieten jeglichen Komfort. Sehr beliebt ist die Brasserie im Haus, beeindruckend gestaltet der Spa-Club.

Les pages et le concierge en costume et livrée ne sont qu'un indice des exigences que s'impose ce Grand Hôtel sur la Potsdamer Platz. Derrière l'élégante façade de cette construction neuve s'ouvre un monde traditionnel de luxe : des colonnes en marbre, des escaliers princiers, un mobilier classique en cuir, des cheminées et des décors dorés. Les chambres et le service offrent tout le confort imaginable. La Brasserie de l'hôtel est très appréciée et l'aménagement du Spa-Club très impressionnant.

Los botones y conserjes vestidos con frac y librea son sólo una muestra de lo exigente que es consigo mismo el hotel de la Potsdamer Platz. Tras la encantadora fachada de nueva construcción se abre un mundo de lujo consciente de la tradición. Las columnas son de mármol, las escaleras majestuosas, el mobiliario de cuero clásico, hay chimeneas y adornos de oro. Las habitaciones y el servicio ofrecen todo el confort posible. La brasería de la casa es muy apreciada y el diseño del spa es impresionante.

Facchini e portieri in frack e livrea sono solo una caratteristica del Grandhotel situato sulla Potsdamer Platz. Dietro la facciata di questa nuova costruzione aggraziata, si apre un mondo di lusso consapevole delle tradizioni: colonne in marmo, ascensori signorili, mobili classici in pelle, camini e decorazioni in oro. Le camere e i servizi offrono ogni tipo di comfort. Molto amata è la Brasserie all'interno dell'edificio, costruito in maniera impressionante è lo Spa-Club.

The golden lady in the entranceway—as the first building on the square, the hotel ensures a dignified reception.

Die goldene Dame im Entree – als erstes Haus am Platz bereitet das Hotel einen würdevollen Empfang.

La dame aux clefs d'or à l'entrée – en tant que premier hôtel de la place, la maison offre un accueil plein de dignité.

Como primera casa de la plaza, el hotel tiene una recepción maravillosa, la dama de oro de la entrada.

Quale primo edificio sulla piazza, l'hotel, con la sua signora dorata all'ingresso, offre il benvenuto degno di un re.

The marble work by Bisazza in the spa represent a visual masterpiece.

Eine Augenweide sind die Marmorarbeiten von Bisazza im Spa.

Les œuvres en marbre de Bisazza dans le Spa sont un régal pour les yeux.

Los trabajos en mármol de Bisazza en el spa son un regalo para la vista.

Un incanto per gli occhi sono le opere di marmo di Bisazza nella Spa.

Jagdschloss Bellin

Bellin, Germany

The Jagdschloss is among the many hidden jewels in the wonderful countryside surrounding the Mecklenburg Lakes. Following the political transition, the buildings, park and numerous pavilions were carefully restored without disturbing the discreet antique charm. The apartments make a somewhat traditional impression, but with a sense of class. And what's more, they measure 1,900-square feet.

Das Jagdschloss gehört zu den vielen, versteckten Juwelen in der landschaftlich so reizvollen Gegend rund um die mecklenburgische Seenplatte. Nach der politischen Wende wurden die Gebäude, der Park und die zahlreichen Pavillons sorgfältig renoviert, ohne den diskreten Charme des Alters gänzlich zu vertreiben. Die Apartments wirken leicht gediegen, doch mit Sinn für Klasse. Extraklasse ist: Sie messen sage und schreibe 180 m².

Ce pavillon de chasse fait partie des nombreux trésors cachés dans le paysage si charmant de la région des lacs de Mecklembourg. Après la chute du régime communiste, les bâtiments, le parc et les nombreux pavillons ont été restaurés avec soin sans pour autant occulter entièrement le charme discret de l'âge. Les appartements paraissent un peu massifs, mais dans le sens de la classe. La première classe : ils font 180 m² au sol !

El Jagdschloss forma parte de las muchas joyas escondidas en el excitante paisaje de la región alrededor de los lagos de Mecklemburgo. Tras el cambio político, los edificios, el parque y los numerosos pabellones fueron renovados minuciosamente, sin eliminar completamente el discreto encanto del paso del tiempo. Los apartamentos parecen casi genuinos, sin embargo mantienen el sentido de clase. Son de una clase extraordinaria los apartamentos de 180 m².

Il castello di caccia è uno dei molti gioielli nascosti nei dintorni di un paesaggio così attraente come quello attorno alla terra lacustre della regione del Meclenburgo. Dopo la caduta del muro, gli edifici, il parco ed i numerosi padiglioni sono stati restaurati con molta attenzione, senza però cancellare completamente lo charme così discreto delle epoche. Gli appartamenti sono accurati e di classe. Grandioso: avere una dimensione di ben 180 m².

The Jagdschloss, which was established in 1912, offers a tranquil getaway on the boundaries of Bellin.

Ein Refugium der Stille bietet das 1912 errichtete Jagdschloss am Rande der Gemarkung Bellin.

Le pavillon de chasse, construit en 1912 aux abords du canton de Bellin, est un havre de paix.

El Jagdschloss, construido en 1912, ofrece un refugio para la calma en los límites del territorio de Bellin.

Il castello di caccia costruito nel 1912, ai confini del comune di Bellin offre un rifugio silenzioso.

Despite the bountifulness—a blazing fire in the fireplace underscores the pleasant atmosphere of the rooms.

Trotz der Großzügigkeit – ein loderndes Feuer im Kamin unterstreicht die angenehme Atmosphäre der Räume.

Malgré les espaces généreusement dimensionnés – un feu dans la cheminée ouverte souligne encore l'ambiance agréable des chambres.

A pesar de la amplitud, el fuego llameante en la chimenea subraya el ambiente agradable de los espacios.

Nonostante l'arredamento grandioso il fuoco acceso nel camino sottolinea l'atmosfera piacevole degli spazi.

Villa Kennedy

Frankfurt, Germany

The first luxury hotel of the Rocco Forte Collection opened in Germany in 2006 exhibits what otherwise characterizes the hotels of the British investor: noble materials, paired with a certain urban understatement; elegance, which never appears opulent, but tends towards the sophisticated. The heart of the 163 room hotel including 29 suites is the historical Villa Speyer built in 1904, to which three new wings were added grouped around a peaceful green inner-courtyard featuring a terrace.

Das erste, 2006 in Deutschland eröffnete, Luxushotel der Rocco Forte Collection zeigt, was auch sonst die Hotels des britischen Investors auszeichnet: edle Materialien, gepaart mit einem gewissen urbanen Understatement; Eleganz, die nie opulent, sondern eher anspruchsvoll anmutet. Kernstück des 163 Zimmer-Hotels inklusive 29 Suiten ist die historische, 1904 erbaute, Villa Speyer, die drei neue Flügelanbauten bekam, die sich um einen begrünten ruhigen Innenhof mit Terrasse gruppieren.

Le premier hôtel de luxe de la Collection Rocco Forte en Allemagne, inauguré en 2006, fait aussi état de ce qui caractérise toujours les hôtels de cet investisseur britannique : des matériaux nobles, combinés à un certain minimalisme urbain ; une élégance qui n'est jamais opulente, mais plutôt distinguée. Le cœur de cet hôtel de 163 chambres et 29 suites est la Villa Speyer, construite en 1904, à laquelle ont été ajoutées trois ailes nouvelles disposées autour de la cour intérieure calme et arborée avec sa terrasse.

El primer hotel de lujo del Rocco Forte Collection en Alemania, inaugurado en el 2006, muestra lo que caracteriza comúnmente a los hoteles de este inversor británico: materiales nobles unidos a una cierta atenuación urbana, es decir, elegancia que no evoca la opulencia sino más bien la exquisitez. El objeto principal de este hotel de 163 habitaciones, de las cuales 29 son suites, es la histórica Villa Speyer, construida en 1904 a la que se le han añadido tres alas nuevas que se agrupan en torno a un tranquilo patio interior con terraza y jardín.

Il primo hotel di lusso del Rocco Forte Collection, aperto nel 2006 in Germania, mette in evidenza gli hotel del tipico investitore britannico: materiali nobili, abbinati ad un certo understatement urbano; eleganza, che non diventa mai soffocante ma piuttosto pretenziosa. Parte centrale dell'hotel, che conta 163 camere — 29 suite incluse — è la storica Villa Speyer, costruita nel 1904, alla quale sono state aggiunte tre nuove costruzioni laterali che si raggruppano intorno al tranquillo e verde cortile interno con terrazzo.

The spa with a 15-meter pool, quiet room, saunas, and eight treatment rooms cultivates noble minimalism.

Edler Minimalismus kultiviert der Spa mit 15-Meter-Pool, Ruheraum, Saunen und acht Behandlungsräumen.

Le spa avec sa piscine de 15 m, ses salles de repos, ses saunas et ses huit salles de massage cultive un minimalisme noble.

El minimalismo noble se aprecia en el spa, en su piscina de 15 metros, su área de reposo, sus saunas y sus ocho salas de tratamiento.

La Spa con una piscina di 15 metri, una sala relax, una sauna e otto sale per i trattamenti è caratterizzata da un minimalismo deciso.

The very special style of the London designer Martin Brudnizki is apparent in the fireplace room, JFK bar and the suites.

In Kaminzimmer, JFK-Bar und den Suiten zeigt sich der sehr spezielle Stil des Londoner Designers Martin Brudnizki.

La salle de réception et sa cheminée, le bar JFK et les suites affichent le style très spécifique du designer londonien Martin Brudnizki.

En el salón de la chimenea, el Bar JFK y en las suites se aprecia el estilo tan especial del diseñador londinense Martin Brudnizki.

Nella sala con camino, nel JFK-Bar e nelle suite si evidenzia lo stile tipico del designer londinese Martin Brudnizki.

Mandarin Oriental, Munich

Munich, Germany

The credo of the Californian architect Peter Remedios while redesigning the former ballroom building was: "The historical character of the neo-renaissance construction must remain in tact". Thus, French and Italian marble, cherry and ebony wood dominate the appearance of the noble hotel: the guests particularly enjoy the exquisite dishes of one of the Munich's five leading gourmet restaurants based here.

Das Credo des kalifornischen Architekten Peter Remedios bei der Umgestaltung des ehemaligen Ballhauses lautete: „Der historische Charakter des Neo-Renaissance-Baus muss bewahrt bleiben". So dominieren französischer und italienischer Marmor, Kirsch- und Ebenholz das Erscheinungsbild der Nobel-Herberge: Die Gäste genießen insbesondere die edlen Speisen eines der fünf führenden und hier beherbergten Gourmet-Restaurants Münchens.

Le credo que l'architecte californien Peter Remedios s'est approprié lors de l'aménagement de cet ancien édifice de danse est le suivant : « Le caractère historique du bâtiment du style néo-renaissance doit être préservé. » Ainsi, le marbre français et italien, les bois de merisier et d'ébène dominent l'aspect de cet hôtel de luxe. Les hôtes apprécient particulièrement les mets raffinés de l'un des cinq meilleurs restaurants gastronomiques de Munich, situé dans les murs de l'hôtel.

El credo del arquitecto californiano, Peter Remedios, durante la remodelación de la antigua casa de bailes era: "Hay que conservar el carácter histórico del edificio neorrenacentista". En consecuencia, en la nueva apariencia del noble hotel dominan el mármol francés e italiano y la madera de cerezo y de ébano. Los huéspedes pueden disfrutar especialmente de los platos nobles de uno de los cinco mejores restaurantes gourmet de Munich, situado en el hotel.

L'architetto californiano Peter Remedios, durante la trasformazione dell'ex edificio da ballo, ha puntato a mantenere intatto il carattere storico della costruzione neorinascimentale. Per questo, l'immagine della residenza di lusso è dominata da marmo francese e italiano, legno di ciliegio ed ebano. Gli ospiti possono gustare, in particolare, le ricche pietanze di uno dei cinque ristoranti-gourmet qui raccolti, vere icone a Monaco.

Not only for epicurians—pure luxury reigns supreme in this noble domicile situated between the Hofbräuhaus and Maximilianstraße.

Nicht nur für Gourmets – in der Nobelherberge zwischen Hofbräuhaus und Maximilianstraße herrscht Luxus pur.

Pas seulement pour les gourmets – C'est le luxe par excellence qui règne dans cet hôtel situé entre la Hofbräuhaus et la Maximilianstraße.

No sólo para gourmets; en el noble hospedaje situado entre el Hofbräuhaus y la Maximilianstraße reina el auténtico lujo.

Non solo per buongustai: nella residenza nobiliare situata tra Hofbräuhaus e Maximilianstraße regna il lusso puro.

The hustle and bustle of the city is completely forgotten in the swimming pool high above the roofs of Munich.

Das Treiben der Stadt ist im Swimmingpool hoch über den Dächern Münchens schnell vergessen.

L'agitation citadine s'oublie très rapidement lorsqu'on est à la piscine qui domine les toits de Munich.

El ajetreo de la ciudad se olvida rápidamente en la piscina, con vistas a los tejados de Munich.

Nella piscina, situata in alto sopra i tetti di Monaco, ci si dimentica velocemente della frenesia della città.

Mandarin Oriental, Munich *Munich, Germany* 173

Hotel Imperial

Vienna, Austria

On the occasion of the world's fair in Vienna, the noble hotel was opened by Emperor Franz Josef himself on April 28th, 1873. It is obvious that this was always a place where the rich and powerful met. And even today, all official visitors to Austria stay in this luxury hotel. 138 rooms and 32 suites offer enough space to sit back and relax after strenuous negotiations. Valuable antiques and an opulent collection of paintings endow the hotel with atmosphere reminiscent of 19th century Vienna.

Kaiser Franz Josef höchstpersönlich eröffnete am 28. April 1873 das Nobelhotel anlässlich der Weltausstellung in Wien. Klar, dass es immer ein Ort gewesen ist, wo sich Reiche und Mächtige trafen. Auch heute noch residieren alle Staatsgäste Österreichs in der Luxusherberge. 138 Zimmer und 32 Suiten bieten genügend Platz, um sich nach anstrengenden Verhandlungen gemütlich zurückzulehnen. Wertvolle Antiquitäten und eine üppige Gemäldesammlung verleihen dem Haus eine Atmosphäre, die an das Wien des 19. Jahrhunderts erinnert.

L'empereur François Joseph en personne inaugura le 28 avril 1873 cet hôtel de luxe dans le cadre de l'exposition universelle de Vienne. Il a bien sûr toujours été un lieu de rencontre des riches et des puissants. Aujourd'hui encore tous les hôtes d'état d'Autriche sont logés entre ses murs luxueux. 138 chambres et 32 suites offrent l'espace nécessaire pour se détendre après de difficiles négociations. Des antiquités précieuses et une grande collection de tableaux confèrent à l'hôtel une ambiance qui rappelle la Vienne du 19ème siècle.

El emperador Francisco José inauguró personalmente este noble hotel con motivo de la exposición mundial de Viena el 28 de abril de 1873, por lo que es normal que siempre fuera un lugar de encuentro para ricos y poderosos. Incluso hoy en día se alojan en este alojamiento de lujo todos los huéspedes del Estado austriaco. Sus 138 habitaciones y 32 suites ofrecen suficiente espacio para retirarse cómodamente después de negociaciones difíciles. Las valiosas antigüedades y una suntuosa colección de pinturas otorgan a la casa una atmósfera que recuerda la Viena del siglo XIX.

Il 28 aprile 1873 l'Imperatore Francesco Giuseppe in persona inaugurò questo nobile hotel durante l'Esposizione mondiale di Vienna. È chiaro che si è sempre trattato di un punto di incontro per ricchi e potenti. Ancora oggi vi risiedono tutti gli ospiti illustri provenienti dall'Austria. 138 camere e 32 suite offrono abbastanza spazio per riposare comodamente dopo estenuanti trattative. Antichità di grande valore ed una raccolta di quadri danno all'edificio un'atmosfera che ricorda la Vienna del XIX secolo.

This noble hotel in the Viennese Ringstraße not to mention its pompous suites house an exceedingly royal atmosphere.

Königlich geht es in diesem Nobelhotel an der Wiener Ringstraße zu — auch in den pompösen Suiten.

Cet hôtel de luxe dans la Wiener Ringstraße est royal — tout comme ses suites fastueuses.

La atmósfera en este noble hotel de la Ringstraße vienesa es también majestuosa en las pomposas suites.

In questo nobile hotel sulla Wiener Ringstraße si vive in maniera regale così come nelle pompose suite.

Chandeliers, stucco ceilings, *antiques and paintings. Royal grandeur in Franz Josef and Sissi flair emanates from every corner.*

Kronleuchter, Stuckdecken, *Antiquitäten und Gemälde. Königlicher Prunk mit Franz Josef und Sissi Flair strahlt aus allen Winkeln.*

Lustres, plafonds en stuc, *antiquités et tableaux caractérisent cet hôtel de luxe. Le luxe ostentatoire avec en filigrane l'aura de l'Empereur François Joseph et de Sissi est omniprésent.*

Candelabros, techos de estuco, *antigüedades y cuadros, todas las esquinas irradian pompa real con el estilo de Francisco José y Sissi.*

Lampadari a corona, *soffitti in stucco, antichità e dipinti. Sfarzosità regale dove il fascino di Francesco Giuseppe e di Sissi risplende in ogni angolo.*

Palais Coburg

Vienna, Austria

After three years of restoration, the palace built by Ferdinand of Saxony-Coburg-Gotha between 1840 and 1845 stands out as an exquisite hotel jewel in the heart of Vienna's historical center. The splendor of the neo-classical rooms with their gilded stuccowork and gorgeous crystal chandeliers was deliberately contrasted with simple architectural details. The mere 35 suites are individually arranged in different styles and furnished with the most up-to-date technical equipment.

Als kostbares Hoteljuwel präsentiert sich das in den Jahren 1840–1845 von Ferdinand von Sachsen-Coburg-Gotha erbaute Palais im Herzen der Wiener Altstadt nach einer drei Jahre dauernden Restaurierung. Bewusst wurde der Prunk in den neoklassizistischen Räumen mit ihren vergoldeten Stuckaturen und prachtvollen Kristalllüstern mit schlichten Baudetails kontrastiert. Die nur 35 Suiten sind individuell in unterschiedlichen Stilrichtungen gestaltet und mit dem neuesten technischen Equipment ausgestattet.

Le palais construit dans les années 1840–1845 par Ferdinand de Sachse-Coburg-Gotha dans le coeur de la vielle ville de Vienne se présente après trois années de restauration comme un joyau. Le faste des pièces néoclassiques avec leurs stucs dorés et leurs magnifiques lustres en cristal constitue un contraste voulu avec la sobriété de certains détails de construction. Les quelque 35 suites ont été réalisées individuellement dans différents styles et pourvues des équipements techniques les plus modernes.

El palacio, construido entre 1840 y 1845 por Fernando de Sajonia Coburgo y Gotha en el corazón del casco antiguo vienés, se presenta como una preciosa joya hotelera tras una restauración que ha durado tres años. Se buscó a propósito el contraste entre la pompa de los espacios neoclásicos, con sus estucos dorados y sus espléndidas arañas de cristal, y la sencillez de los detalles arquitectónicos. Tan sólo tiene 35 suites, que están decoradas individualmente siguiendo diferentes estilos y equipadas con la técnica más moderna.

Il palazzo, costruito nel cuore della Vienna antica negli anni 1840–1845 da Ferdinando di Sassonia-Coburgo-Gotha, si presenta oggi come un gioiello prezioso dopo un restauro durato 3 anni. La sfarzosità nelle sale neo-classiche con i loro stucchi dorati ed i sfarzosi lucernai di cristallo contrasta volontariamente con gli essenziali dettagli edili. Le 35 suite sono arredate in maniera personalizzata seguendo stili diversi e tutte dotate di apparecchiature tecniche.

The staircase reflects the historical-modern concept of the hotel, in which six centuries of architectural history can be experienced.

Der Treppenaufgang spiegelt das historisch-moderne Konzept des Hauses wider, in dem sechs Jahrhunderte Baugeschichte erlebbar sind.

L'escalier reflète le concept historique et moderne de l'hôtel, faisant paraître 6 siècles d'histoire de l'architecture.

La escalinata refleja el concepto histórico pero a la vez moderno de la casa, que se puede apreciar en sus seis siglos de historia arquitectónica.

La scalinata rispecchia il concetto storico-moderno del palazzo, in cui si possono rivivere 6 secoli di storia edilizia.

The full grandeur of the 19th century unfolds in the representative conference rooms.

In den repräsentativen Veranstaltungsräumen entfaltet sich die ganze Pracht des 19. Jahrhunderts.

Tout le faste du 19ème siècle se déploie dans les salles de réunion et de réception.

En los espacios más representativos, reservados para eventos, se revela todo el esplendor del siglo XIX.

Nelle sale destinate agli avvenimenti rappresentativi risplende tutto lo sfarzo del XIX secolo.

Over 3,000 wines *from vineyards all around the world are offered in the restaurant Coburg and the Coburg wine bistro; the oldest of them date back to the year 1795.*

Im Restaurant Coburg *und dem Coburg Wein Bistro werden über 3.000 Weine von Gütern aus aller Welt angeboten; die ältesten stammen aus dem Jahrgang 1795.*

Le restaurant Coburg *et le Coburg Wein Bistro proposent plus de 3 000 vins en provenance des grands domaines viticoles du monde entier. Les vins les plus âgés datent de 1795.*

En el restaurante Coburg *y en el Coburg Wein Bistro se ofrecen más de 3.000 vinos de bodegas de todo el mundo. Los más antiguos pertenecen a la cosecha de 1795.*

Nel ristorante Coburg *e nel Coburg Wein Bistro vengono offerti più di 3.000 vini provenienti dalle vigne di tutto il mondo; i vini più antichi risalgono al 1795.*

Badrutt's Palace Hotel

St. Moritz, Switzerland

Set in the center of St. Moritz behind a chiseled stone facade and a series of mock Gothic towers, Badrutt's Palace Hotel remains an enduring symbol of wealth, prestige, and pampered luxury. Most of the 165 distinctive rooms are designed with an international style with sumptuous furnishings, state-of-the-art technologies, Italian marble bathrooms, and have magnificent views of the spectacular, jagged scenery of the mountains enveloping Lake St. Moritz.

Das mitten in St. Moritz hinter einer Fassade aus gemeißeltem Stein und einer Reihe nachgemachter gotischer Türme gelegen Badrutt's Palace Hotel bleibt ein beständiges Symbol für Reichtum, Ansehen und Luxus. Die meisten der 165 unverwechselbaren Zimmer sind in einem internationalen Stil mit prächtigen Möbeln, modernster Technologie und Badezimmern aus italienischem Marmor ausgestattet und bieten einen wunderbaren Ausblick auf die eindrucksvollen, zerklüfteten Berge, die den St. Moritz See umgeben.

Situé dans le centre de St. Moritz derrière une façade en pierre sculptée et une série d'imitations de tourelles gothiques, le Badrutt's Palace Hotel reste un symbole durable de la richesse, du prestige et du luxe douillet. La majeure partie des 165 chambres sont conçues dans un style international avec des meubles somptueux, des technologies de pointe, des salles de bains en marbre italien, et disposent de vues magnifiques sur les montagnes spectaculaires et découpées entourant le lac de St. Moritz.

El Badrutt's Palace Hotel, situado en el centro de St. Moritz, se esconde detrás de una fachada de piedra cincelada y una fila de torres a imitación del estilo gótico. Este hotel es un símbolo estable de riqueza, prestigio y lujo refinado. La mayoría de sus 165 habitaciones inconfundibles están diseñadas en un estilo internacional y magníficamente decoradas. Están dotadas de la tecnología más moderna y los cuartos de baño son de mármol italiano. Tienen además unas vistas maravillosas a las impresionantes montañas escarpadas que rodean el lago St. Moritz.

Posizionato nel centro di San Moritz dietro ad una facciata di pietra cesellata e ad una serie di torri ad imitazione gotica, il Badrutt's Palace Hotel rappresenta un simbolo di ricchezza duratura, di prestigio e di lusso che vizia. La maggior parte delle 165 camere è concepita in uno stile internazionale con arredi sontuosi, tecnologie all'avanguardia, bagni in marmo italiano, e con delle magnifiche viste sullo scenario spettacolare asimmetrico del lago di San Moritz circondato dalle montagne.

A World-renowned resort with view of lake and mountains is the prime location for the winter see-and-be-seen jet-set circuit.

Ein weltbekanntes Resort mit Blick auf See und Berge, das im Winter ein erstklassiger Ort für den Sehen-und-gesehen-werden-Jetset ist.

Ce lieu de villégiature connu dans le monde entier avec sa vue sur le lac et les montagnes est pour la jet-set un endroit privilégié pour voir et être vu.

Este resort con vistas al lago y a las montañas goza de fama internacional y es un lugar de primera clase para los famosos que quieren ver y dejarse ver en invierno.

Un resort famoso in tutto il mondo, con vista sul lago e sulle montagne, rappresenta la località invernale emergente dove il jet-set internazionale desidera ammirare e essere ammirato.

The Great Hall soars in Gothic dimensions above twin black-marble fireplaces and clusters of antique furniture.

Die Große Halle erhebt sich in gotischen Dimensionen über zwei Feuerstellen aus schwarzem Marmor sowie Gruppen antiker Möbel.

Le grand hall s'élance dans des dimensions gothiques au dessus de cheminées ouvertes doubles en marbre et de groupes de meubles anciens.

El gran vestíbulo adquiere dimensiones góticas debido a sus dos hogares de mármol negro y los conjuntos de muebles antiguos.

Nella sua hall spiccano due camini gemelli in marmo nero e un insieme di mobili d'antiquariato.

Suvretta House

St. Moritz, Switzerland

Like a beautiful fairytale castle, Suvretta House was built in 1912 on a plateau surrounded by mountains and lakes. Its Edwardian facade has two neo-medieval towers and a baroque central gable that has become the hotel's trademark. This five-star-rated hotel is a citadel of subdued elegance and conservative charm, with areas of richly grained oak paneling and interiors covered with plaster and pierced with an endless series of vaulted arches.

Das Suvretta House erscheint wie ein wunderschönes Märchenschloss und wurde 1912 auf einem von Bergen und Seen umgebenen Plateau erbaut. Seine edwardianische Fassade hat zwei neomittelalterliche Türme und einen barocken Mittelgiebel, der zur Marke des Hotels geworden ist. Das Fünf-Sterne-Hotel ist eine Zitadelle unaufdringlicher Eleganz und zurückhaltenden Charmes mit Bereichen, die mit reich gemaserter Eichenvertäfelung geschmückt sind, und Interieuren, die mit Stuck verziert und mit unzähligen Bögen dekoriert sind.

Tel un superbe château de conte de fée, le Suvretta House a été construit en 1912 sur un plateau entouré de montagnes et de lacs. Sa façade edwardienne dispose de deux tours néo-médiévales et d'un pignon central baroque qui est devenu l'emblème de l'hôtel. Cet hôtel à cinq étoiles est une citadelle d'élégance discrète et de charme conservateur, dont certaines parties disposent d'un habillage en chêne et d'aménagements intérieurs en stuc, ainsi que de rangées interminables d'arches voûtées.

La Suvretta House, construida en 1912 sobre una meseta rodeada de montañas y lagos, parece un castillo maravilloso salido de un cuento. Su fachada de estilo eduardiano tiene dos torres neomedievales y un hastial central barroco que se ha convertido en el símbolo del hotel. Este hotel de cinco estrellas es una ciudadela de elegancia y encanto discretos que tiene zonas decoradas con revestimientos de roble granulado muy adornados e interiores enlucidos y con innumerables arcos.

Simile ad un meraviglioso castello delle fiabe, il Suvretta House fu eretto nel 1912 su un'area circondata da laghi e montagne. La sua facciata edwardiana ha due torri neomedievali ed un frontone centrale barocco che è il logo dell'hotel. Questo hotel a cinque stelle è una cittadella dall'eleganza discreta e dal fascino conservatore, con zone dai pannelli artistici in quercia, gli interni rivestiti e una serie infinita di archi a volta.

The hotel is embedded in the alpine landscape of the Upper Engadine with magical views.

Das Hotel ist in die alpine Landschaft des oberen Engadins eingebettet und bietet magische Ausblicke.

L'hôtel est logé dans le paysage alpestre du haut Engadine et bénéficie de vues imprenables.

El hotel forma parte del paisaje alpino del Oberengadin y ofrece unas vistas mágicas.

L'hotel è parte del paesaggio alpino dell'Alta Engadina ed offre viste magiche.

The spacious guest rooms in traditional or alpine style are luxurious with contemporary touches without being glitzy.

Die geräumigen Gästezimmer im traditionellen oder alpinen Stil sind luxuriös und haben einen zeitgenössischen Touch, ohne glamourös zu wirken.

Les chambres spacieuses dans le style traditionnel ou alpestre sont luxueuses et disposent de touches contemporaines sans pour autant être extravagantes.

Las amplias habitaciones de estilo tradicional o alpino son de lujo y tienen un toque contemporáneo sin llegar a ser glamouroso.

Le spaziose camere per gli ospiti, in stile tradizionale o alpino, sono lussuose, con tocchi contemporanei, ma senza mai diventare pompose.

Park Hyatt Zurich

Zurich, Switzerland

The Park Hyatt in the world village of Zurich regards itself as a contemporary five-star destination. With its steel-glass construction, the architecture makes a striking mark on the city's distinguished banking district. In the interior, the architecture of past eras echoes in harmony with modern design. 142 rooms are available, all generously spaced and equipped. The hotel's Onyx Bar is also chic.

Das Park Hyatt im Weltdorf Zürich versteht sich als eine zeitgemäße Fünf-Sterne-Destination. Die Architektur setzt mit der Stahl-Glas-Konstruktion ein markantes Zeichen im ehrwürdigen Bankenviertel der Stadt. Die Inneneinrichtung bietet architektonische Anklänge an vergangene Epochen im Einklang mit modernem Design. 142 Zimmer stehen zur Verfügung, allesamt großzügig geschnitten und ausgestattet. Schick ist aber auch die Onyx Bar des Hauses.

Le Park Hyatt dans la capitale villageoise de Zurich se conçoit comme une destination cinq étoiles contemporaine. L'architecture en acier et en verre constitue un ensemble remarquable dans l'honorable quartier bancaire de la ville. L'aménagement intérieur marie des détails d'architecture d'époques révolues avec un design moderne. 142 chambres sont à la disposition des hôtes, toutes très spacieuses et équipées à souhait. L'Onyx Bar de l'hôtel est très chic.

El Park Hyatt en Zurich, se describe como un destino contemporáneo de cinco estrellas. Su arquitectura, con su construcción de acero y vidrio, marca un estilo a seguir en el respetable barrio banquero de la ciudad. La decoración de sus interiores tiene reminiscencias arquitectónicas de épocas pasadas, que se compenetran con un diseño moderno. Las 142 habitaciones disponibles son amplias y están generosamente equipadas. El Onyx Bar de la casa es también muy elegante.

Il Park Hyatt nella città di Zurigo rappresenta una destinazione contemporanea a cinque stelle. Grazie alla costruzione in acciaio-vetrato, l'architettura evidenzia il quartiere delle banche della città. L'arredamento interno offre rimandi architettonici ad epoche passate ma in armonia con il design moderno. Sono a disposizione 142 camere, tutte pensate ed arredate in maniera grandiosa. Altrettanto elegante è anche l'Onyx Bar che si trova all'interno.

The lounge of the hotel—a true goldmine for classics in objective design.

Die Lounge des Hotels – geradezu eine Fundgrube für Klassiker des Objektdesigns.

Le hall de l'hôtel – une vraie mine d'or pour les objets classiques du design.

El lounge del hotel es casi una mina de obras clásicas del diseño de objetos.

Le lounge dell'hotel rappresenta una vera e propria miniera d'oro per il design classico degli oggetti.

A feast for the eyes and seduction all in one: the free-standing bathtubs.

Augenweide und Verführung in einem: die freistehenden Badewannen.

Plaisir pour les yeux et tentation : les baignoires centrales.

Un regalo para la vista y a su vez una tentación son las bañeras con patas.

Piacere per gli occhi e seduzione: le vasche da bagno fuori terra.

Le Dokhan's

Paris, France

The Dokhan's, located between Tracadéro and the Arc de Triomphe, cultivates the elegance and the charm of a noble Parisian private home. The 45-room hotel is regarded as a well-kept secret of the metropolis on the Seine. Star architect Frédéric Méchiche had the entire interior designed as a "one-of-a-kind": carpets weaved according to 18th century motives, old parquet arranged artistic patterns, the walls painted by hand or covered with heavy materials and an original Louis Vuitton wardrobe trunk is used as an elevator.

Die Eleganz und den Charme eines noblen Pariser Privathauses kultiviert das Dokhan's, zwischen Trocadéro und Arc de Triomphe gelegen. Das 45-Zimmer-Haus gilt als ein gut gehütetes Geheimnis der Seine-Metropole. Starinnenarchitekt Frédéric Méchiche ließ das gesamte Interieur als Unikat fertigen: Teppiche nach Motiven aus dem 18. Jahrhundert gewebt, altes Parkett in kunstvollen Mustern verlegt, die Wände von Hand bemalt oder mit schweren Stoffen bespannt und als Aufzug dient ein original Louis Vuitton Schrankkoffer.

Le Dokhan's, situé entre le Trocadéro et l'Arc de Triomphe, cultive l'élégance et le charme d'un noble hôtel particulier parisien. Avec ses 45 chambres, cet hôtel est l'un des secrets bien gardés de la capitale française. Le grand architecte Frédéric Méchiche a fait aménager l'ensemble de l'hôtel avec des objets uniques: des tapis ornés de motifs du 18ème siècle, des parquets anciens posés en dessins complexes, des murs peints à la main ou tendus de lourdes étoffes, et l'ascenseur qui a été réalisé avec une malle-armoire originale de Louis Vuitton.

El Dokhan's apuesta por la elegancia y el encanto de la noble casa privada parisina que se encuentra entre el Trocadero y el Arco del Triunfo. Esta casa de 45 habitaciones se considera uno de los secretos mejor guardados de la metrópolis francesa. El famoso arquitecto de interiores, Frédéric Méchiche, diseñó modelos exclusivos para todos los interiores. Se tejieron alfombras siguiendo la línea de motivos del siglo XVIII, se puso parqué antiguo con muestras artísticas, las paredes se pintaron a mano o se cubrieron con elementos pesados y el ascensor es un armario original de Louis Vuitton.

L'eleganza e lo charme di una nobile casa privata di Parigi viene coltivato dal Dokhan's, posizionato tra il Trocadero e l'Arco di Trionfo. L'edificio con 45 camere viene considerato come un segreto ben custodito della metropoli della Senna. Il famoso architetto d'interni, Frédéric Méchiche, fece costruire gli interni come qualcosa di unico: tappeti tessuti a motivi del XVIII secolo, antico parquet posato in modelli artistici, pareti dipinte a mano o tappezzate da pesanti stoffe e un baule originale Louis Vuitton che fa da ascensore.

The facade in the style of the era of Baron Haussmann is made of Pierre de Taille sandstone, characteristic of Paris.

Die Fassade im Stil der Zeit Baron Haussmanns ist aus dem für Paris charakteristischen Pierre de Taille-Sandstein.

La façade dans le style de l'époque du Baron Haussmann est érigée dans la pierre de taille calcaire typique de Paris.

La fachada, al estilo de los tiempos del Barón Haussmann, es del sillar de arenisca que caracteriza a París.

La facciata, nello stile del periodo del Barone Haussmann, è in pietra arenaria tipica di Parigi.

The Suite Eiffel *features a spectacular view of the Eiffel Tower.*

Von der Suite Eiffel *genießt man einen traumhaften Blick auf den Eiffelturm.*

La suite Eiffel *dispose d'une vue imprenable sur la Tour Eiffel.*

Desde la suite Eiffel *se disfruta de una vista de ensueño de la Torre Eiffel.*

Dalle suite Eiffel *si gode di una vista fantastica sulla Tour Eiffel.*

Every suite was elaborately and individually designed down to the slightest detail.

Jede Suite wurde bis ins kleinste Detail aufwändig und individuell gestaltet.

Chaque suite a été aménagée individuellement avec soin jusque dans le moindre détail.

Cada suite fue diseñada minuciosamente hasta el más mínimo detalle.

Ogni suite è stata arredata con impegno ed in maniera personalizzata, nel più piccolo dettaglio.

Murano Urban Resort

Paris, France

"When a good sleep is not enough"—the motto of the hotel is hardly an understatement. The design hotel, which was opened in spring 2004, knows how to radiate casual and debonair glamour. All the rooms are individually furnished, dominated by a modern purism. The sesame of the suites opens by fingerprint. Before this, a futuristic elevator brings the guests to the right floor. As dazzling as it is tasteful: the bar and restaurant of the urban resort.

„Wem Schlafen allein nicht reicht" – von Understatement zeugt das Motto des Hauses kaum. Das Designhotel, das im Frühjahr 2004 eröffnete, versteht lässig-schönen Glanz zu verströmen. Alle Räume sind individuell eingerichtet, dominiert von einem modernen Purismus. Per Fingerabdruck öffnet sich der Sesam der Suiten. Zuvor bringt die Gäste ein futuristischer Aufzug in den richtigen Stock. Ebenso schillernd wie geschmackvoll: Bar und Restaurant des Stadt-Resorts.

« Si dormir ne vous suffit pas »** – la devise de ce lieu de villégiature ne fait pas vraiment preuve d'une modestie exagérée. Cet hôtel design inauguré au printemps 2004 répand une ambiance d'élégance belle et décontractée. Toutes les chambres ont été conçues individuellement et équipées avec un purisme contemporain. Les hôtes ouvrent leurs suites à l'aide de leurs empreintes digitales, après avoir accédé à leur étage grâce à un ascenseur futuriste. Le bar et le restaurant de l'hôtel sont aussi brillants qu'élégants.

"Cuano el sueño no llega fácilmente"… este es el lema inacabado de la casa. Este hotel de diseño, que se inauguró en la primavera de 2004, sabe como difundir un brillo relajado y bello. Todos los espacios están decorados individualmente, dominados por un purismo moderno. Las puertas de las suites se abren mediante la lectura de las huellas dactilares, pero antes, un ascensor futurista lleva al huésped a su planta. Tan deslumbrantes como refinados son el bar y el restaurante del resort de la ciudad.

"Chi dorme non piglia pesci" – il motto dell'edificio non è una forma di riduzione. L'hotel di stile, aperto nella primavera del 2004, è in grado di trasmettere uno splendore piacevole. Le camere sono arredate in modo personalizzato, caratterizzate da un purismo moderno. Con una leggera pressione delle dita si apre la porta delle suite. Prima di giungervi un ascensore futuristico porta gli ospiti al piano giusto. Altrettanto scintillanti e di gusto sono il Bar e il ristorante del Resort-cittadella .

Contemporary interior defines the ambiance. The best proof of this is the atrium in the entrance area of the hotel.

Zeitgenössisches Interieur bestimmt das Ambiente. Der beste Beleg dafür ist das Atrium im Eingangsbereich des Hotels.

L'ambiance est dominée par l'intérieur contemporain. L'Atrium dans l'espace d'accueil de l'hôtel en est le meilleur exemple.

La decoración interior moderna determina el ambiente y la mejor prueba de ello es el atrio en el vestíbulo del hotel.

Gli interni contemporanei caratterizzano l'ambiente. La migliore testimonianza è l'atrio nella zona d'entrata dell'albergo.

Every room bears its own name. The bar and restaurant of the hotel are also popular among the "citoyens", though.

Jedes Zimmer trägt einen eigenen Namen. Beliebt bei den Citoyens sind aber auch Bar und Restaurant des Hotels.

Chaque chambre dispose de son propre nom. Les citoyens, quant à eux, apprécient le bar et le restaurant de l'hôtel.

Cada habitación tiene su propio nombre. Los ciudadanos también aprecian el bar y el restaurante del hotel.

Ogni camera ha un proprio nome. I francesi adorano anche il bar ed il ristorante dell'hotel.

Plaza Athénée

Paris, France

The popular Parisian interior designer Patrick Jourin redesigned the "Bar du Plaza". Ever since, it has been a must for Parisian society and a crowd-puller for the legendary hotel. This deluxe establishment, founded in 1911, is situated on Avenue Montaigne, surrounded by trendy boutiques, fine restaurants and businesses. Despite comprehensive renovation, one can still perceive the radiance of times gone by in the Plaza Athénée. Furniture and accessories in the hotel are reminiscent of the classical French style. A few of the 430-square feet deluxe suites offer an idyllic view of the garden.

Der angesagte Pariser Designer Patrick Jourin gestaltete die „Bar du Plaza" neu. Seitdem ist sie eine Muss-Adresse für die Pariser Gesellschaft und ein Aushängeschild des legendären Hotels. Die 1911 in Betrieb genommene Luxusherberge liegt an der Avenue Montaigne, umgeben von Trendboutiquen, feinen Restaurants und Geschäfts- häusern. Trotz einer umfangreichen Sanierung ist im Plaza Athénée der Glanz vergangener Zeiten zu spüren. Möbel und Accessoires im Hotel greifen den klassischen, französischen Stil auf. Einige der 40 m² großen Deluxe-Zimmer bieten einen idyllischen Blick in den Garten.

Patrick Jourin, un designer parisien renommé, a remanié le « Bar du Plaza ». Depuis lors, cette adresse est un must pour la société parisienne et sert d'image de marque à cet hôtel légendaire. Cette résidence de luxe, qui a ouvert ses portes en 1911, se trouve dans l'Avenue Montaigne, entourée de boutiques au top de la tendance, de restaurants fins et d'immeubles de bureaux. Malgré les travaux d'assainissement de très grande envergure qui y ont été effectués, on ressent au Plaza Athénée la splendeur du passé. Les meubles et accessoires à l'intérieur de l'hôtel reprennent le style classique français. Certaines des grandes chambres « Deluxe », d'une superficie de 40 m², offrent une vue idyllique sur le jardin.

El famoso diseñador parisino de interiores Patrick Jourin efectuó la reestructuración del "Bar du Plaza". El mismo constituye desde entonces un lugar de destino para la sociedad parisina y un estandarte del legendario hotel. El hospedaje de lujo inaugurado en 1911 se encuentra en la avenida Montaigne, rodeado de boutiques de moda, finos restaurantes y establecimientos comerciales. A pesar de haber sufrido una amplia restauración, en el Plaza Athénée puede percibirse el brillo de épocas pasadas. Los muebles y accesorios del hotel se asocian al estilo clásico francés. Algunas de las habitaciones de lujo de 40 m² ofrecen una visión idílica del jardín.

L'ammirato designer parigino, Patrick Jourin, ricreò in maniera nuova il "Bar du Plaza". Da allora, rappresenta una meta obbligatoria per la società parigina, ed un biglietto da visita del leggendario hotel. La residenza di lusso, aperta nel 1911, si trova sulla Avenue Montaigne, attorniata da boutique trendy, eleganti ristoranti e centri commerciali. Nonostante il risanamento completo, nel Plaza Athénée si percepisce ancora lo splendore di tempi passati. I mobili e gli accessori dell'hotel riprendono lo stile classico francese. Alcune delle camere deluxe, grandi 40 m², offrono una vista idilliaca sul giardino.

The hotel offers enough places to spend a couple of relaxing hours. In the summer, guests often sit in the courtyard.

Das Hotel bietet genügend Plätze für schöne Stunden. Im Sommer sit- zen die Gäste gerne im Innenhof.

L'hôtel offre suffisamment de places pour passer des heures agréables. En été, les hôtes se prélassent avec plaisir sur les bancs de la cour intérieure.

El hotel ofrece suficiente espacio para horas agradables. En verano los clientes suelen sentarse en el patio interior.

L'hotel offre abbastanza spazio per trascorrere ore piacevoli. D'estate gli ospiti si siedono volentieri nel cortile interno.

All rooms were modernized and technically upgraded. The restaurant is also marked by cool elegance and atmosphere.

Alle Zimmer wurden modernisiert und technisch aufgerüstet. Kühle Eleganz und Atmosphäre findet sich auch im Restaurant.

Toutes les chambres ont été modernisées et rééquipées sur le plan technique. L'élégance et l'ambiance sobres se reflètent également dans le restaurant.

Todas las habitaciones fueron modernizadas y equipadas técnicamente. La elegancia y un ambiente sobrio también se pueden hallar combinados en el restaurante.

Tutte le camere sono state ristrutturate e dotate di tecnologie. Una notevole eleganza ed un ambiente raffinato si trovano anche nel ristorante.

Le Meurice

Paris, France

For over two centuries already, Le Meurice can be found on the list of the world's most outstanding hotels. No wonder! The hotel resembles a palace and this can be felt from the foyer up to the very last corners of the upper floor. The classicistic style from the era of Louis XVI dominates the interior, but the hotel understands the art of facing modern demands. The 2,300-square feet large "Belle Étoile"-Suite with its 360-degree panoramic view of Paris is unparalleled.

Über zwei Jahrhunderte schon findet Le Meurice in der Liste der weltweit herausragenden Hotels Erwähnung. Wen wundert es! Das Haus gleicht einem Palast, was vom Foyer bis in die letzten Winkel der obersten Etage zu spüren ist. Der klassizistische Stil aus der Zeit des Louis XVI dominiert das Interieur, doch das Haus versteht es, sich den Ansprüchen der Moderne zu stellen. Ihresgleichen sucht die 210 m² große „Belle Etoile"-Suite mit ihrem 360-Grad-Panorama über Paris.

Depuis plus de deux siècles déjà, Le Meurice figure dans la liste des meilleurs hôtels du monde. Il n'y a rien de surprenant ! L'hôtel ressemble à un palais, et cela se sent du foyer jusqu'au dernier recoin du dernier étage. Le style classique de l'époque Louis XVI domine l'intérieur, mais le bâtiment a su s'adapter aux exigences modernes. La suite « Belle Etoile » de 210 m², depuis laquelle on bénéficie d'une vue panoramique à 360 degrés sur Paris, n'a pas son égal.

Hace ya más de dos siglos que se incluye al hotel Le Meurice en la lista de los hoteles internacionales excelentes. ¿Y a quién le extraña? La casa se asemeja a un palacio, cosa que se puede apreciar desde el vestíbulo hasta el último rincón de la planta superior. El estilo clasicista de la época de Luís XVI domina el interior, sin embargo, este hotel sabe como hacer frente a las exigencias de la modernidad. No hay suite comparable a la gran "Belle Etoile", con sus 210 m² y los 360 grados de su vista panorámica de París.

Da più di due secoli il Le Meurice viene citato nella lista degli hotel migliori del mondo. Ciò non stupisce nessuno! L'edificio assomiglia ad un palazzo, questo è visibile dalla lounge fino agli ultimi angoli del piano più alto. Lo stile classicistico del periodo di Luigi XVI domina gli interni, ma contemporaneamente l'edificio soddisfa le esigenze attuali. La suite "Belle Etoile", grande 210 m² e con il suo panorama a 360 gradi sopra Parigi, non teme rivali.

Nearly all stars and starlets of the world have bathed in these tubs and resided in these rooms.

In diesen Wannen und Zimmern badeten und residierten nahezu alle Stars und Sternchen dieser Welt.

Ces baignoires et ces chambres ont accueilli presque toutes les stars et starlettes du monde.

En sus bañeras y habitaciones se bañaron y residieron casi todas las estrellas y estrellas menores de este mundo.

In queste vasche e camere hanno fatto il bagno ed hanno soggiornato quasi tutte le star del mondo.

Hotel de Crillon

Paris, France

The palace completed in 1758 under Louis XV has been a hotel since 1909 and is thus one of the oldest grand hotels in Paris. It lies in the heart of Paris, directly at the Place de la Concorde. Both politicians and artists have always enjoyed staying in these representative luxury scenic quarters. Those who walk into the entrance hall are immersed into a different world: floors as smooth as glass, meter-high flower bouquets, and massive columns of marble mirror the French savoir vivre.

Das 1758 unter Ludwig XV. realisierte Palais ist seit 1909 ein Hotel und gehört somit zu den ältesten Pariser Grandhotels. Es liegt im Herzen von Paris, direkt an der Place de la Concorde, und Politiker und Künstler haben seit jeher gerne in dieser repräsentativen Kulisse Quartier bezogen. Wer die Eingangshalle betritt, taucht ein in eine andere Welt: spiegelglatte Fußböden, mannshohe Blumenbuketts und massive Säulen aus Marmor spiegeln französische Lebenskunst.

Ce palais construit en 1758 sous Louis XV a été transformé en hôtel en 1909 et fait ainsi partie des plus anciens grands hôtels parisiens. Il est situé dans le cœur de Paris, sur la Place de la Concorde, et accueille depuis toujours les politiciens et les artistes derrière sa façade représentative. Lorsqu'on entre dans le hall d'entrée, on pénètre dans un autre monde : les sols brillants comme des miroirs, les compositions florales à hauteur d'homme et les colonnes massives reflètent l'art de vivre français.

El palacio, que se realizó en 1758 bajo el mandato de Luís XV, se convirtió en 1909 en un hotel, pasando así a formar parte de los grandes hoteles más antiguos de París. Se encuentra en el corazón de París, junto a la Plaza de la Concordia, y desde los comienzos, tanto políticos como artistas se han alojado en este representativo bastidor. Quien entra en el vestíbulo se sumerge en otro mundo, sus suelos brillantes, sus decoraciones florales de dimensiones humanas y sus enormes columnas de mármol reflejan la forma de vivir francesa.

Il palazzo, realizzato nel 1758 da Ludovico XV, è diventato un hotel nel 1909, ed è per questo uno dei grandhotel più antichi di Parigi. Si trova nel cuore di Parigi, direttamente su Place de la Concorde, e, da sempre, politici e artisti risiedono con piacere in questo luogo strategico. Chi entra nella halle, si immerge in un altro mondo: pavimenti che sembrano specchi, bouquet di fiori dalle dimensioni uomane e colonne massicce di marmo rispecchiano l'arte del bon vivre.

The shiny polished stones are silent testimonies of revolutions and affairs.

Die blank polierten Steine sind stumme Zeitzeugen von Revolutionen und Affären.

Les pierres polies sont les témoins historiques muets des révolutions et des affaires.

Las piedras pulidas son testigos mudos de revoluciones y aventuras amorosas.

Le pietre bianche sono dei testimoni silenti di rivoluzioni e amori.

It is here where the old splendor of long-past eras shines and the mundane elegance of the French metropolis unfurls.

Hier glänzt die alte Pracht längst vergangener Epochen und entfaltet sich die mondäne Eleganz der französischen Metropole.

L'élégance mondaine de la métropole française s'y fond dans le faste d'époques depuis longtemps révolues.

En este hotel reluce la pompa antigua de épocas ya pasadas y se revela la elegancia mundana de la metrópolis francesa.

Qui risplende l'antica ricchezza di epoche ormai trascorse e si sviluppa l'eleganza mondana della metropoli francese.

Villa d'Este

Como, Italy

The master builder Pellegrino Pellegrini already began constructing a cardinal residence in 1568 directly on wonderful Lake Como. Three centuries later the Queen's Pavilion was added and in 1873 both villas were finally combined and the grand hotel "Villa d'Este" opened its gates. Nowadays it offers guests 154 rooms and suites dominated by the materials brocade and linen. Some rooms feature a terrace or balcony, and a walk around the 26 hectare large private park is always a worthwhile experience.

Schon 1568 macht sich Baumeister Pellegrino Pellegrini direkt am herrlichen Comer See an den Bau einer Kardinalsresidenz. Drei Jahrhunderte später kommt der Queen's Pavillon dazu, und 1873 werden die beiden Villen schließlich vereint und das Grand Hotel Villa d'Este eröffnet seine Pforten. Heute präsentieren sich den Gästen 154 Zimmer und Suiten, in denen die Materialien Brokat und Leinen dominieren. Manche Zimmer sind mit Terrasse oder Balkon ausgestattet, ein Spaziergang im 26 Hektar großen Privatpark lohnt sich immer.

Dès 1568, le maître d'œuvre Pellegrino Pellegrini a entrepris la construction d'une résidence de cardinal sur les rives superbes du lac de Côme. Trois siècles plus tard, le Queen's Pavillon vient s'y ajouter, et en 1873, les deux villas sont finalement réunies et ouvrent leurs portes sous le nom de Grand Hôtel Villa d'Este. Aujourd'hui, 154 chambres et suites décorées de brocarts et de lin sont à la disposition des hôtes. Certaines chambres disposent d'une terrasse ou d'un balcon. Une promenade dans le parc privé de 26 hectares est toujours agréable.

En 1568, el arquitecto Pellegrino Pellegrini se encargó de la construcción de una residencia cardenalicia frente al majestuoso Lago de Como. Tres siglos después se construyó el Pabellón de la Reina y en 1873 se unieron ambas villas y abrió sus puertas el gran hotel Villa d'Este. Hoy en día, los huéspedes tienen a su disposición 154 habitaciones y suites en las que dominan el brocado y el lino, algunas de ellas con terraza o balcón. Merece la pena pasear por el enorme jardín privado de 26 hectáreas.

Già nel 1568 il maestro delle costruzioni Pellegrino Pellegrini si costruisce, sullo sfondo dello stupendo Lago di Como, una residenza cardinalesca. Tre secoli più tardi aggiunge il Queen's Pavillon, e nel 1873 le due ville vengono unite, ed il Grand Hotel Villa d'Este apre le sue porte. Oggi agli ospiti si presentano 154 camere e suite, nelle quali dominano materiali quali il broccato ed il lino. Alcune camere hanno una terrazza o un balcone, vale sempre la pena fare una passeggiata nel parco privato grande 26 ettari.

Two villas unite to become a hotel. The lobby with its colonnade is impressive.

Zwei Villen vereinen sich zu einem Hotel. Imposant ist die Lobby mit ihrem Säulengang.

Deux villas s'unissent ici pour former un hôtel. Le hall avec sa colonnade est particulièrement imposant.

Dos villas unidas forman un Hotel. El vestíbulo, con su pasillo de columnas, es imponente.

Due ville si uniscono in un unico hotel. La lobby è maestosa con il suo corridoio a colonne.

There is a direct view of Lake Como from the swimming pool.

Vom Swimmingpool aus kann man direkt auf den Comer See schauen.

La piscine dispose d'une vue directe sur le lac de Côme.

Desde la piscina se puede ver directamente el lago Comer.

Dalla piscina ci si può direttamente affacciare sul lago di Como.

Grand Hotel a Villa Feltrinelli

Gargnano, Italy

The luxury that awaits guests here is truly beyond all stars. Located on the lovely western shore of Lake Garda in the middle of a spacious park with a century-old precious tree population, the American Bob Burns, the earlier owner of the Regent Group, created a hideaway of superlatives. The private villa of the legendary Italian family of publishers Feltrinelli, which was built in 1892 in Liberty style, was restored in an enormously expensive procedure in accordance with strict monument protection guidelines.

Jenseits aller Sterne ist der Luxus, der Gäste hier erwartet. Am feinen Westufer des Gardasees inmitten eines weitläufigen Parks mit jahrhundertealtem kostbaren Baumbestand gelegen, hat der Amerikaner Bob Burns, der frühere Besitzer der Regent-Gruppe, ein Refugium der Superlative geschaffen. Unter strengen Auflagen des Denkmalschutzes wurde die 1892 im Liberty-Stil erbaute Privatvilla der legendären italienischen Verlegerfamilie Feltrinelli mit einem ungeheuren finanziellen Aufwand restauriert.

Le luxe qui attend les hôtes ici est au-delà de toutes les étoiles. L'américain Bob Burns, l'ancien propriétaire du Groupe Regent, a créé sur la majestueuse rive occidentale du lac de Garde, un refuge des superlatifs au milieu d'un grand parc parsemé de précieux arbres anciens. Sous le regard attentif et strict des services responsables des monuments historiques, cette villa privée appartenant à la légendaire famille d'éditeurs italiens Feltrinelli, construite en 1892 dans le style Liberty, a été restaurée à très grands frais.

El lujo del que gozarán los huéspedes supera todas las expectativas. El americano Bob Burns, antiguo propietario del grupo Regent, ha creado un refugio impresionante en la elegante orilla oeste del Lago de Garda, en medio de un amplio parque de árboles centenarios majestuosos. Esta villa privada, construida en 1892 al estilo liberty y que perteneció a la legendaria familia de editores Feltrinelli, fue restaurada respetando las estrictas normas de protección de monumentos y con un presupuesto muy elevado.

Dietro ad ogni stella c'è il lusso. E qui attende gli ospiti. Sull'elegante riva occidentale del Lago di Garda, posizionato al centro di un grande parco con alberi secolari e di inestimabile valore, l'americano Bob Burns, ex proprietario del Gruppo Regent, ha creato un complesso superlativo. Seguendo le rigide disposizioni imposte dalla tutela monumentale, la villa privata, della leggendaria famiglia proprietaria della casa editrice italiana Feltrinelli, e costruita nel 1892 in stile liberty, è stata restaurata con immensi costi.

The entrance area, which offers a view all the way to Lake Garda, is reminiscent of a Venetian Palazzo.

An einen venezianischen Palazzo erinnert der Eingangsbereich, der einen Durchblick bis auf den Gardasee gewährt.

L'entrée, qui bénéficie d'une vue allant jusqu'au lac de Garde, rappelle un palazzo vénitien.

La zona de la entrada recuerda a un palacio veneciano y ofrece unas vistas que abarcan hasta el Lago de Garda.

La zona dell'entrata ricorda un palazzo veneziano. Da qui è possibile scrogere il Lago di Garda.

The grand opulence of the historical rooms and the precious original furniture were meticulously restored.

Mit Akribie hat man die prachtvolle Opulenz der historischen Räume samt den kostbaren Originalmöbeln wieder hergestellt.

L'opulence fastueuse des salles historiques avec leurs précieux meubles d'origine a été reconstituée avec précision.

Con meticulosidad se ha recuperado la magnífica opulencia de los espacios históricos, además de los preciosos muebles originales.

Con meticolosità è stata ricreata l'opulenza sfarzosa degli spazi storici e dei mobili originali di alto valore.

Grand Hotel a Villa Feltrinelli *Gargnano, Italy* 225

St. Regis Grand Hotel, Rome

Rome, Italy

After an elaborate restoration that cost millions, the luxurious hotel again shines in its original splendor. With its frescos, lofty ceilings, crystal lights from Murano, marble columns and antique treasures, the St. Regis is a true jewel of the Belle Époque. The magnificently decorated rooms and suites are painted in shades of cream-color and red, adorned with gold stucco and equipped with antique furniture and marble baths.

Nach einer aufwändigen, millionenteuren Restaurierung erstrahlt das luxuriöse Hotel wieder im alten Glanz. Mit seinen Fresken, hohen Decken, Kristallleuchtern aus Murano, Marmorsäulen und antiken Kostbarkeiten ist das St. Regis ein wahres Juwel der Belle Époque. Die prunkvoll ausgestatteten Zimmer und Suiten sind in Creme- und Rottönen gehalten, mit Goldstuck verziert und mit antiken Möbeln und Marmorbädern ausgestattet.

Après une restauration minutieuse et extrêmement coûteuse, ce luxurieux hôtel a retrouvé son faste d'origine. Avec ses fresques, ses plafonds hauts, ses lustres en cristal de Murano, ses colonnes en marbre et ses trésors d'antiquités, le St. Regis est un vrai joyau de la Belle Epoque. Les chambres et suites fastueuses sont décorées dans les tons crème et rouge avec des stucs dorés, et équipées de meubles antiques et de salles de bains en marbre.

Tras una restauración minuciosa que contó con un presupuesto millonario, este hotel de lujo vuelve a resplandecer con todo su antiguo brillo. Con sus frescos, sus techos altos, sus lámparas de cristal de Murano, sus columnas de mármol y sus valiosos objetos antiguos, el St. Regis es una verdadera joya de la Belle Époque. Las habitaciones y suites mantienen los tonos color crema y rojos y están decoradas pomposamente con piezas de oro y muebles antiguos. Sus bañeras son de mármol.

Dopo il restauro impegnativo costato milioni, il lussuoso hotel risplende ora di nuova luce. Con i suoi affreschi, alti soffitti, lampadari in vetro di Murano, colonne di marmo e preziosità antiche, il St. Regis è un vero gioiello della Belle Époque. Le camere e le suite, arredate in maniera sfarzosa, hanno tonalità cremisi e rosse, sono decorate con stucchi dorati e arredate con mobili antichi e bagni in marmo.

Pompous interior spaces and a strict facade contribute to the special atmosphere of this unique hotel.

Prunkvolle Innenräume und eine strenge Fassade tragen zur besonderen Atmosphäre dieses einzigartigen Hotels bei.

Des espaces intérieurs fastueux et une façade sévère contribuent à l'ambiance particulière de cet hôtel unique en son genre.

La suntuosidad de los espacios interiores y la fachada sobria aportan un toque especial al ambiente de este hotel único.

Sale interne sfarzose ed una rigida facciata contribuiscono a creare la particolare atmosfera di questo hotel così unico.

The grand hotel, which was built in 1894, is only a short walk away from many historical sights such as the Spanish Stairs, the Trevi Fountain and the Via Veneto.

Das 1894 erbaute Grandhotel ist nur ein Spaziergang von vielen historischen Sehenswürdigkeiten, wie der Spanischen Treppe, dem Trevi-Brunnen und der Via Veneto entfernt.

Le Grand Hôtel, construit en 1894, ne se situe qu'à deux pas de nombreux monuments historiques, tels que l'Escalier espagnol, la fontaine de Trevi et la Via Veneto.

Este gran hotel, construido en 1894, está tan sólo a un paseo de muchos de los monumentos históricos dignos de ver, como las escaleras de la Piazza di Spagna, la Fontana de Trevi y la Via Veneto.

Il grandhotel, costruito nel 1894, dista solo un paio di passi dalle numerose bellezze storiche, come la Scalinata di Piazza di Spagna, la Fontana di Trevi e Via Veneto.

Bulgari Hotel, Milan

Milan, Italy

The design metropolis of Milan constitutes the choice of exclusive jeweler, Bulgari, for the location of his first hotel. Within walking distance of Milan's La Scala in the historic quarter of Brera and nestled in a 43,000-square foot garden, the luxury hotel perfectly reflects the philosophy of this exclusive lable. Only heavy, precious materials were used: black marble from Zimbabwe, bronze and gold mosaics for the indoor pool. In the spa, a special lighting effect creates a particularly relaxing atmosphere.

Die Design-Metropole Mailand hat sich der Nobel-Juwelier Bulgari zum Standort für sein erstes Hotel erkoren. In Gehweite zur Mailänder Scala im historischen Stadtteil Brera, eingebettet in einen 4000 m² großen Garten, spiegelt das Luxushotel perfekt die Philosophie des Nobel-Labels wider. Verarbeitet wurden nur schwere, kostbarste Materialien: schwarzer Marmor aus Simbabwe, Bronze, Goldmosaiken für den Innenpool. Im Spa sorgt eine spezielle Lichttechnik für eine besonders entspannende Atmosphäre.

Pour son premier hôtel, le bijoutier de luxe Bulgari a choisi Milan, métropole du design. A quelques minutes de marche de la Scala de Milan, dans le quartier historique de la ville Brera, intégré dans un jardin de 4000 m², cet hôtel de luxe reflète parfaitement la philosophie de la marque de prestige. Seuls des matériaux imposants et extrêmement précieux ont été retenus : marbre noir du Zimbabwe, bronze, mosaïques en or pour la piscine intérieure. Dans le spa, une technique de lumière spéciale crée une atmosphère particulièrement reposante.

El joyero de élite Bulgari ha escogido Milán, la metrópoli del diseño, para albergar a su primer hotel. La filosofía de la prestigiosa marca se ve reflejada a la perfección en este hotel de lujo inmerso en 4000 m², de jardín y ubicado en el barrio histórico de Brera, muy cerca a pie del teatro de la Scala. El interior está compuesto de materiales pesados y costosos: mármol negro de Zimbabue, bronce y mosaicos de oro en la piscina cubierta. El spa cuenta con una técnica especial de iluminación destinada a proporcionar un exclusivo ambiente de relax.

Il designer dei gioielli di lusso, Bulgari, ha scelto Milano, la metropoli del design, come sede del suo primo hotel. Vicinissimo alla Scala, situato nello storico quartiere Brera, nel mezzo di un parco di 4000 m², questo lussuoso hotel rispecchia perfettamente la filosofia del prestigioso marchio. Per costruirlo sono stati utilizzati soltanto i materiali più solidi e preziosi: marmo nero dello Zimbawe, bronzo, e mosaici d'oro per la piscina interna. Una speciale tecnica d'illuminazione crea nella Spa un'atmosfera particolarmente rilassante.

Black dominating marble and clear lines create a contemporary, luxurious ambiance in the lobby.

Schwarzer dominanter Marmor und klare Linienführung kreieren ein zeitgemäßes, luxuriöses Ambiente in der Lobby.

Le marbre noir prédominant et les contours précis créent une ambiance contemporaine et luxueuse dans le lobby.

El penetrante mármol negro y la claridad de líneas envuelven al vestíbulo con una atmósfera actual y lujosa.

Il marmo nero è il materiale dominante i cui contorni ben definiti creano un ambiente lussuoso e moderno all'interno della lobby.

Reduction and elegance enter into a congenial relationship.

Reduktion und Eleganz gehen eine kongeniale Verbindung ein.

L'alliance de la réduction et de l'élégance offre un résultat fabuleux.

Minimalismo y elegancia se fusionan en perfección pura.

Essenzialità ed eleganza in perfetta sintonia.

Four Seasons Hotel Milano

Milan, Italy

Once a cloister and today a luxury hotel close to the Via Montenapoleone, Milan's noble shopping street. This elaborately restored hotel with its frescos and paintings is one of the gems of Italian art. The large French windows of the suites offer a wonderful view of the private garden. Guests may feast on excellent northern Italian specialties in the restaurant Il Teatro and in La Veranda, Sergio Mei's team of chefs serves Mediterranean cuisine.

Einst ein Kloster, heute eine Luxusherberge unweit der Via Montenapoleone, der edelsten Shoppingmeile Mailands. Dieses aufwändig restaurierte Haus mit seinen Fresken und Bildern zählt zu den Schmuckstücken italienischer Kunst. Die großen französischen Fenster der Suiten bieten einen herrlichen Blick auf den Privatgarten. Im Restaurant Il Teatro schlemmen die Gäste exzellente norditalienische Speisen und im La Veranda serviert das Team um Sergio Mei mediterrane Küche.

Jadis un monastère, aujourd'hui un hôtel de luxe à proximité de la Via Montenapoleone, la rue où se trouvent les boutiques les plus chics de Milan. Cet hôtel restauré avec soin avec ses fresques et ses tableaux compte parmi les trésors de l'art italien. Les grandes fenêtres à la française des suites offrent une vue magnifique sur le jardin privé. Le restaurant Il Teatro propose des mets exquis typiques de l'Italie du Nord, tandis que dans le La Veranda, l'équipe qui entoure Sergio Mei sert une cuisine méditerranéenne.

Lo que antaño fue un monasterio, hoy es un parador de lujo cercano a la Via Montenapoleone, la milla para ir de compras más aristocrática de todo Milán. Esta casa, que ha sido restaurada con minuciosidad, es junto con sus frescos y cuadros una de las joyas del arte italiano. Las grandes ventanas francesas de las suites ofrecen una vista magnífica al jardín privado. Los huéspedes disfrutan de los excelentes platos del norte de Italia en el restaurante Il Teatro y el equipo de Sergio Mei sirve cocina mediterránea en La Veranda.

In passato un chiostro, oggi un hotel di lusso vicino a Via Montenapoleone, una delle vie per lo shopping sfrenato di Milano. Questo edificio ristrutturato, con molto impegno, con i suoi affreschi e immagini è uno dei gioielli dell'arte italiana. Le grandi finestre alla francese delle suite offrono un panorama fantastico sul giardino privato. Nel ristorante Il Teatro gli ospiti possono gustare eccellenti specialità del Italia settentrionale e nel ristorante La Veranda il team di Sergio Mei serve cucina mediterranea.

While praying monks wandered through the cloister in the 15th century, it now invites hotel guests to go for a stroll.

Im 15. Jahrhundert wanderten betende Mönche durch den Kreuzgang, heute lädt er Hotelgäste zum Flanieren ein.

Au 15ème siècle, des moines en prière déambulaient dans le cloître, aujourd'hui il invite les hôtes à la flânerie.

En el siglo XV caminaban los monjes rezando por el claustro, hoy éste invita a los huéspedes del hotel a pasear sin rumbo fijo.

Nel XV secolo i monaci in preghiera passavano di qui durante la via crucis, oggi lo stesso percorso è seguito dagli ospiti dell'albergo.

Whether round arches in the foyer or stucco ceilings in the rooms—this elegant hotel houses the evidence of times gone by.

Ob Rundbögen in der Eingangshalle oder Stuckdecken in den Zimmern – die Nobelherberge liefert ein Zeugnis vergangener Epochen.

Qu'il s'agisse des arcades ou des plafonds en stuc dans les chambres, cette résidence de luxe témoigne d'époques prestigieuses du passé.

Bien sean los arcos de medio punto en el hall de entrada o los techos de estuco en las habitaciones, el albergue noble es un testimonio de épocas pasadas.

Dalle arcate nella hall,— fino ai soffitti stuccati delle camere, la residenza di lusso è una testimonianza delle epoche passate.

Bauer Venezia

Venice, Italy

Royal families, actors, and the international "jet set" enjoy coming to this hideaway located directly on the Canal Grande time and time again. According to the regular guests, the grand hotel founded in 1880 is the best address in Venice to sleep and dine. Perhaps it is also the successful stylistic mixture from rococo to Art Deco, which enchants the guests and passers-by. From the terraces, one may experience the savoir-vivre of Venice: gondolas, the tranquility between the houses, elegant people and abundant history.

Königsfamilien, Schauspieler und der internationale Jetset kommen immer wieder gerne in das direkt am Canal Grande gelegene Refugium. Das 1880 gegründete Grandhotel ist nach Meinung der Stammgäste die erste Adresse zum Schlafen und Schlemmen in Venedig. Vielleicht ist es aber auch die gelungene Stilmischung von Rokoko bis Art déco, der die Gäste und Flaneure begeistert. Von den Terrassen aus erlebt man das Savoir-vivre von Venedig: Gondeln, die Stille zwischen den Häusern, elegante Menschen und viel Geschichte.

Les familles royales, les actrices et acteurs et la jet-set internationale aiment venir se réfugier dans cet hôtel situé directement sur le Canal Grande. Ce Grand Hôtel inauguré en 1880 est, selon l'avis des hôtes réguliers, la première adresse à Venise, tant pour dormir que pour manger. Mais c'est peut-être aussi le mariage très réussi de tous les styles, du Rococo à l'art déco, qui fascine les hôtes et les promeneurs. Des terrasses, on aperçoit l'art de vivre vénitien : les gondoles, le calme entre les maisons, les personnes habillées avec élégance et beaucoup d'histoire.

En este refugio, situado frente al Canal Grande, se alojan siempre familias reales, actores y la jet set internacional. Según la opinión de sus huéspedes habituales, este hotel fundado en 1880 es el mejor lugar para dormir y comer en Venecia. Quizás se deba también a su lograda mezcla de estilos, que abarca desde el Rococó hasta el el art déco, que encanta tanto a los huéspedes como a los peatones que pasan por al lado. Desde la terraza se disfruta del saber vivir veneciano: góndolas, la calma de las casas, personas elegantes y mucha historia.

Famiglie reali, attori ed il jetset internazionale tornano sempre con piacere in questo rifugio, che si trova direttamente sul Canal Grande. Il Grandhotel, costruito nel 1880, è, secondo l'opinione degli ospiti fissi, una meta obbligata per chi desidera riposare e darsi all'ozio a Venezia. Forse è anche grazie al miscuglio riuscito di stili, dal rococó fino all'art deco, ad appassionare gli ospiti ed i giramondo Dalle terrazze si vede il savoir-vivre di Venezia: le gondole, la quiete tra le casette, le persone eleganti e tanta storia.

The hotel is located in the middle of the city of lagoons. The panoramic view which unfurls in front of the windows is unparalleled.

Das Hotel liegt mitten in der Lagunenstadt. Unvergleichlich ist das Panorama Venedigs, das sich vor den Fenstern ausbreitet.

L'hôtel est situé au centre de la ville sur le lagon. Le panorama de Venise qui s'étale devant les fenêtres est incomparable.

El hotel se ubica en medio de la ciudad de los canales. El panorama de Venecia que se avista desde la ventana es incomparable.

L'hotel è sito al centro della città lagunare. Il panorama di Venezia che si apre di fronte alle finestre non ha eguali.

The guest rooms of the grand hotel are characterized by high ceilings and inlay work in the floor.

Hohe Decken und Intarsienarbeiten im Boden kennzeichnen die Gästeräume des Grandhotels.

Des plafonds hauts et des sols en marqueterie caractérisent les chambres de ce Grand Hôtel.

Los techos altos y los grabados en el suelo caracterizan los espacios de los huéspedes del gran hotel.

Soffitti alti e lavorazioni ad intarsio nel pavimento caratterizzano le camere degli ospiti del grandhotel.

Hotel Cala di Volpe

Sardinia, Italy

Those who think that luxury is only pomp may walk away disappointed from the Resort Cala di Volpe. No need to worry though—that will not happen. The charm of this hotel is too ingratiating, as its construction reminds us of a village that lives from its picturesque and serene ambiance. And the countryside around the Costa Smeralda is also too beautiful to turn away from. Many of the pieces of furniture are the product of traditional handwork and ideally complement the casual charm of the interior. And the hotel restaurant also has an excellent reputation.

Wer unter Luxus ausschließlich Prunk versteht, mag sich enttäuscht abwenden vom Resort Cala di Volpe. Doch keine Sorge, das passiert nicht. Zu einnehmend ist der Charme dieser Anlage, deren Bau bewusst an ein Dorf erinnert, das von seinem malerisch-heiteren Ambiente lebt. Zu schön ist auch das landschaftliche Umfeld der Costa Smeralda. Viele der Möbel stammen aus traditioneller Handarbeit und ergänzen ideal den lässigen Charme des Interieurs. Und auch die Küche besitzt einen exzellenten Ruf.

Celui qui considère que seul le faste justifie l'appellation de luxe pourrait être déçu par l'hôtel Cala di Volpe. Mais cela n'arrive jamais. Le charme de cet ensemble, dont le style rappelle un village qui vit de son ambiance picturale et joyeuse, est trop envoûtant. Le paysage environnant de la Costa Smeralda est également d'une exceptionnelle beauté. Bon nombre des meubles ont été fabriqués par des artisans selon les préceptes traditionnels et complètent le charme décontracté des aménagements intérieurs. La cuisine aussi bénéficie d'une excellente réputation.

Quien piense que el lujo es sólo consiste en pomposidad posiblemente quede decepcionado con el resort Cala di Volpe. Pero no se preocupe, porque no va a ser así. Hay que admitir el encanto de este complejo, cuya construcción recuerda intencionadamente a un pueblo que vive de su ambiente pintoresco y alegre. El paisaje de la Costa Smeralda es también muy bello. Muchos de los muebles están hechos a mano según la tradición y complementan perfectamente el encanto relajado de los interiores. Y también la cocina tiene una fama excelente.

Chi per lusso intende esclusivamente sfarzosità, se ne andrà deluso dal Resort Cala di Volpe. Ma niente paura, ciò non avverrà di certo. Lo charme di questo complesso è incredibile, la sua costruzione ricorda volutamente un paesino vivace e pittoresco. Particolarmente bella è anche la zona rurale circostante la Costa Smeralda. Molti dei mobili sono stati creati tradizionalmente a mano e completano in maniera ideale lo charme leggero degli interni. Ed anche la cucina gode di un' eccellente reputazione.

Serene elegance—this successful mixture of authenticity and exclusiveness is rarely found.

Heitere Eleganz – diese gelungene Melange von Ursprünglichkeit und Exklusivität ist selten.

Une élégance joyeuse – ce mélange réussi du naturel et de l'exclusivité est rare.

Esa elegancia alegre, esa mezcla lograda entre lo originario y lo exclusivo se encuentra pocas veces.

Eleganza vivace: un raro mix di successo tra semplicità ed esclusività.

Architect Jaques Couelle designed the hotel premises like a village with towers, terraces, arcades and old landing stages.

Architekt Jaques Couelle gestaltete die Anlage wie ein Dorf mit Türmen, Terrassen, Arkaden und alten Anlegestellen.

L'architecte Jaques Couelle a conçu cet ensemble comme un village avec des tourelles, des terrasses, des arcades et d'anciens pontons.

El arquitecto Jaques Couelle diseñó el complejo como un pueblo con torres, terrazas, arcadas y viejos atracaderos.

L'architetto Jaques Couelle lo ha ideato come se si trattasse di un paesino con torri, terrazze, arcate e vecchi imbarcaderi.

Hotel Arts Barcelona

Barcelona, Spain

From the upper floors of the modern Hotel Arts guests may enjoy an impressive view over the Port Olimpic and neighboring districts of Barcelona. The luxury hotel offers 482 rooms and suites—those located in the upper floors form the Club Level. The occupants of these rooms may visit a Club Lounge in the 33rd floor and make use of an individual concierge service. For beauty purposes, guests can take the elevator upwards to the Six Senses Spa.

Von den oberen Etagen des modernen Hotel Arts haben Gäste einen beeindruckenden Blick über den Port Olimpic und die angrenzenden Stadtteile von Barcelona. 482 Zimmer und Suiten bietet das Luxushotel – die in den oberen Stockwerken befindlichen Räume bilden das Club Level: Bewohner dieser Zimmer können sich in einer Club Lounge im 33. Stock aufhalten und einen eigenen Concierge-Service in Anspruch nehmen. Zu Beauty-Anwendungen fährt man per Lift ganz nach oben in das Six Senses Spa.

Des étages supérieurs de l'hôtel moderne Arts, les hôtes ont une vue imprenable sur le Port Olimpic et les quartiers attenants de Barcelone. Cet hôtel de luxe dispose de 482 chambres et suites – celles situées dans les étages supérieurs constituent le Club Level : leurs hôtes sont admis dans un Club Lounge au 33ème étage et peuvent faire appel à un service de conciergerie particulier. Les soins de beauté sont disponibles dans le Six Senses Spa situé au dernier étage et accessible par un ascenseur.

Desde las plantas más altas del moderno hotel Arts, los huéspedes disfrutan de una vista impresionante del Port Olimpic y las periferias de Barcelona. El hotel de lujo ofrece 482 habitaciones y suites. Los espacios que se encuentran en las plantas superiores forman el Club Level. Los huéspedes de estas habitaciones pueden frecuentar el Club Lounge en la planta 33 y solicitar un servicio de conserje individualizado. Con el ascensor se accede al área de tratamientos de belleza, el Six Senses Spa, que se encuentra en la planta superior.

Dai piani più alti del moderno Hotel Arts gli ospiti hanno una vista da capogiro sul Port Olimpic e sui quartieri periferici di Barcellona. Questo hotel di lusso offre 482 camere e suite. Le camere che si trovano ai piani più alti costituiscono il Club Level: coloro che risiedono in queste camere possono trascorrere del tempo in una Club Lounge al 33° piano ed usufruire di un servizio Concierge personalizzato. Per i trattamenti di bellezza si raggiunge il centro benessere Six Senses Spa in ascensore.

Dream location: the Mediterranean in front of the window and surrounded by the best shops and restaurants Barcelona has to offer.

Traumlage: das Mittelmeer vor dem Fenster und ringsherum die besten Shops und Restaurants von Barcelona.

Une situation de rêve : la Mer Méditerranéenne fait face aux fenêtres et, tout autour, les meilleurs magasins et restaurants de Barcelone.

Una zona de ensueño: el mediterráneo en frente y en sus alrededores los mejores comercios y restaurantes de Barcelona.

Posizione da sogno: il Mediterraneo davanti alla finestra e attorno i migliori negozi e ristoranti di Barcellona.

Warm colors convey a modern sense of comfort. Spa and wellness activities take place at lofty altitudes.

Warme Farben vermitteln eine moderne Behaglichkeit. Spa- und Wellness-Anwendungen finden in luftiger Höhe statt.

Les couleurs chaudes créent une ambiance de confort moderne. Les soins de balnéo et de bien-être sont disponibles au dernier étage.

Los colores cálidos transmiten un moderno bienestar. Los tratamientos de spa y wellness se encuentran en un piso alto, a donde llega la brisa.

I colori caldi trasmettono una comodità moderna. I trattamenti del centro benessere sono effettuati ai piani superiori.

Hotel Ritz

Madrid, Spain

Many significant luxury hotels of the world bear the name Ritz. And since Madrid did not want to lag behind London and Paris, King Alfonso XIII initiated the construction of this baroque palace hotel, which was opened in 1910. The impressive facade only offers a preview of the equally pompous interior: 137 rooms and 30 suites, each featuring an individual design. The renowned Restaurant Goya in the hotel is an attraction for the eyes and senses in its own right.

Viele bedeutende Luxushotels der Welt tragen den Namen Ritz. Und da Madrid den Vorbildern aus London und Paris nicht nachstehen wollte, stieß König Alfons XIII. die Errichtung dieses barocken Palasthotels an, das 1910 eröffnet wurde. Die imposante Fassade gibt dabei nur einen Vorgeschmack auf die nicht minder pompöse Innenwelt: 137 Zimmer und 30 Suiten, die individuell ausgestaltet sind. Eine eigene Attraktion für Augen und Sinne ist das viel gerühmte Restaurant Goya im Haus.

De nombreux grands hôtels de luxe portent le nom de Ritz. Comme Madrid ne voulait pas céder le pas aux modèles de Londres et de Paris, le Roi Alfonso XIII a lancé la construction de ce palace baroque, qui a été inauguré en 1910. La façade impressionnante ne constitue qu'un avant-goût de son intérieur non moins fastueux : 137 chambres et 30 suites, toutes aménagées individuellement. Le fameux restaurant Goya, situé dans l'hôtel, est déjà par lui-même une attraction pour les yeux et les sens.

Muchos de los hoteles de lujo importantes del mundo llevan el nombre Ritz y como Madrid no quería quedarse atrás respecto a los modelos londinenses y parisienses, el rey Alfonso XIII impulsó la construcción de este palacio barroco que se inauguró en 1910. La imponente fachada es tan sólo una muestra del mundo interior que no es menos pomposo con sus 137 habitaciones y 30 suites, decoradas individualmente. El famosísimo restaurante Goya es una atracción propia de la casa para que gocen todos los sentidos.

Molti importanti hotel di lusso al mondo portano il nome Ritz. E poiché Madrid non voleva essere da meno rispetto a Londra e Parigi, il Re Alfonso XIII propone la costruzione di questo hotel-palazzo barocco, inaugurato nel 1910. L'imponente facciata rappresenta solo un assaggio degli interni non meno sfarzosi con 137 camere e 30 suite arredate in maniera personalizzata. Una vera e propria attrazione per gli occhi ed i sensi è il famoso ristorante interno Goya.

For more than a century, the Ritz in Madrid has been one of the city's most glamorous addresses.

Seit mehr als einem Jahrhundert zählt das Madrider Ritz zu den glamourösesten Adressen der Stadt.

Depuis près d'un siècle, l'Hôtel Ritz de Madrid compte parmi les adresses les plus glamours de la ville.

Desde hace más de un siglo, el Ritz madrileño se incluye entre los lugares más glamourosos de la ciudad.

Da più di un secolo il Ritz di Madrid è uno degli indirizzi più glamour della città.

Embroidered bed linen, hand-woven carpets, and marble baths.

Bestickte Bettwäsche, handgewebte Teppiche und Bäder aus Marmor.

Des draps de lit brodés, des tapis tissés à la main et des salles de bains en marbre.

Las sábanas están bordadas, las alfombras hechas a mano y las bañeras son de mármol.

Lenzuola ricamate, tappeti fatti a mano e bagni in marmo.

Santo Mauro

Madrid, Spain

Once the palace of the Marquis of Santo Mauro, nowadays an elegant hotel in the center of Madrid, near the Paseo de la Castellana. The splendid construction from the 19th century was renovated in 1999 and now combines classical French style with contemporary elements. In the elegant rooms of the once palace library, the restaurant Santo Mauro offers local specialties and a broad selection of top-class international wines.

Einst der Palast des Marquis von Santo Mauro, heute ein elegantes Hotel im Zentrum von Madrid, nahe des Paseo de la Castellana. Die prachtvolle Anlage aus dem 19. Jahrhundert wurden 1999 renoviert und kombiniert jetzt klassischen französischen Stil mit zeitgenössischen Elementen. In den eleganten Räumen der ehemaligen Palast-bibliothek bietet das Restaurant Santo Mauro einheimische Spezialitäten und eine umfangreiche Auswahl internationaler Spitzenweine an.

C'était autrefois le palais du Marquis de Santo Mauro, c'est aujourd'hui un hôtel élégant dans le centre de Madrid, à proximité du Paseo de la Castellana. Cet ensemble magnifique du 19ème siècle a été rénové en 1999 et associe maintenant avec succès le style classique français à des éléments modernes. Dans les salles élégantes de l'ancienne bibliothèque du palais, le restaurant Santo Mauro propose des spécialités locales et un grand choix de vins internationaux de première qualité.

El que antaño fuera el palacio del Marqués de Santo Mauro es hoy un elegante hotel del centro de Madrid, cercano al Paseo de la Castellana. Las magníficas instalaciones del siglo XIX fueron renovadas en 1999 y ahora combinan el estilo clásico francés con elementos modernos. En los elegantes espacios de lo que antes fuera la biblioteca de palacio, el restaurante Santo Mauro ofrece especialidades regionales y una amplia selección de los mejores vinos internacionales.

Una volta il palazzo del Marchese di Santo Mauro, oggi un elegante hotel nel centro di Madrid, vicino al Paseo de la Castellana. Il complesso sfarzoso del XIX secolo è stato rinnovato nel 1999 e combina oggi lo stile classico francese a degli elementi contemporanei. Nelle eleganti sale della ex biblioteca del palazzo, il ristorante Santo Mauro offre specialità tipiche ed una vasta scelta di eccellenti vini internazionali.

Antique and contemporary elements are cleverly combined with one another.

Alte und zeitgenössische Elemente werden gekonnt miteinander kombiniert.

Des éléments anciens et modernes ont été intégrés avec goût.

Los elementos antiguos y modernos se combinan con el saber hacer.

Elementi antichi e contemporanei vengono combinati in maniera eccellente.

Former ballrooms with large windows and the modern lounges provide for an exquisite atmosphere.

Ehemalige Ballsäle mit großen Fenstern und die modernen Lounges bieten eine exquisite Atmosphäre.

Les anciennes salles de bal avec leurs grandes fenêtres et les Lounges modernes offrent une ambiance exquise.

Los antiguos salones de baile de grandes ventanas y los lounges modernos ofrecen un ambiente exquisito.

Ex sale da ballo, con grandi finestre e moderne lunge, regalano un'atmosfera squisita.

Mardavall Hotel & Spa

Majorca, Spain

The famous yacht port of Puerto Portals lies right around the corner, while the Tramuntana mountain range protrudes into the blue sky behind the luxury hotel. The hotel is surrounded by Majorca at its best. The resort offers the largest spa in Europe with a surface of 5,600-square yards. All 133 rooms and 89 suites have a private terrace with a view of the sea. Those with a liking for the exclusive may take advantage of the "luxury butler service": 24-hour care from teatime in the suite to guided tours around the island.

Der berühmte Yachthafen von Puerto Portals liegt gleich um die Ecke, hinter dem Luxushotel ragt das Tramuntana-Gebirge in den blauen Himmel. Um das Hotel zeigt sich Mallorca von seiner schönsten Seite. Mit 4.700 m² Fläche bietet das Resort das größte Spa in Europa. Alle 133 Zimmer und 89 Suiten haben eine private Terrasse mit Meerblick. Wer es ganz exklusiv mag, nimmt den „Luxury-Butler-Service" in Anspruch: 24-Stunden-Betreuung von Teatime in der Suite bis hin zu geführten Touren über die Insel.

Cet hôtel de luxe est situé à proximité du fameux port de plaisance de Puerto Portals. Derrière lui, dans le ciel bleu, s'élèvent les monts du Tramuntana. L'hôtel est situé dans la plus belle partie de Majorque. Avec une superficie de 4700 m², il offre le plus grand spa d'Europe. Chacune des 133 chambres et 89 suites dispose de sa propre terrasse avec vue sur la mer. Si vous souhaitez entourer votre séjour d'un luxe tout à fait exclusif, vous pouvez faire appel au « Luxury Butler Service » : un service 24/24, qui s'étend du thé dans votre suite jusqu'à des excursions guidées à travers l'île.

El famoso Puerto Portals está muy cerca y detrás del hotel de lujo se extiende la Sierra de Tramontana hacia el cielo azul. En torno al hotel Mallorca exhibe su mejor cara. Con sus 4.700 m² de superficie, el resort ofrece el spa más grande de Europa. Cada una de las 133 habitaciones y 89 suites tienen una terraza privada con vistas al mar. Quién guste de lo exclusivo puede solicitar el "Luxury Butler Service": asistencia las 24 horas del día, desde la hora del té en la suite hasta visitas guiadas por la isla.

Il famoso porto Puerto Portals dove si ormeggiano gli yacht, si trova proprio dietro l'angolo e dietro l'hotel lussuoso ci sono le montagne Tramuntana che si innalzano al cielo. Attorno all'hotel, Maiorca mostra il suo lato migliore. Con una superficie di 4.700 m² il resort offre il centro benessere più grande d'Europa. Le 133 camere e le 89 suite hanno un terrazzo privato con vista sul mare. Chi desidera una vera esclusività, usufruisce del servizio "Luxury-Butler-Service" in poche parole un servizio 24 ore su 24, con un ventaglio di offerte che va dal tè nella suite fino alle gite guidate attorno all'isola.

No conventional finca style, rather a bountiful and open construction with many outside surfaces.

Kein üblicher Finca-Stil, sondern eine großzügige und offene Anlage mit viel Außenfläche.

Pas le style Finca habituel, mais une installation spacieuse et ouverte avec de nombreux espaces extérieurs.

El estilo no es el habitual de una finca, sino que se trata de un amplio complejo con muchas superficies exteriores.

Non si tratta del solito stile maiorchino, ma è un complesso generoso e aperto con molte superfici esterne.

The hotel spa and its pools are the ideal place for thalassic activities.

Im Hotel-Spa mit seinen Pools finden auch Thalasso-Anwendungen statt.

Le spa de l'hôtel et ses piscines propose également des soins de thalassothérapie.

En el spa y sus piscinas se aplica también la terapia thalasso.

Nel centro benessere dell'hotel, con le sue piscine, si effettuano anche trattamenti di talassoterapia.

View of the sea included: the rooms and suites offer abundant space and are equipped with marble baths and modern office technology.

Meerblick inklusive: Zimmer und Suiten bieten viel Platz und sind mit Marmorbädern und moderner Bürotechnik ausgestattet.

Avec vue sur la mer : les chambres et suites sont très spacieuses et disposent de salles de bains en marbre et d'équipements de bureaux modernes.

Vistas al mar incluidas: las habitaciones y suites ofrecen mucho espacio y están equipadas con bañeras de mármol y técnologías modernas de oficina.

Vista mare inclusa: le camere e le suite offrono molto spazio e sono arredate con bagni in marmo e la più moderne tecnologie per l'ufficio.

Hotel Alfonso XIII

Seville, Spain

A spectacular palace in Neomudéjar style rises in the heart of the city, not far from the Guadalquivir River and the cathedral. King Alfonso XIII, who initiated construction in 1928, gave the royal hotel its name. 147 rooms and 19 suites are divided among the floors of the noble hotel. They include not only Moorish elements but also an air of classical baroque. The restaurant San Fernando serves regional cuisine, while Japanese dishes are offered in the Kaede.

Ein spektakulärer Palast im Neomudéjar-Stil erhebt sich im Herzen der Stadt, nicht weit vom Fluss Guadalquivir und der Kathedrale entfernt. König Alfonso XIII., der 1928 den Bau veranlasste, verlieh der königlichen Herberge seinen Namen. 147 Zimmer und 19 Suiten verteilen sich auf den Etagen des noblen Hauses. In ihnen finden sich neben maurischen Elementen auch Akzente des klassischen Barocks. Das Restaurant San Fernando serviert regionale Küche, im Kaede werden japanische Speisen angeboten.

Un palace spectaculaire dans le style néomudéjar s'élève dans le coeur de la ville, non loin du Guadalquivir et de la cathédrale. Le Roi Alfonso XIII, qui en a décidé la construction en 1928, a donné son nom à cette auberge royale. 147 chambres et 19 suites se répartissent sur les étages de ce noble édifice. On y trouve, outre des éléments mauresques, également des accents du baroque classique. Le restaurant San Fernando sert une cuisine régionale, tandis que le Kaede propose des mets japonais.

Un espectacular palacio de estilo neomudéjar levantado en el corazón de la ciudad, no muy lejos del río Guadalquivir y de la catedral. El rey Alfonso XIII, que ordenó la construcción en el año 1928, bautizó el albergue real con su propio nombre. Por las plantas de la noble casa se reparten 147 habitaciones y 19 suites. En ellas se encuentran junto a los elementos árabes también acentos del barroco clásico. En el restaurante San Fernando se sirve cocina regional y en el Kaede se ofrecen platos japoneses.

Un palazzo spettacolare in stile Neomudéjar si erige nel cuore della città, non lontano dal fiume Guadalquivir e dalla cattedrale. Il Re Alfonso XIII che, nel 1928 ne ordinò la costruzione, diede il proprio nome a questa residenza regale. 147 camere e 19 suite si suddividono sui diversi piano del nobile edificio. In essi si trovano, oltre ad elementi mauriziani, anche accenti di barocco classico. Il ristorante San Fernando serve una cucina regionale, il Kaede offre specialità giapponesi.

The King, who gave his name to the hotel, wanted it to be the most luxurious in Europe.

Das luxuriöseste Hotel Europas sollte es nach Wunsch des Königs werden, der dem Luxushotel seinen Namen verlieh.

Cet hôtel de luxe qui porte le nom du roi devait devenir selon ses vœux l'hôtel le plus luxueux d'Europe.

El rey tuvo el deseo de que el hotel fuera el más lujoso de Europa, prestándole al mismo su nombre.

Avrebbe dovuto diventare l'hotel più lussuoso d'Europa: questo era il desiderio del Re che diede a questo hotel il proprio nome.

Built in Moorish style, round arches are a continual dominant feature of the house. Guests enjoy the Spanish air at the "El Patio" fountain.

Im maurischen Stil erbaut, dominieren stets Rundbögen das Erscheinungsbild des Hauses. Spanische Luft genießen die Gäste am Brunnen „El Patio".

Des arcades mauresques dominent l'ensemble architectural de cet établissement royal. Les hôtes profiteront de l'air espagnol assis près de la fontaine « El Patio ».

Construido al estilo morisco, el aspecto del hotel está constantemente marcado por arcos de medio punto. En la fuente "El Patio" pueden disfrutar sus clientes del aire español.

Costruito in stile mauriziano, dove le arcate dominano nell'immagine totale. Gli ospiti respirano aria spagnola sulle fontane de „El Patio".

Hotel Grande Bretagne

Athens, Greece

Only a select number of hotels are surrounded by as many myths as this "kingly box" in the middle of Athens. Since its opening in 1874, the dignified hotel has accommodated just about all the kings, presidents and rulers that the previous century had to offer. In 2003 the aged magnificent building underwent a thorough renovation. Since then, a modern spa and wellness offer awaits the guests.

Nur wenige Hotels umranken so viele Mythen wie diese „königliche Box" mitten in Athen. Denn das ehrwürdige Haus beherbergte seit seiner Eröffnung im Jahre 1874 so ziemlich alles an Königen, Präsidenten und Herrscherinnen, die das letzte Jahrhundert hervorbrachte. 2003 erfuhr der in die Jahre gekommene Prunkbau eine Generalsanierung. Seitdem warten moderne Spa- und Wellnessangebote auf die Gäste.

Peu d'hôtels peuvent se prévaloir d'autant de mythes que cette « Boîte royale » au centre d'Athènes. Cet hôtel vénérable a hébergé depuis son inauguration en 1874 à peu près toutes les têtes royales, présidentielles et impériales que le dernier siècle a pu générer. Les bâtiments luxueux quelque peu vétustes ont été entièrement rénovés en 2003. Depuis, des installations de spa et de remise en forme modernes sont à la disposition des hôtes.

A muy pocos hoteles les rodean tantos mitos como a esta "Caja Real" en medio de Atenas, pues la respetable casa alojó, desde su inauguración en 1874, a muchos de los reyes, presidentes y gobernantes protagonistas del siglo pasado. En 2003 se realizó un saneamiento general en este edificio castigado por el tiempo. Desde entonces, se ofrece a los huéspedes un moderno spa y tratamientos de wellness.

Solo pochi hotel sono circondati da così tanti miti come questa "scatola reale" nel centro di Atene. Infatti, dalla sua inaugurazione nel 1874, il nobile edificio ha ospitato praticamente tutti i regnanti, i presidenti e le donne al potere dell'ultimo secolo. Nel 2003, la vecchia costruzione sfarzosa è stata risanata. Da allora sono presenti offerte di spa e di wellness che attendono gli ospiti.

A feeling of freshness in a historic building. The spa also brought the modern spirit into the hotel.

Spürbare Frische in einem geschichtsträchtigen Gebäude. Mit dem Spa zog auch die Moderne in das Haus ein.

Une fraîcheur notable dans des bâtiments historiques. Avec le spa, la modernité a fait son entrée dans ces murs.

Un viento fresco palpable en un edificio cargado de historia. Con el spa llegó también la modernidad a la casa.

Una freschezza percepibile in un edificio ricco di storia. Assieme al centro benessere è arrivata anche la modernità.

Whether it is the view of the Acropolis from the terrace or the feudal décor—the hotel is replete with history.

Ob Terrassenblick auf die Akropolis oder feudale Ausstattung – die Geschichte winkt von überall her.

Que ce soit par la vue de la terrasse sur l'Acropole ou par l'aménagement intérieur fastueux – l'histoire se manifeste dans tous les détails.

Se respira historia por doquier, ya sea al mirar desde la terraza a la Acrópolis o por su elegante decoración.

Dalla vista sull'acropoli regalata da un terrazzo o in un pezzo di arredo feudale: tutto fa percepire la storia.

Ciragan Palace Kempinski

Istanbul, Turkey

The palace combines rich history. The sultans of Istanbul had their residence here for more than two centuries and the building thus reflects the splendor of a past, but impressive era. With its exposed location on the Bosphorus and the park, which surrounds the palace, the 284 guest rooms and 31 suites offer first-class views. The restaurant Tugra is among the world's most famous addresses. The outright classical Turkish bath is completely made of marble and nacre.

Der Palast vereint eine reiche Geschichte. Mehr als zwei Jahrhunderte residierten hier die Sultane von Istanbul und so spiegelt das Gebäude den Prunk einer zwar verflossenen, gleichwohl eindrucksvollen Zeit wider. Mit der exponierten Lage am Bosporus und dem Park, der den Palast umrahmt, bieten die 284 Gästezimmer und 31 Suiten erstklassige Aussichten. Das Restaurant Tugra gehört zu den weltweit berühmten Adressen. Das ganz und gar klassisch türkische Bad ist ganz aus Marmor und Perlmutt.

Le palais bénéficie d'une riche histoire. Durant plus de deux siècles, il a servi de résidence aux sultans d'Istanbul, et ses bâtiments reflètent le faste d'une époque révolue, mais néanmoins impressionnante. Grâce à sa situation sur le Bosphore et au parc qui entoure le palais, les 284 chambres et 31 suites offrent des vues extraordinaires. Le restaurant Tugra fait partie des meilleures adresses du monde. Les bains turcs tout à fait traditionnels sont entièrement ornés de marbre et de nacre.

En el palacio converge una riqueza histórica. Durante más de dos siglos residieron aquí los sultanes de Estambul y así refleja el edificio la pompa de una época en realidad ya acabada, pero igualmente impresionante. Las 284 habitaciones y 31 suites ofrecen vistas de primera clase gracias a su ubicación expuesta al Bósforo y al parque que rodea al palacio. El restaurante Tugra está entre los más famosos del mundo. El baño turco es absolutamente clásico y está hecho de mármol y madreperla.

Il palazzo è ricco di storia. Qui vi hanno risieduto per più di due secoli i sultani di Istambul, di cui l'edificio rispecchia lo sfarzo di un periodo passato. Grazie alla posizione sul Bosforo e sul parco che circonda il palazzo, le 284 camere per gli ospiti e le 31 suite offrono una vista grandiosa. Il ristorante Tugra è uno dei più rinomati al mondo. Il bagno turco, completamente classico, è in marmo e madreperla.

Whether it is the giant chandelier, the rich adornments or the staircases completely made of marble—every corner of the palace radiates a manorial aura.

Ob riesiger Kronleuchter, reiche Verzierungen oder Treppenaufgänge ganz aus Marmor – überall verströmt der Palast einen herrschaftlichen Anspruch.

Qu'il s'agisse des lustres gigantesques, des riches décorations ou des escaliers entièrement en marbre – tout le palais exhale une ambiance princière.

El palacio irradia por doquier una exquisitez majestuosa, palpable en sus arañas de cristal, en sus ricos adornos o en sus escalinatas construidas totalmente de mármol.

Dall'enorme lampadario, alle ricche decorazioni fino alle scalinate in marmo: ovunque il palazzo trasmette l'esigenza della signorilità.

The **hammam** *or the rooms are places where the nobility used to amuse themselves or rested their heads.*

Das **Hammam** *oder die Zimmer sind Orte, an denen sich früher der Adel vergnügte oder sein Haupt bettete.*

C'est dans ce **hammam** *ou ces chambres-mêmes que festoyaient et dormaient les nobles de l'époque.*

El **Hammam** *o las habitaciones son los lugares en los que antaño los nobles se complacían o descansaban.*

L' **hammam** *e le camere sono dei luoghi in cui in passato i nobili si divertivano e riposavano.*

276   Ciragan Palace Kempinski *Istanbul, Turkey*

Amanjena

Marrakech, Morocco

A 12 acre desert refuge for very private spheres complete with walls and passages is located in a remote oasis nestled between date palms and olive groves, cultivated gardens with a variety of plants, traditional Turkish lagoons and discreet walkways composed of meticulously designed tiles. A mere 40 deluxe rooms and a staff of over 200 guarantee every guest his/her own, unforgettable experience.

Ein 5 Hektar großes Wüstenrefugium liegt für absolute Privatsphäre mit Mauern und Gängen versehen in einer abgelegenen Oase zwischen Dattelpalmen und Olivenhainen, gepflegten Gärten mit vielen Pflanzen, ursprünglichen türkisen Lagunen und dezenten Gängen sorgfältig bearbeiteter Fliesen. Mit nur 40 großzügigen Gästezimmern und über 200 Angestellten erhält jeder Gast sein persönliches, unvergessliches Erlebnis.

Ce lieu de villégiature du désert de 5 hectares est clos et entouré de colonnades afin d'assurer une intimité absolue, et se situe dans une oasis reculée de palmiers dattiers et d'oliviers, de jardins de plantes luxuriantes paysagés, de bassins turquoise d'origine et de couloirs discrets dallés avec soin avec des terres cuites. Comme l'hôtel ne dispose que de 40 chambres spacieuses, mais de plus de 200 employés, chaque hôte est certain de vivre une expérience personnelle mémorable.

Un refugio de 5 hectáreas en el desierto que garantiza una privacidad absoluta con sus muros y columnatas. Se asienta en un oasis apartado, entre palmeras de dátiles y olivares, jardines cuidados con muchas plantas, lagunas originales color turquesa y caminos discretos de baldosas. Tan sólo tiene 40 habitaciones espaciosas y más de 200 empleados que hacen que cada huésped viva una experiencia personal e inolvidable.

Più di 5 ettari di deserto, protetto e circondato da mura e colonnati per un'assoluta privacy, e sito in un'oasi ricca di palme da dattero e olivi, i giardini curati, con ricche piante, le originali lagune turchesi, e i corridoi tranquilli costruiti con un meticoloso lavoro di piastrellatura. Le sole 40 camere per gli ospiti ma tutte dalle dimensioni generose e più di 200 impiegati, assicurano ad ogni ospite un'esperienza personale memorabile.

The architect Ed Tuttle invented the mosque architecture combining a nomadic element with Islamic architecture.

Der Architekt Ed Tuttle erfand die Moscheenarchitektur neu und brachte ein Nomadengefühl in die islamische Bauweise.

L'architecte Ed Tuttle a réinventé l'architecture des mosquées en ajoutant un feeling nomade au design islamique.

El arquitecto, Ed Tuttle, reinventó la arquitectura de las mezquitas aportando un toque nómada al estilo arquitectónico islámico.

L'architetto Ed Tuttle ha reinventato l'architettura della moschea aggiungendo un tocco di nomadismo al design islamico.

The unmistakable Moorish style is integrated in the Moroccan culture to a moderate extent, yet in an authentic and harmonious manner.

Der unverkennbar maurische Stil ist in zurückhaltendem Maße zeitgenössisch, aber trotzdem authentisch und harmonisch in die marokkanische Kultur integriert.

Son style nettement mauresque est modérément contemporain, mais authentique et intégré avec harmonie dans la culture marocaine.

El inconfundible estilo morisco es modéstamente contemporáneo, pero se integra con autenticidad y armonía en la cultura marroquí.

Il suo caratteristico stile moresco è modestamente contemporaneo, ma autentico e armoniosamente integrato nella cultura marocchina.

Dar Ahlam

Skoura, Morocco

In the southeast of the country, where the offshoots of the Sahara begin, stands a "house of dreams"—this is the translation by Dar Ahlam. The luxury hotel, lodged in what used to be a castle, combines French savoir-vivre with oriental traditions. The Parisian landscape architect Louis Benech created an oasis within an oasis with the five acre garden surrounding the Kasbah. Lush bougainvilleas twine around the bathhouse and tents for outdoor massages lure you to relax en plein air.

Im Südosten des Landes, wo die Ausläufer der Sahara beginnen, steht ein „Haus der Träume" – so die Übersetzung von Dar Ahlam. Die Luxusherberge, untergebracht in einer ehemaligen Burg, verbindet französisches Savoir-vivre mit orientalischen Traditionen. Eine Oase in der Oase hat der Pariser Landschaftsarchitekt Louis Benech mit dem zwei Hektar umfassenden Garten rund um die Kasbah geschaffen. Üppige Bougainvilleen ranken sich am Badehaus empor, Zelte für die Outdoor-Massage locken zur Entspannung unter freiem Himmel.

Dans le Sud-Ouest du pays, là où commencent les premières dunes du Sahara, se trouve une « maison des rêves » – telle est la traduction de Dar Ahlam. Cet hôtel de luxe, logé dans un ancien château-fort, conjugue le savoir-vivre à la française et les traditions orientales. Le paysagiste parisien Louis Benech a créé dans les jardins de deux hectares qui entourent la kasbah une oasis dans l'oasis. Des bougainvillées opulentes grimpent sur les murs de la maison des bains, des tentes pour les massages à l'extérieur invitent à la détente à ciel ouvert.

En el sudeste del país, donde comienza el Sáhara, se levanta la "casa de los sueños", esa es la traducción de Dar Ahlam. El alojamiento de lujo, ubicado en una antigua alcazaba, aúna el arte de vivir francés con las tradiciones orientales. Louis Benech, arquitecto de paisajes parisino, creó un oasis dentro de un oasis con sus dos hectáreas de jardín en torno al kasbah. Las buganvilias exuberantes se extienden por la casa de baños y las tiendas para masajes, situadas en el exterior, invitan a relajarse al aire libre.

Nella zona a sud est del paese, dove iniziano i confini del Sahara, si trova la "casa dei sogni"– questa è la traduzione di Dar Ahlam. La residenza di lusso, sita su una ex roccaforte, unisce il savoir-vivre francese alle tradizioni orientali. Un'oasi nell'oasi, creata dall'architetto paesaggista parigino Louis Benech grazie ad un giardino di due ettari attorno alla Kasbah. Dei rigogliosi bougainville si arrampicano lungo le cabine, e le tende dove si eseguono massaggi richiamano al relax all'aperto.

Quiet areas with an oriental flair are located behind thick walls.

Hinter dicken Mauern befinden sich Ruhebereiche mit orientalischem Flair.

Derrière les murs épais se trouvent des espaces de repos à l'ambiance orientale.

Detrás de los gruesos muros se encuentran las áreas de descanso con el típico ambiente oriental.

Dietro a delle spesse mura si trovano le zone di riposo dal fascino orientale.

All rooms of the Kasbah hotel are bright and bountiful. Many of them are equipped with a terrace, where the guests may spend the evening.

Alle Zimmer des Kasbah-Hotels sind hell und großzügig. Viele sind mit einer Terrasse ausgestattet, wo die Gäste den Abend verbringen können.

Toutes les chambres de l'hôtel Kasbah sont lumineuses et spacieuses. Beaucoup disposent d'une terrasse, sur laquelle les hôtes peuvent passer la soirée.

Todas las habitaciones del kasbah son luminosas y amplias y muchas tienen terraza, donde el huésped puede pasar la tarde.

Tutte le camere dell'Hotel-Kasbah sono luminose e generose. Molte hanno una terrazza dove gli ospiti possono trascorrere una serata.

Madinat Jumeirah

Dubai, United Arab Emirates

Waterways meander through the Madinat, built like a traditional Arabian village, with the three destinations Mina A'Salam, Al Qasr, Dar Al Masyaf and its cheery and colorful Madinat Jumeirah souk. The Jumeirah Group's hotel village stretches for almost four kilometers along the sea. Guests can reach the 44 different restaurants and bars via wooden water taxis. Or they can visit the Six Senses Spa, with its 30 freestanding treatment rooms, surrounded by luscious and blooming gardens and one of the largest fitness areas in the Middle East.

Wasserwege mäandern durch das wie ein traditionelles arabisches Dorf gebaute Madinat mit den drei Destinationen Mina A'Salam, Al Qasr, Dar Al Masyaf und seinem farbenfrohen Madinat Jumeirah Suk. Fast vier Kilometer zieht sich das Hoteldorf der Jumeirah Gruppe am Meer entlang. Gäste können mit Wassertaxis aus Holz die 44 verschiedenen Restaurants und Bars erreichen. Oder den Six Senses Spa, der mit seinen 30 freistehenden Behandlungsräumen, umgeben von üppig blühenden Gärten, als der größte Wellness-Bereich im Mittleren Osten gilt.

Des canaux artificiels sillonnent le Madinat, ensemble construit comme un village arabe traditionnel et comprenant les trois destinationes Mina A'Salam, Al Qasr, Dar Al Masyaf, ainsi que le souk bariolé Madinat Jumeirah. Le complexe hôtelier de la chaîne Jumeirah s'étire sur presque quatre kilomètres le long du littoral. Les hôtes sont emmenés par des bateaux en bois jusqu'aux 44 restaurants et bars. Ou au Six Senses Spa, le centre de fitness considéré comme le plus grand du Moyen-Orient avec ses 30 salles de soins autonomes, entouré de jardins fleuris luxuriants.

Las acequias, que discurren formando meandros, atraviesan el Madinat, una instalación construida imitando un pueblo árabe y compuesta por tres destinaciones, Mina A'Salam, Al Quasr y Dar Al Masyaf, y Madinat Jumeirah, un colorido suk o plaza del mercado. Este pueblo hotel del grupo Jumeirah se extiende a lo largo de la costa durante casi cuatro kilómetros. Los huéspedes pueden dirigirse a los 44 restaurantes y bares a bordo de taxis de madera. O pueden visitar el Six Senses Spa que, con sus 30 zonas independientes de tratamiento rodeadas de exuberantes jardines, está considerado como el centro de salud y bienestar más grande de Oriente Medio.

Vie d'acqua formano meandri attraverso il Madinat, costruito come un tipico paese arabo, con i tre destinazioni Mina A'Salam, Al Qasr, Dar Al Masyaf ed il suo souk Madinat Jumeirah dai colori vivaci. La struttura del gruppo Jumeirah si estende lungo il mare per quasi quattro chilometri. Gli ospiti possono raggiungere, con piccole imbarcazioni-taxi in legno, i 44 diversi ristoranti e bar oppure essere accompagnati alla Six Senses SPA, che con i suoi 30 locali e i vari trattamenti, in mezzo a giardini lussureggianti, è considerata il più grande centro benessere del Medio Oriente.

A delightful contrast: the view over the hotel village with its waterways to Dubai's spectacular landmark, the Burj al Arab by Jumeirah.

Ein reizvoller Kontrast: Der Blick über das Hoteldorf mit seinen Wasserwegen auf das spektakuläre Wahrzeichen Dubais, das Burj al Arab von Jumeirah.

Un contraste plein de charme : la vue au-dessus du complexe hôtelier avec son réseau de canaux sur le spectaculaire emblème de Dubai, le Burj al Arab de Jumeirah.

Un contraste encantador: la vista sobre el pueblo hotel y sus acequias con el espectacular símbolo de Dubai, el Burj al Arab de Jumeirah, al fondo.

Un affascinante contrasto: la vista dal centro residenziale, con le sue vie d'acqua, è sullo spettacolare Burj al Arab di Jumeirah, che con la sua forma di vela spiegata è diventato il simbolo di Dubai.

The inspiration for the interior design is none other than the palatial style, featuring an abundance of marble and carvings. The Six Senses Spa, on the other hand, remains resolutely modern.

Die Innenraumgestaltung ist – wie könnte es anders sein – einem Palast nachempfunden, mit viel Marmor und Schnitzarbeiten. Sachlich modern gibt sich dagegen das Six Senses Spa.

La réalisation des intérieurs ressemble – comment pourrait-il en être autrement – à celle d'un palais, avec beaucoup de marbre et de sculptures sur bois. Le Six Senses Spa est, quant à lui, résolument moderne et fonctionnel.

El diseño interior del espacio está inspirado, como no, en el de un palacio, con abundancia de mármol y tallas de madera. En contraste, el Six Senses Spa ha sido concebido con una línea más moderna.

L'arredamento all'interno è – ovviamente – adeguato ad un palazzo, con tanto marmo e lavori d'intaglio. Razionale e moderno si presenta invece il centro benessere Six Senses SPA.

One&Only Royal Mirage
Dubai, United Arab Emirates

Domes made from clay slates, low walls and date palms swaying in the wind define the silhouette of the luxury hotel village on the blinding white Jumeirah beach, which strictly speaking consists of three different resorts. A fountain in the inner courtyard, around which generous divans are positioned, emphasizes the Arabian appearance. The Givenchy spa, a traditional hammam and the pool landscape, sheltered by palms, offer perfect relaxation.

Kuppeln aus Lehmziegeln, niedrige Mauern und sich im Wind wiegende Dattelpalmen bestimmen die Silhouette des luxuriösen Hoteldorfs am blendend weißen Jumeirah Beach, das genau genommen aus drei unterschiedlichen Resorts besteht. Ein Brunnen im Innenhof, um den sich ausladende Diwane gruppieren, unterstreicht die arabische Anmutung. Der Givenchy-Spa, ein traditionelles Hammam und die von Palmen beschattete Poollandschaft bieten perfekte Entspannung.

Des coupoles constituées de tuiles en argile, des murets et des dattiers se balançant au gré du vent dessinent la silhouette de ce complexe hôtelier luxueux au bord de la plage d'un blanc éblouissant de Jumeirah, composé en fait de trois resorts distincts. L'atmosphère arabe est soulignée par une fontaine au milieu du patio autour duquel se trouvent des divans invitant au repos. Le Spa Givenchy, un hammam traditionnel et la piscine ombragée de palmiers assurent une parfaite détente.

Las cúpulas de ladrillo de adobe, los muros bajos y las palmeras de dátiles mecidas por el viento, forman la línea del contorno de este lujoso pueblo hotel compuesto, en realidad, por tres centros levantados en la luminosa playa blanca Jumeirah Beach. La fuente, situada en el centro del patio interior y rodeada de amplios divanes, subraya el acento árabe. El balneario Givenchy, un hamman tradicional y la piscina rodeada de palmeras, ofrecen el escenario perfecto para la relajación.

Cupole in mattoni d'argilla, basse mura e palme da datteri che ondeggiano al vento caratterizzano la silhouette del lussuosissimo complesso residenziale del Jumeirah Beach. È caratterizzato da un candore splendente e composto da tre strutture. Una fontana nel cortile interno, attorno alla quale si raggruppano ampi e invitanti divani ne accentua la grazia araba. La Givenchy-SPA, un hammam tradizionale e il susseguirsi di piscine, ombreggiate da palme, offrono puro relax.

Spacious shadowed garden areas with palm trees and an aquatic landscape give the hotel premises the appearance of an oasis.

Weitläufige Gartenanlagen mit Schatten spendenden Palmen und mehreren Pools lassen die Hotelanlage wie eine Oase wirken.

Grâce à ses grands jardins ombragés par des palmiers et plusieurs piscines, l'ensemble de l'hôtel ressemble à un oasis.

Los vastos terrenos del jardín a la sombra de las palmeras y varias piscinas hacen que las instalaciones del hotel parezcan un oasis.

Grandi giardini con palme che danno ombra, e diverse piscine rendono l'hotel una vera oasi.

The rooms and suites as well as the hammam with its various steam baths and jacuzzis have been kept in the traditional Arabic style.

Zimmer und Suiten wie auch der Hammam mit seinen unterschiedlichen Dampfbädern und Jacuzzis sind im traditionellen arabischen Stil gehalten.

Les chambres et les suites, ainsi que le hammam avec ses différents bains à vapeur et jacuzzis, ont été réalisés dans le style arabe traditionnel.

Las habitaciones y suites, así como el Hammam, con sus diversos baños de vapor y bañeras, se han mantenido con el estilo árabe tradicional.

Camere e suite ed anche l'hammam con i suoi diversi bagni di vapore e idromassaggi, sono tutti arredati in tradizionale stile arabo.

Emirates Palace Abu Dhabi

Abu Dhabi, United Arab Emirates

Like a palace out of Thousand and One Nights—this encompasses the appearance Abu Dhabi's newest, top-class luxury hotel. Located in the middle of an almost 200 acre park landscape, the two wings of the building measure one kilometer in length. 114 domes define its silhouette. The majestic oriental luxury of the interior is matched by the gigantic exterior appearance. Even the technical equipment sets standards: the 394 rooms, suites and public hotel spaces boast 755 plasma screens.

Wie ein Palast aus Tausendundeiner Nacht mutet Abu Dhabis neuestes Luxushotel der Superlative an. Inmitten einer 80 Hektar großen Parklandschaft gelegen, misst das Gebäude mit seinen zwei Flügeln einen Kilometer in der Länge. 114 Kuppeln bestimmen seine Silhouette. Der gigantischen äußeren Erscheinung entspricht der prunkvolle orientalische Luxus des Interieurs. Selbst die technische Ausstattung setzt Maßstäbe: Allein 755 Plasma-Bildschirme befinden sich in den 394 Zimmern, Suiten und öffentlichen Hotelbereichen.

Tel un palais des Mille et Une Nuits, ce nouvel établissement d'un luxe extrême se trouve à Abou Dhabi. Situé au cœur d'un immense parc de 80 hectares, le bâtiment constitué de deux ailes mesure un kilomètre de long. Sa silhouette est marquée par 114 coupoles. Les fastes orientaux des intérieurs sont à l'égal de cette apparition gigantesque. Mêmes les équipements technologiques servent de référence : 755 écrans plasma viennent équiper les 394 chambres, suites et les espaces publics de l'hôtel.

Como un palacio sacado de las Mil y una noches, el Abu Dhabis, el último hotel de lujo construido, alcanza el grado de superlativo. En medio de un parque de 80 hectáreas, el edificio junto a sus dos alas llega al kilómetro de longitud. 114 cúpulas determinan su contorno. Su gigantesca apariencia exterior refleja el suntuoso lujo oriental de su interior. Incluso su equipamiento tecnológico establece nuevas pautas: un total de 755 pantallas de plasma se reparten entre sus 394 habitaciones, suites y en las áreas del hotel abiertas al público.

Come un palazzo da Mille e una notte ecco l'albergo di lusso costruito di recente. In un parco il cui paesaggio si estende per ben 80 ettari, l'edificio con le sue due ali è lungo un chilometro. La sua silhouette è formata da 114 cupole. All' imponente aspetto esterno corrisponde lo sfarzoso lusso orientale degli interni. La tecnologia non è da meno: ben 755 schermi al plasma, per esempio, sono posizionati nelle 394 camere, nelle suite e nelle zone comuni dell'hotel.

Even in the corridors—here in the eastern wing—the oriental opulence thrives with its rich array of ornaments.

Selbst in den Korridoren – hier im Ostflügel – entfaltet sich die orientalische Opulenz mit ihrer reichen Ornamentik.

Dans les couloirs aussi — comme ici dans l'aile Est — le faste oriental se déploie avec ses riches ornements.

En los mismos corredores, situados aquí en el ala este, revela la opulencia oriental con sus ricos ornamentos.

Persino nei corridoi qui in oriente si nota l'opulenza, nei ricchi ornamenti.

The ceiling mosaics in the Blue Salon make a striking mark on the luxury hotel, which is otherwise kept in desert colors.

Das Deckenmosaik im Blue Salon setzt einen markanten Akzent im ansonsten ganz in Wüstenfarben gehaltenen Luxushotel.

La mosaïque au plafond du Blue Salon constitue un élément marquant dans cet hôtel de luxe dont les teintes sont celles du désert.

El mosaico del techo del Blue Salon pone un marcado acento en el hotel, que ha mantenido en el resto de los espacios los colores del desierto.

Il mosaico del soffitto nel salone blu è una variente per un hotel di lusso solitamente qui arredato nei colori del deserto.

The Oberoi Mauritius

Turtle Bay, Mauritius

The unique cultural mix of African, Asian and European influence on Mauritius is reflected in the architecture and design of this hotel complex, with its 72 villas and terrace-pavilions. The roofs are thatched with dried sugar cane, the walls are constructed of volcanic rock, and African art objects set the tone in the rooms. This refuge lies in total seclusion on the island's northwest coast, directly on Turtle Bay, although the busy island capital of Port Louis is only 20 minutes away by car.

Der einzigartige kulturelle Mix aus afrikanischen, asiatischen und europäischen Einflüssen auf Mauritius spiegelt sich in der Architektur und dem Design der Hotel-anlage mit ihren 72 Villen und Terrassen-Pavillons wider. Die Dächer wurden mit getrocknetem Zuckerrohr gedeckt, die Mauern sind aus Vulkangestein gefertigt, afrika-nische Kunstgegenstände setzen in den Zimmern Akzente. Das Refugium liegt in völliger Abgeschiedenheit an der Nordwestküste der Insel, direkt am Baie aux Tortues, trotzdem erreicht man die quirlige Inselhauptstadt Port Louis in nur 20 Autominuten.

Le mélange culturel unique des influences africaines, asiatiques et européennes sur l'île Maurice se reflète dans l'architecture et la conception de cet ensemble de 72 villas et petits pavillons. Les toits sont recouverts de cannes à sucre séchées, les murs sont édifiés en pierre volcanique et des objets d'art africains créent le contraste dans les chambres. Ce havre de paix est complètement isolé sur la côte nord-ouest de l'île, directement au bord de la baie aux tortues ; on rejoint pourtant Port Louis, la remuante capitale de l'île, en seulement 20 minutes en voiture.

La excepcional mezcla cultural de influencias africanas, asiáticas y europeas presente en Mauricio, se refleja en la arquitectura y en el diseño de este complejo hotelero con sus 72 villas y sus pabellones. Los tejados están recubiertos con cañas de azúcar secas, los muros han sido elaborados con piedras volcánicas y los objetos de arte afri-canos ponen el acento artístico en las habitaciones. Este refugio se encuentra en un lugar completamente apartado, en la costa noroeste de la isla, en la Baie aux Tortues. Aún así es posible llegar a la animada capital de la isla, Port Louis, en sólo 20 minutos en coche.

La singolare mescolanza tra cultura africana, asiatica ed europea si rispecchia nell'architettura e nel design del complesso residenziale con le sue 72 ville e terrazze-pa-diglioni. I tetti sono stati, coperti con canna da zucchero essiccata, per la costruzione delle mura è stata usata pietra lavica, ed oggetti d'arte africana danno alle camere un tocco particolare. Il rifugio giace completamente isolato sulla costa nord ovest dell'isola, direttamente sulla baia delle Tartarughe, ma in soli 20 minuti d'auto è possibile raggiungere la vivacissima capitale dell'isola Port Louis.

Natural materials and bright, finely graded hues provide for a light atmosphere.

Natürliche Materialien und helle, fein abgestufte Farbschattierungen verleihen eine lichte Atmosphäre.

Des matériaux naturels et des teintes claires et nuancées sont à l'ori-gine de l'ambiance lumineuse.

Los materiales naturales y los contrastes de color proporcionan una atmósfera clara.

Materiali naturali e giochi di chiaro scuro donano un ambiente lu-minoso.

Here water becomes an element of architectural design: the surface of the pool and ponds around the restaurant optically merge with the Indian Ocean.

Hier wird Wasser zum architektonischen Gestaltungselement: die Oberfläche des Pools und der Teiche um das Restaurant verschmelzen optisch mit dem Indischen Ozean.

Ici, l'eau fait partie intégrante de la conception architecturale : la surface de la piscine et des bassins autour du restaurant se fondent visuellement dans l'océan Indien.

Aquí el agua se convierte en un elemento arquitectónico: la superficie de la piscina y de los estanques que rodean al restaurante parece fundirse con el Océano Índico.

Qui l'acqua è un elemento di creazione architettonica: la superficie della piscina e degli stagni attorno al ristorante sembrano fondersi nell'Oceano Indiano.

Banyan Tree Seychelles

Mahé Island, Seychelles

Whether located in the rainforest or on the beach, one sees the Indian Ocean and the fine-grained sandy bay from the white villas. Colonial architecture, ethno-fabrics, and Creole delicacies exude exotic charms. The furniture and accessories were gathered from Africa and Southeast Asia. The legendary Coco de Mer, the largest nut in the world, inspired a great deal of the artwork featured. Even larger are the giant turtles that one may encounter on stroll along the beach.

Ob im Regenwald oder direkt am Strand gelegen, von den weißen Villen aus sieht man den Indischen Ozean und die feinsandige Bucht. Koloniale Architektur, Ethnostoffe und kreolische Delikatessen verbreiten exotischen Charme. Die Möbel und Accessoires sind aus Afrika und Süd-Ost-Asien zusammengetragen. Inspiration für viele Kunstwerke war die legendäre Coco de Mer, die größte Nuss der Welt. Noch größer sind die Riesenschildkröten, denen man beim Strandspaziergang begegnen kann.

Qu'elles soient situées dans la forêt vierge ou directement en bord de mer, toutes les villas blanches donnent sur l'océan Indien et les baies de sable fin – le cliché carte postale typique. L'architecture coloniale, les tissus ethniques et les mets créoles transmettent aux espaces un charme exotique. Les meubles et les accessoires sont originaires d'Afrique ou du Sud-Est asiatique. La coco de mer légendaire, la plus grosse noix du monde, sert d'inspiration à de nombreuses oeuvres d'art. Les tortues géantes que l'on peut voir à l'occasion d'une promenade sur la plage sont encore plus gigantesques.

Independientemente estando en la selva lluviosa o en la playa, desde los blancos chalés se divisa el Océano Índico y la bahía de arena fina. La arquitectura colonial, las telas étnicas y los platos preparados criollos irradian el encanto exótico. Los muebles y los accesorios provienen de África y el sureste asiático. Muchas obras de arte están inspiradas en el legendario coco-de-mer, la nuez más grande del mundo. Más grandes aún son las tortugas gigantes con las que uno se puede encontrar al salir a pasear.

Dalla foresta pluviale come dalla spiaggia, dalle ville bianche si vedono l'Oceano Indiano e la baia dalla sabbia fine. Architettura coloniale, stoffe e prelibatezze creole diffondono lo charme esotico. I mobili e gli accessori provvengono dall'Africa e dal sud est asiatico. Ispirazione per molte delle opere d'arte è la leggendaria Coco de Mer, la più grande noce al mondo. Ma più grandi sono le tartaruge giganti che si possono incontrare durante passeggiate sulla spiaggia.

The magnificent aquatic landscape extends all the way to the ocean waves in the protected bay.

Die grandiose Poollandschaft reicht bis zur Meeresbrandung in der geschützten Bucht.

Le grandiose paysage de bassin s'étend jusqu'au déferlement des vagues dans la baie protégée.

El grandioso paisaje de piscinas se extiende hasta las olas de la bahía protegida.

Il paesaggio grandioso delle piscine arriva fino alla risacca del mare in una baia riparata.

Lost footsteps in the sand—a symbol of a spot where every villa offers an highly intimate escape together with the stimulus of an exotic culture and spiritual world.

Verlorene Fußspuren am Strand – Sinnbild für einen Ort, an dem jede Villa einen ganz intimen Platz bietet, verbunden mit dem Reiz einer exotischen Kultur und Geisteswelt.

Des pas perdus sur la plage – une image pleine de sens pour un lieu où chaque villa offre un espace très intime ; le tout associé à la découverte d'une culture exotique et de son environnement spirituel.

Pasos perdidos en la playa –símbolo de un lugar, en el que cada chalé ofrece un espacio íntimo, unido al atractivo de una cultura y un mundo espiritual exóticos.

Pace perduta sulla spiaggia: metafora per un luogo dove ogni villa offre uno spazio privato, oltre al fascino esotico della cultura e dello spirito.

North Island

North Island, Seychelles

4° 22' **South**, 55° 13' East—coordinates worth noting. That's because the resort on this small island gives rise to visions of heavenly climes. Nestled in the greenery of the trees, each of the eleven villas comprises over 4800-square feet. There, every conceivable comfort together with private refreshing pool, designer furniture, and a lawn in front of the terrace await. Yet, the lodge presents itself as environmentally-friendly and original: in half African, half Balinese style.

4° 22' **Süd**, 55° 13' Ost – eine Positionsbestimmung zum Vormerken. Denn das Resort dieses kleinen Eilandes lässt Erinnerungen an paradiesische Zustände aufkommen. Versteckt im Grün der Bäume, misst jede der elf Villen 450 m². Darin wartet jeglicher Komfort mit eigenem Erfrischungspool, Designermöbeln und Liegewiese vor der Terrasse. Gleichwohl präsentiert sich die Lodge umweltschonend und ursprünglich: im Stil halb afrikanisch, halb balinesisch.

4° 22' **Sud**, 55° 13' Est – une position dont on doit se souvenir. En effet, le domaine de cette petite île réveille des souvenirs de conditions paradisiaques. Cachées dans le vert des arbres, chacune des onze villas possèdent une superficie de 450 m². Là vous attend un confort complet et une piscine privée pour vous rafraîchir, des meubles de designers et une pelouse de détente devant la terrasse. Le pavillon a une apparence naturelle et originelle : de style moitié africain, moitié balinais.

4° 22' **Sur**, 55° 13' Este –una posición a tener en cuenta, ya que el resort en esta pequeña isla evoca sensaciones paradisíacas. Escondidos tras el verde de los árboles, cada una de los once villas tiene 450 m². Aquí se encuentran todo tipo de comodidades: Una piscina propia, muebles de diseño y un prado para tumbarse delante de la terraza. No obstante, el diseño es auténtico y compatible con el medio ambiente: Un estilo mitad africano, mitad balinés.

4° 22' **sud**, 55° 13' est: una posizione da ricordare. Il resort di questa piccola isola rammenta, non a caso, il paradiso. Nascoste nel verde degli alberi, ognuna delle undici ville ha un'area di 450 m². Al loro interno si trova ogni genere di confort: una piscina per rinfrescarsi, mobili di design e un solarium davanti alla terrazza. Allo stesso tempo il lodge rispetta l'ambiente con la sua originalità: uno stile misto tra l'africano ed il balinese.

The resort contributes to the preservation of a unique natural environment, while simultaneously offering the greatest level of seclusion possible.

Das Resort trägt zum Erhalt einer einzigartigen Natur bei — und bietet gleichzeitig eine größtmögliche Abgeschiedenheit.

Le domaine participe à la préservation de la nature exceptionnelle qui l'entoure — et offre un isolement total.

El resort contribuye a la conservación de una naturaleza única y, al mismo tiempo, permite un gran recogimiento.

Il resort contribuisce alla conservazione di una natura unica offrendo contemporaneamente il massimo dell'isolamento.

Living like *Robinson Crusoe without having to sacrifice western luxury—that's the special charm of North Island.*

Leben wie *Robinson Crusoe ohne auf westlichen Luxus verzichten zu müssen – darin liegt der besondere Reiz von North Island.*

Vivre comme *Robinson Crusoé, sans renoncer cependant au luxe occidental – c'est le défi relevé par North Island.*

Vivir como *Robinson Crusoe sin tener que renunciar al lujo occidental, eso es lo que hace especialmente atractiva la North Island.*

Vivere come *Robinson Crusoe senza dover rinunciare al lusso occidentale: è questo il fascino particolare della North Island.*

Vumbura Plains

Okavango Delta, Botswana

For several years now, hunting has been strictly prohibited in the Okavango Delta in southern Africa. The antelope, buffalo, elephants and lions living here in the reservation can often be observed from just a few meters away. The two Vumbura Camps are the starting point for photo safaris. The South African architect couple Silvio Rech and Lesley Carsten have created here a nearly perfect mixture of untouched wilderness and purist luxury.

Seit einigen Jahren schon herrscht im Okavango Delta im südlichen Afrika ein striktes Jagdverbot. Antilopen, Büffel, Elefanten und Löwen leben hier und können in dem Reservat aus oft nur wenigen Metern Entfernung beobachtet werden. Ausgangspunkt für Fotosafaris sind die zwei Vumbura Camps. Das südafrikanische Architekten-Ehepaar Silvio Rech und Lesley Carsten hat hier eine nahezu perfekte Mischung aus unberührter Wildnis und puristischem Luxus geschaffen.

Depuis quelques années déjà, le delta de l'Okavango dans le Sud de l'Afrique bénéficie d'une interdiction de chasse stricte. Des antilopes, des buffles, des éléphants et des lions vivent ici et peuvent être observés souvent à une distance de quelques mètres seulement. Les deux Camps Vumbura sont les points de départ des safaris photo. Le couple d'architectes Sud-Africain Silvio Rech et Lesley Carsten a créé ici un mariage presque parfait entre la nature sauvage et un luxe puriste.

Desde hace ya algunos años impera una estricta prohibición de caza en el delta de Okavango, en el sur de África. Los antílopes, búfalos, elefantes y leones viven ahí y se les puede observar en la reserva, a menudo a pocos metros de distancia. Los dos Vumbura Camps son el punto de partida para los safaris fotográficos. El matrimonio de arquitectos sudafricanos, Silvio Rech y Lesley Carsten ha conseguido una mezcla casi perfecta de naturaleza intacta y lujo purista.

Già da alcuni anni vige nel delta del Okavango nell'Africa del Sud un severo divieto di caccia. Antilopi, bufali, elefanti e leoni vivono qui dove è spesso possibile osservarli anche da pochi metri di distanza. Il punto di partenza per safari fotografici è rappresentato dai due Vumbura Camps. La coppia sudafricana di architetti Silvio Rech e Lesley Carsten vi ha creato un mix quasi perfetto tra natura selvaggia ed incontaminata e vero lusso.

Seven villas on wooden platforms make up the complex. They are connected with the main building by means of footbridges.

Sieben Villen auf Holzplattformen gehören zur Anlage. Mit dem Haupthaus sind sie durch Stege verbunden.

Sept villas sur des plates-formes en bois font partie des installations. Elles sont reliées au bâtiment principal par des passerelles.

Siete villas sobre plataformas de madera forman parte del complejo y están unidas con la casa principal por caminos.

Il complesso è composto da sette ville, poste su delle piattaforme di legno, collegate ad una casa principale grazie a dei sentieri.

Nature and glassless rooms nearly melt into one. Each of the seven accommodations has its own terrace, a refreshment pool as well as an outdoor shower.

Natur und glaslose Räume verschmelzen schier. Jede der sieben Unterkünfte hat eine eigene Terrasse, einen Erfrischungspool sowie eine Freiluftdusche.

La nature et les espaces sans vitres semblent se confondre. Chacun des sept logements dispose de sa propre terrasse, d'une piscine et d'une douche en plein air.

La naturaleza y los espacios sin cristales casi se confunden. Cada uno de los siete alojamientos tiene su propia terraza, una pequeña piscina para refrescarse y una ducha al aire libre.

La natura e gli spazi aperti si fondono. Ognuna delle sette abitazioni ha un terrazzo proprio, una piscina dove rinfrescarsi ed una doccia all'aperto.

Mount Nelson Hotel
Cape Town, South Africa

The well up to a century-old hotel, itself a legend, is located at the foot of Table Mountain, Cape Town's landmark. After extensive renovations, the "Pink Lady", as it is affectionately referred to by guests due its pink facade, can once again welcome guests with a one of a kind colonial charm. The 201 rooms and suites are distributed in the main building and the restored historical summerhouses in the park nearly 7,5 acres in size, planted in 1843 and still home to the original variety of trees.

Am Fuße des Tafelbergs, dem Wahrzeichen Kapstadts, gelegen ist das gut hundert Jahre alte Hotel selbst eine Legende. Nach umfangreicher Renovierung kann die „Pink Lady", wie die Gäste das Hotel wegen seiner rosaroten Fassade liebevoll nennen, wieder mit einem ganz besonderen kolonialen Charme aufwarten. Die 201 Zimmer und Suiten verteilen sich auf das Hauptgebäude und die restaurierten historischen Gartenhäuser im schon 1843 angelegten, drei Hektar großen Park mit seinem wertvollen alten Baumbestand.

Au pied de la Table Mountain, l'emblème du Cap, cet hôtel largement centenaire est une véritable légende. Après une importante réfection, la « Dame Rose », comme le surnomment gentiment ses hôtes en raison de sa façade rose, peut de nouveau se présenter avec un charme colonial tout particulier. Les 201 chambres et suites se répartissent sur le bâtiment principal et les maisons de jardin historiques restaurées, dans un parc de trois hectares aménagé dès 1843 et planté de grands arbres aux essences rares.

A los pies de la meseta, el símbolo de la Ciudad del Cabo, se encuentra este centenario hotel, toda una leyenda. Después de profundas reformas, el "Pink Lady", como le llaman con cariño sus huéspedes por su fachada rosa, ha recuperado su especial encanto colonial. Las 201 habitaciones y suites están ubicadas en el edificio principal, y los históricos pabellones, levantados en 1843 y actualmente restaurados, se reparten por el jardín de tres hectáreas con viejos y valiosos árboles.

Ai piedi della Table Mountain, simbolo di Città del Capo, è ubicato questo Hotel che esiste da ben cento anni, tanto da rappresentare una leggenda. La "Pink Lady", come viene amorevolmente chiamato dagli ospiti per la sua facciata color rosa, si ripresenta nel suo fascino coloniale particolare dopo essere stato restaurato da cima a fondo. Le 201 camere e suite si suddividono fra l'edificio principale ed i padiglioni storici nel parco di tre ettari, realizzato già nel 1843 e dal pregiato e antico patrimonio arboreo.

Tender pastel colors accent the colonial charm of the South African grand hotel.

Zarte Pastelltöne betonen den kolonialen Charme des südafrikanischen Grandhotels.

Des tons pastel doux soulignent le charme colonial de ce Grand Hôtel Sud-Africain.

Los suaves tonos pastel acentúan el encanto colonial del gran hotel sudafricano.

Toni pastello delicati evidenziano lo charme coloniale del grand hotel sudafricano.

The newly opened Planet Champagne Bar by the South African designer Graham Viney quickly rose to become a "place to be" in Cape Town.

Die neu eröffnete Planet Champagne Bar des südafrikanischen Designers Graham Viney avancierte schnell zum „Place to be" in Kapstadt.

Le bar Planet Champagne du concepteur sud-africain Graham Viney qui a récemment ouvert ses portes est vite devenu le dernier « lieu à la mode » du Cap.

El recién inaugurado Planet Champagne Bar, del diseñador sudafricano Graham Viney, se ha convertido en poco tiempo en uno de las mejores "lugares donde estar" de la Ciudad del Cabo.

Il bar Planet Champagne, aperto da poco e ideato dal designer sudafricano Graham Viney, si è velocemente trasformato in un luogo d' eccellenza a Città del Capo.

Birkenhead House

Hermanus, South Africa

As lucent as the wave crests, the hotel rises from a cliff above "Walker Bay". Light shell tones characterize the interior with its nostalgic baths, antiques and chaise-longues that would only leave to take a refreshing dip in one of the three pools and on the beautiful bathing beach. From the terrace, guests can watch the Southern Right Whales, which come into the bay to calf. In the evening, when the lanterns on the patio have been lit and the sea air wafts through the dining room, the young hotel team serves freshly caught fish, lobster and sushi.

Leuchtend wie die Schaumkronen der Wellen erhebt sich das Hotel auf einem Felsen über der „Walker Bay". Helle Muscheltöne prägen auch das Interieur mit nostalgischen Bädern, Antiquitäten und Chaiselonguen, die man höchstens verlässt, um sich in einem der drei Pools und am schönen Badestrand zu erfrischen. Von der Terrasse aus können Gäste Southern Right Wale beobachten, die zum Kalben in die Bucht kommen. Abends, wenn die Laternen im Patio leuchten und Meeresluft in den Speisesaal weht, serviert das junge Hotelteam fangfrischen Fisch, Hummer und Sushi.

Rayonnant comme la couronne d'écume des vagues, l'hôtel se dresse sur un rocher au-dessus de la « Walker Bay ». Des tons coquillage clair caractérisent les intérieurs, avec des salles de bains nostalgiques, des antiquités et des chaises longues que l'on ne quitte que pour aller se rafraîchir dans une des trois piscines ou sur la magnifique plage. De la terrasse, les hôtes peuvent observer la baleine australe venue mettre bas dans la baie. Le soir, quand les lanternes s'allument dans le patio et qu'une brise marine souffle dans la salle à manger, la jeune équipe de l'hôtel sert des poissons fraîchement pêchés, du homard et des sushis.

Este hotel, brillante como el resplandor de la espuma de las crestas de las olas, se levanta en la roca por encima de la "Walker Bay". Los colores claros de las conchas impregnan el interior, con cuartos de baños nostálgicos, antigüedades y sillones chaise longue que el visitante sólo abandonará para refrescarse en una de las tres piscinas o en la playa. Desde la terraza, los huéspedes pueden observar a las ballenas Southern Right, que se dirigen a las bahías a dar a luz. Por la tarde, cuando las farolas del patio se iluminan y el aire del mar recorre el comedor, el joven equipo del hotel sirve el pescado, las langostas recién pescados y el sushi.

L'albergo, scintillante come la schiuma delle onde, si impone sulla scogliera della "Walker Bay". Chiari toni dai colori delle conchiglie danno la loro impronta anche agli interni: i bagni nostalgici dal sapore antico, i pezzi d'antiquariato e le sdraio che si abbandonano solo per rinfrescarsi in una delle tre piscine o per spostarsi verso la magnifica spiaggia. Dalla terrazzo, gli ospiti possono osservare le balene Southern Right che vengono nella baia per figliare. La sera, quando sono accese le lanterne nel patio e la brezza del mare aleggia nella sala ristorante, il giovane team dell'albergo serve pesce fresco, astici e sushi.

Guests can dive into the pool not to mention into the sheltered bay extending from right in front of the hotel.

Abtauchen können Gäste im Pool und in der geschützten Bucht, die sich gleich vor dem Hotel erstreckt.

Les hôtes peuvent plonger dans la piscine ou dans la baie protégée qui s'étend juste devant l'hôtel.

Los huéspedes pueden bañarse en la piscina y en la bahía protegida que se extiende delante del hotel.

Gli ospiti si possono immergere nella piscina e nella baia protetta che si stende davanti al hotel.

The comfortable suites ensure instant relaxation.

Sofortige Entspannung garantieren die komfortablen Suiten.

La détente immédiate est garantie par les bains de soleil sur la véranda et dans les confortables lits à baldaquin des suites.

Las tumbonas de la terraza acristalada y las cómodas camas con dosel de las suites, garantizan una relajación inmediata.

Relax immediato è garantito dalla comodità delle suite.

Earth Lodge
Sabi Sabi Private Game Reserve, South Africa

Like a chameleon, the walls of the Eco Lodge with their clay plaster blend in with the sand-colored surroundings. The South African architect, Mohammed Hans, built them in the middle of the Sabi Sabi-Reserve, a region that boasts one of Africa's most abundant animal populations. The hotel's interior presents itself extravagantly with furniture created especially the lodge itself including tables with Impala horn legs and bathtubs reminiscent of giant, halved ostrich eggs. At dinner in the open loggia, the wilderness begins right in front of festively laid tables.

Wie ein Chamäleon passen sich die lehmverputzten Mauern der Eco-Lodge der sandfarbenen Umgebung an. Der südafrikanische Architekt Mohammed Hans hat sie mitten im Sabi Sabi-Reservat, einer der tierreichsten Regionen Afrikas, errichtet. Extravagant präsentiert sich das Interieur des Hotels mit einer eigens für die Lodge entworfenen Ausstattung wie Tische mit Impalahorn-Beinen und Badewannen, die an riesige halbierte Straußeneier erinnern. Beim Dinner in der offenen Loggia beginnt die Wildnis direkt vor der festlich gedeckten Tafel.

Comme le caméléon, les murs enduits d'argile de l'éco-lodge se camouflent dans l'environnement couleur de sable. L'architecte sud-africain Mohammed Hans l'a placé au coeur de la réserve Sabi Sabi, l'une des régions les plus peuplées d'animaux d'Afrique. L'intérieur de l'hôtel se présente extravagant, avec des meubles dessinés spécifiquement pour le lodge, tels que des tables aux pieds en cornes d'impala et des baignoires faisant penser à d'énormes moitiés d'oeufs d'autruche. Au dîner, sur la loggia en plein air, le désert commence face aux tables festivement dressées.

Los muros de adobe del pabellón Eco se adaptan al entorno de color de la arena de forma camaleónica. El arquitecto sudafricano Mohammed Hans diseñó este hotel en medio de la reserva Sabi Sabi, una de las regiones con mayor fauna de África. El interior de la instalación se presenta extravagante con un mobiliario diseñado especialmente para el pabellón, como mesas con patas de astas de impala y bañeras parecidas a gigantescos medios huevos de avestruz. Durante la cena en la galería abierta, la selva empieza justo delante de la fastuosa mesa.

Come un camaleonte, le mura dell'eco-lodge, rivestite in argilla si mimetizzano nell'ambiente circostante, con i suoi colori tipici del deserto. L'architetto sudafricano Mohammed Hans ha costruito il lodge in mezzo alla riserva Sabi Sabi, una delle regioni più ricche di fauna. Gli interni dell'Hotel sono stravaganti con un arredamento creato appositamente per il lodge, come i tavoli dalle gambe in corno di impala e le vasche da bagno, che richiamano la forma di gigantesche uova di struzzo dimezzate. Cenando nella loggia all'aperto è visibile la vegetazione selvaggia della regione direttamente dalla tavola festosamente apparecchiata.

The bungalows in their perfect camouflage are situated behind tall Acacias along a watering hole where elephants quench their thirst.

Perfekt getarnt liegen die Bungalows hinter hohen Akazien an einem Wasserloch, wo Elefanten ihren Durst löschen.

Parfaitement dissimulés, les bungalows se dressent derrière de hauts acacias au bord du point d'eau où les éléphants viennent étancher leur soif.

Los bungalows se levantan, perfectamente camuflados, detrás de unas grandes acacias, a orillas de una laguna a la que los elefantes se acercan para saciar su sed.

Perfettamente mascherati, i bungalow si trovano dietro ad alti alberi d'acacia vicino ad una riserva d'acqua, dove gli elefanti vanno a dissetarsi.

The clay facade *houses twelve luxury suites. Cape Town designers created the reception area with native woods.*

Hinter der Lehmfassade *verbergen sich zwölf Luxussuiten. Den Empfangsbereich gestalteten Kapstädter Designer mit heimischen Hölzern.*

Derrière leur façade *d'argile se cachent douze luxueuses suites. Des designers originaires du Cap ont décoré la réception avec les essences locales.*

Detrás de la fachada *de adobe se ocultan doce suites de lujo. La zona de la recepción ha sido elaborada por diseñadores de Ciudad del Cabo, que emplearon maderas autóctonas.*

Dietro alla facciata *in argilla si celano dodici suites di lusso. I designer di Città del Capo crearono i locali della reception con legname locale.*

Singita Sweni Lodge
Kruger National Park, South Africa

The intimate lodge on the Sweni River sets new standards in terms of style and luxury: six suites designed in gentle shades of khaki are encircled by glass walls. The effect: the boundaries between the loft-like suites and nature melt into one. Traditional woodcraft, clay vessels, and batik material are contrasted with modern furniture made of kudu leather, baste meshwork and chrome. Wood-covered terraces await guests for breakfast in the outdoors. The outdoor shower is a hidden location for observing wildlife.

Neue Maßstäbe im Hinblick auf Stil und Luxus setzt die intime Lodge am Sweni Fluss: Gläserne Wände umgeben sechs Suiten, die in sanften Khakitönen gestaltet sind. Der Effekt: die Grenzen zwischen den loftartigen Suiten und der Natur verschmelzen. Traditionelle Schnitzkunst, Tongefäße und Batikstoffe kontrastieren mit modernen Möbeln aus Kuduleder, Bastgeflechten und Chrom. Holz gedeckte Terrassen laden zum Frühstück im Freien ein. Ein versteckter Ort für Wildbeobachtungen ist die Outdoor-Dusche.

Le lodge intime sur la rivière Sweni définit de nouvelles normes en matière de style et de luxe. Des murs en verre entourent les six suites, aménagées dans des teintes kaki douces. L'effet : les limites entre les suites de type loft et la nature deviennent floues. Les sculptures sur bois traditionnelles, les terres cuites et les tissus batikés contrastent avec les meubles modernes en cuir de koudou, les nattages en fibres et le chrome. Des terrasses couvertes en bois invitent à prendre le petit déjeuner à l'extérieur. La douche extérieure est un lieu privilégié pour observer les animaux sauvages.

El pabellón a orillas del río Sweni aporta nuevas dimensiones de cara al estilo y al lujo: las paredes de cristal que rodean seis suites en suaves tonos caqui. El efecto: se funden los contornos de las suites tipo loft y la naturaleza. Las tradicionales tallas artísticas, los recipientes de arcilla y los batiks contrastan con los muebles modernos de piel de kudu, las enredaderas de líber y el cromo. Las terrazas, cubiertas con techos de madera, invitan a desayunar al aire libre. La ducha al aire libre sirve de escondite para observar a los animales salvajes.

La lodge intima sul fiume Sweni inventa nuovi criteri per quanto riguarda lo stile ed il lusso: pareti di vetro circondano sei suite arredate in toni soft color kaki. L'effetto è la fusione tra le delimitazioni delle suite, simili a loft, e la natura. Arte dell' intaglio tradizionale, vasi di terracotta e stoffe batik contrastano con i mobili moderni in pelle di kudu, intrecci di raffia e cromo. Le terrazze rivestite in legno invitano alla colazione all'aperto. Un luogo nascosto per delle osservazioni selvagge è la doccia all'aperto.

The lounge, bathtub and terrace are places to lounge along the Sweni River. From here, one can hear the mystic symphony of the savannah.

*Lounge, **Badewanne** und Terrasse sind Logenplätze am Sweni River. Von hier aus hört man die geheimnisvolle Musik der Savanne.*

Le Lounge, les baignoires et les terrasses sont des endroits privilégiés avec vue sur la rivière Sweni. D'ici on entend la musique mystérieuse de la savane.

El lounge, la bañera y la terraza son como los asientos de primera fila a orillas del río Sweni, desde allí se oye la misteriosa música de la Sabana.

Lounge, vasca da bagno e terrazza sono il posto d'onore davanti al fiume Sweni, dove ascoltare la musica misteriosa della savana.

The veranda, *pool, bush-spa and noble suites are ideal for relaxing and dreaming of exciting safaris.*

Auf der Veranda*, am Pool, im Bush-Spa und in den Nobelsuiten lässt es sich entspannt von aufregenden Safaris träumen.*

La véranda, *la piscine et le Bush-Spa permettent de rêver en toute quiétude de safaris excitants.*

En el mirador*, en la piscina, en el Bush-Spa y en las nobles suites se puede soñar tranquilamente con emocionantes safaris.*

Sulla veranda, *sulla piscina, nel centro benessere immerso nella natura selvaggia e nelle nobili suite è possibile sognare, in tutta tranquillità, di eccitanti safari.*

Royal Malewane

Hoedspruit, South Africa

Royal Malewane is a classic definition of what living and lifestyle culture means: a Victorian bath, prim antique furniture, candelabras and white chaise-longues in Chesterfield style are also included. The owners have place full emphasis on colonial luxury. Nonetheless, this style is combined with the origins of the wilderness: reed roofs, for instance, and exposed-beam ceilings. Individual immersion in the world of the game reserve is at the top of the list in the intimate atmosphere with a mere six suites and the Royal and Malewane Suites.

Royal Malewane definiert auf klassische Weise, was höchste Wohn- und Lebenskultur bedeutet: ein viktorianisches Bad, gedrechselte antike Möbel, Kronleuchter, dazu weiße Chaiselonguen im Chesterfieldstil. Die Besitzer setzen ganz auf kolonialen Luxus. Der allerdings verbindet sich mit den Ursprüngen der Wildnis: Reet gedeckte Dächer etwa und offene Balkendecken. In der intimen Atmosphäre mit nur sechs Suiten sowie den beiden Royal und Malewane Suiten, steht das individuelle Eintauchen in die Welt des Wildreservats an vorderster Stelle.

Royal Malewane témoigne de façon classique de ce qu'une culture de vie et d'habitat poussée à son paroxysme signifie : salle de bains victorienne, meubles antiques façonnés, lustres et chaises longues de style Chesterfield. Les propriétaires jouent à fond la carte du luxe colonial. Celui-ci est étroitement lié aux ressources du désert : par exemple, toits de chaume et plafonds aux poutres apparentes. Dans l'atmosphère intime des quelque six suites, ainsi que les Royal et Malewane Suites, l'immersion individuelle dans l'univers de la réserve est au premier plan.

Royal Malewane define de forma clásica el significado de una exquisita cultura de vida y de vivienda: un cuarto de baño victoriano, antiguos muebles torneados, candelabros y blancos sillones chaise lounge de estilo Chesterfield. Los propietarios apuestan por el lujo colonial, pero fusionándolo con los orígenes de la selva, como los tejados de caña y los techos de vigas. En las atmósferas íntimas, con solo seis suites y las Royal y Malewane Suites, lo más importante es la aproximación individual al mundo de la reserva.

Royal Malewane definisce in modo classico ciò che sono il vero gusto per l'arredamento e l'arte di vivere: un bagno vittoriano, mobili antichi lavorati al tornio, lampadari e sdraio bianche in stile Chesterfield. I proprietari tengono al lusso coloniale, in armonia con la regione deserta. Esempio ne sono i tetti di canne e i bar aperti. Così, in questo ambiente intimo composto da sei suite e dalle suite Royal e Malewane, immergersi nel mondo della riserva è d'obbligo.

Living in the outdoors and dreaming in luxurious and spacious king-size canopy beds.

Openair wohnen und träumen in luxuriösen und geräumigen King-size-Himmelbetten.

Habiter à ciel ouvert et rêver dans les lits à baldaquin luxurieux et spacieux.

Vivir al aire libre y soñar en las lujosas, cómodas y amplias camas con dosel.

Vivere e sognare all'aperto in lussuosi grandi letti a baldacchino.

Feel like the king of the bush—even if it's only at the fireside or enjoying an excellent dinner in a small group on the terrace.

Sich fühlen wie der König des Buschs — sei es nun am Kaminfeuer oder beim ausgezeichneten Dinner in kleiner Runde auf der Terrasse.

Se sentir le roi de la savane — que ce soit au coin d'un feu de cheminée ou autour d'un dîner fin entre amis sur la terrasse.

Para sentirse como el rey de la selva, tanto al fuego de la chimenea como durante la exquisita cena en pequeños grupos en la terraza.

Sentirsi come il re della foresta semplicemente davanti al camino o cenando sulla terrazza in compagnia di pochi intimi.

Saxon

Johannesburg, South Africa

With a unique style mix of African artists' craftsmanship and designer furniture, the Saxon is an impressive sight in the exclusive suburb of Sandhurst. Above the stairway in the lobby looms a glass dome that catches the sunlight arches. Elegant sofas in the piano lounge, library and dining room invite guests to relax, while shady foliage and the pool are nestled in fabulous garden facilities. By the way, the platinum suite is named after Nelson Mandela, who wrote his autobiography "Long Walk to Freedom" here after his release from prison.

Mit einem einzigartigen Stilmix aus afrikanischem Kunsthandwerk und Designermöbeln beeindruckt das Saxon im exklusiven Vorort Sandhurst. Über dem Treppenaufgang in der Lobby wölbt sich eine Glaskuppel, die das Sonnenlicht einfängt. In der Piano-Lounge, der Bibliothek und dem Speisesaal laden elegante Sofas zum Entspannen ein, während schattige Lauben und der Pool in herrliche Gartenanlagen eingebettet sind. Die Platinum-Suite ist übrigens nach Nelson Mandela benannt, der hier nach der Entlassung aus der Haft seine Autobiografie „Long Walk to Freedom" schrieb.

Le mélange unique des styles, conjuguant artisanat africain et meubles de designer, est impressionnant au Saxon situé dans Sandhurst, un quartier très exclusif. Au-dessus des escaliers de la réception s'élève un dôme de verre qui capte le soleil. Dans le salon à musique, la bibliothèque et la salle à manger, d'élégants sofas invitent à la détente, tandis que des tonnelles ombragées et la piscine vous attendent dans de magnifiques jardins. Par ailleurs, la suite Platinum porte le nom de Nelson Mandela puisqu'il y écrivit son autobiographie « Un long chemin vers la liberté » après sa libération.

El Saxon, situado en el exclusivo barrio Sandhurst, impresiona por su excepcional mezcla cultural y sus muebles de diseño. Sobre la escalera del vestíbulo se arquea una cúpula de vidrio que permite el paso de la luz natural. En el salón del piano, la biblioteca y el comedor, los elegantes sofás invitan a relajarse, mientras que los umbríos cenadores y la piscina están integrados en el maravilloso jardín. La suite Platinum lleva el nombre de Nelson Mandela, quien, después de ser puesto en libertad, escribió aquí su autobiografía "El largo camino hacia la libertad".

Il Saxon emerge nel sobborgo di Sandhurst, con la sua fusione di stili unica fra artigianato artistico africano e mobili di design. Il soffitto della scalinata dell'atrio è una cupola di vetro che cattura la luce del sole. Nel piano bar, nella biblioteca e nella sala ristorante eleganti sofà invitano al relax mentre nel giardino alcove ombrose e la piscina richiamano il riposo. La Suite Platinum è stata dedicata a Nelson Mandela che vi scrisse, dopo il rilascio detentivo, la sua autobiografia intitolata "Lungo cammino verso la libertà".

The large hotel pool is harmoniously integrated into the premises.

Der große Hotelpool integriert sich harmonisch in die Anlage.

La grande piscine de l'hôtel s'intègre harmonieusement dans l'ensemble.

La gran piscina del hotel se integra armónicamente en el complejo.

La grande piscina dell'hotel si integra perfettamente nel parco.

The stylish atmosphere is defined by African elegance and bright interior.

Afrikanische Eleganz und helles Interieur prägen die stilvolle Atmosphäre.

L'élégance africaine et un aménagement intérieur lumineux créent une ambiance très stylée.

La elegancia africana y los interiores luminosos determinan el ambiente tranquilo.

Un'eleganza africana e gli interni chiari ne caratterizzano l'atmosfera ricca di stile.

The Westcliff

Johannesburg, South Africa

Like a Mediterranean village, the luxury hotel with its terraces and balconies clings to a hillside with a view of the green Magalies mountains. Cobblestone paths lead to the restaurant and panoramic terrace. Anyone who looks down will discover the elephants in the zoo that is located beneath. The famous South African designer Graham Viney designed the 115 rooms and suites. Lavish floral designs, soft chintz and warm cappuccino tones take care of comfort. The wood-paneled polo lounge quickly advanced to a rendezvous for high society.

Wie ein mediterranes Dorf schmiegt sich das Luxushotel mit seinen Terrassen und Balkonen an einen Hügel mit Blick auf die grünen Magaliesberge. Zu Restaurant und Panoramaterrasse führen Wege aus Pflastersteinen. Wer nach unten schaut, entdeckt Elefanten im darunter liegenden Zoo. Die 115 Zimmer und Suiten hat der bekannte südafrikanische Designer Graham Viney gestaltet. Üppige Blumenmuster, weicher Chintz und warme Cappuccino-Töne sorgen für Behaglichkeit. Die holzgetäfelte Polo Lounge avancierte schnell zu einem Treffpunkt der High Society.

Tel un village méditerranéen, cet hôtel de luxe avec ses terrasses et balcons s'adosse à une colline, offrant une belle vue sur les vertes montagnes de la Magalies. Des chemins pavés conduisent au restaurant et à la terrasse panoramique. En regardant vers le bas, on découvre les éléphants du zoo situé en contrebas. C'est le célèbre designer sud-africain Graham Viney, qui a réalisé les 115 chambres et suites. De généreux motifs floraux, du chintz moelleux, des tons chauds couleur cappuccino créent une impression de bien-être. Le salon Polo aux lambris de bois est vite devenu le point de rencontre de la haute société.

Este hotel de lujo, con sus terrazas y sus balcones, parece un pueblo mediterráneo. Sus casas se agrupan en una colina con vistas a las verdes montañas Magalies. Caminos de adoquín conducen hasta el restaurante y a la terraza panorámica. Si se mira hacia abajo pueden verse los elefantes del zoo. Las 115 habitaciones y suites han sido decoradas por el famoso diseñador sudafricano Graham Viney. Ricos dibujos florales, telas suaves de chintz y colores tostados hacen que las estancias resulten confortables. El salón Polo, revestido de madera, se convirtió rápidamente en el lugar de encuentro de la alta sociedad.

Questo hotel di lusso sembra un paese mediterraneo in cima ad una collina, che con le sue terrazze e i suoi balconi offre una vista meravigliosa delle Magaliesberg. Vie lastricate conducono al ristorante e alla terrazza panoramica. Guardando di sotto si scorgono elefanti nello zoo sottostante. Le 115 camere e suite sono state ideate dal famoso designer africano, Graham Viney. Ricchi disegni a fiori, morbido calancà e caldi toni color cappuccino danno il benvenuto. La Polo Lounge, rivestita di legno, è punto d'incontro per l'alta società.

Despite being in the middle of a large city, the hotel looks more like a resort. Those with a bit of luck may even have the chance to watch elephants from the pool.

Obwohl inmitten der Großstadt, wirkt das Hotel eher wie ein Resort. Vom Pool aus kann man mit etwas Glück sogar Elefanten beobachten.

Bien que situé au centre de la métropole, l'hôtel ressemble plutôt à un lieu de villégiature. Avec un peu de chance, on peut observer des éléphants de la piscine.

Aunque está situado en medio de la gran ciudad el hotel parece más bien un resort. Con un poco de suerte, se pueden observar incluso elefantes desde la piscina.

Nonostante la posizione centrale, questo hotel sembra un resort. Con un po' di fortuna è persino possibile vedere gli elefanti dalla piscina.

Leather sofas, *historic photos and an open fire: the Polo Lounge is the city's most popular "living room" after a civilized dinner.*

Ledersofas, *historische Fotos, Kaminfeuer: Die Polo Lounge ist nach einem gepflegten Dinner das angesagteste „Wohnzimmer" der Stadt.*

Des sofas de cuir, *des photos historiques, un feu de cheminée : le salon Polo est la « salle de séjour » la plus prisée de la ville à la suite d'un dîner raffiné.*

Sofás de cuero, *fotos históricas, el fuego de la chimenea: después de una deliciosa cena, el salón Polo es el "cuarto de estar" más de moda de la ciudad.*

Divani in pelle, *stampe storiche, camino acceso. La Polo lounge, per i suoi pasti prelibati, rappresenta il luogo più ricercato della città.*

One&Only Maledives at Reethi Rah

North Malé Atoll, Maledives

130 villas are discreetly placed amidst beautiful landscaping on one of the largest islands in North Malé Atoll, each occupying its own secluded piece of white sand shores or private deck over crystal turquoise waters of the lagoon. Set in lush vegetation, all villas are spaced 66 feet apart for an unprecedented degree of privacy. A dedicated villa host personalizes service and dining to each guest, as well as booking signature spa treatments in one of the private pavilion suites.

130 Villen liegen dezent mitten in einer wunderschönen Landschaft auf einer der größten Inseln des North Malé Atolls, jede auf einem abgeschiedenen Stück Sandstrand oder mit privater Dachterrasse über den kristalltürkisen Wassern der Lagune. Diese inmitten üppiger Vegetation befindlichen Villen stehen alle wegen einer nie da gewesenen Privatsphäre 20 Meter von einander entfernt. Ein fest zugeordneter Villenbetreuer personalisiert für jeden Gast Service und Speisen und bucht auch charakteristische Wellness-Behandlungen in einer der privaten Pavillonsuiten.

130 villas sont discrètement intégrées à un environnement paysagé de grande beauté sur l'une des plus grandes îles de l'atoll de North Malé, chacune disposant de sa propre plage de sable blanc ou de son ponton privé sur les eaux cristallines turquoises du lagon. Entourées d'une végétation luxuriante, toutes les villas sont disposées à 20 mètres les unes des autres afin d'assurer un degré inégalé d'intimité. Un service particulier pour chaque villa personnalise le service et les repas de chaque hôte, et réserve les traitements balnéaires spécifiques dans l'une des suites aménagées dans les pavillons privés.

Las 130 villas se integran discretamente en el paisaje maravilloso de una de las islas más grandes del North Malé Atoll. Cada una ocupanda una parcela aislada sobre la arena de la playa, con su terraza privada en el tejado, sobre las aguas cristalinas de color turquesa de la laguna. Estas villas, situadas en medio de una vegetación exuberante, están separadas entre sí por 20 metros, garantizando así una esfera privada que no conoce precedentes. Cada villa tiene un asistente fijo que se encarga de los servicios y comidas individualmente para cada huésped y de reservar también los tratamientos de wellness característicos en uno de los pabellones privados.

Le 130 ville sono discretamente situate al centro di un paesaggio fantastico su una delle più grandi isole nell'atollo a nord di Malé, ognuna occupa il proprio spazio sulla sabbia bianca o il proprio terrazzo si affaccia sulle acque cristalline e turchesi della laguna. Situate in una ricca vegetazione, tutte le ville si trovano ad una distanza di 20 metri l'una dall'altra per mantenere una privacy senza precedenti. È possibile personalizzare i servizi e la ristorazione per ogni ospite così come prenotare trattamenti presso il centro benessere nel padiglione delle suite.

Villas have high airy ceilings and generous exterior space, ranging from private verandas overlooking stretches of beach to private swimming pools with large decks.

Die Villen haben hohe luftige Decken und großzügige Außenbereiche von privaten Verandas, von denen aus man Teile des Strandes überblicken kann, bis hin zu privaten Schwimmbädern mit großen Dachterrassen.

Les plafonds des villas sont hauts et aérés, et les espaces extérieurs sont généreux, allant de la véranda privée avec vue sur la plage à des piscines privées avec de grandes terrasses.

Las villas tienen techos altos y amplias áreas exteriores que abarcan desde miradores privados, desde los cuales se pueden ver partes de la playa, hasta piscinas privadas con terrazas grandes en el tejado.

Le ville hanno soffitti alti e generosi spazi all'aperto, dalle verande private che si affacciano su lingue di spiaggia, fino alle piscine private su ampie terrazze.

The interior design is Asian-island contemporary and elegantly tropical, using beautiful natural materials like bamboo arches, coconut shells, sea grass, and silks.

Die Innenausstattung entspricht einer zeitgenössischen asiatischen Insel und eleganter tropischer Umgebung, wozu Naturstoffe wie Bambusbögen, Kokosnussschalen, Seetang und Seidenstoffe verwendet werden.

Le design intérieur est du style insulaire asiatique contemporain et tropical élégant, et fait usage de superbes matériaux naturels tels que les arches en bambou, les noix de coco, l'herbe de dunes et les tissus en soie.

La decoración interior es la de una isla asiática contemporánea y un entorno tropical elegante. Para esta decoración se han utilizado materiales naturales, como arcos de bambú, cáscaras de coco, algas y sedas.

Il design interno è quello tipico di un'isola asiatica contemporanea e sofisticatamente tropicale, grazie a fantastici materiali naturali come gli archi di bambù, le noci di cocco, le alghe e le preziose sete.

The Imperial
New Delhi, India

King palms looming high in the sky above the white hotel walls emphasize the vertical architecture of the grand Art Deco building. The historic hotel was built in 1931 by Sir Edwin Lutyens. The hotel welcomes guests in its atrium adorned with gold leafs in the midst of Delhi's shopping and commercial district. The hotel's collection of antiques, crystal chandeliers and works of art decorate the rooms and halls. The urban-oasis shady veranda offers the perfect setting for an English five o'clock tea.

Königspalmen ragen vor den weißen Mauern des Hotels in den Himmel und betonen die vertikale Architektur des grandiosen Art déco-Baus. Das traditionsreiche Hotel, das der Architekt Sir Edwin Lutyens 1931 errichtete, empfängt seine Gäste im blattgoldverzierten Atrium mitten im Einkaufs- und Geschäftsviertel Delhis. Antiquitäten, Kristallleuchter und Kunstwerke aus der Sammlung des Hotels dekorieren Zimmer und Flure. Die perfekte Kulisse für einen englischen Five o'clock tea bietet die schattige Veranda der Großstadt-Oase.

Les palmiers royaux s'élèvent dans le ciel devant les murs blancs de l'hôtel et soulignent l'architecture verticale du splendide bâtiment en art déco. L'hôtel riche en traditions, réalisé par l'architecte Sir Edwin Lutyens en 1931, reçoit ses hôtes dans un atrium décoré de feuilles d'or en plein centre du quartier commerçant et du quartier des affaires de Delhi. Les antiquités, les lustres en cristal et les oeuvres d'art de la collection de l'hôtel décorent les chambres et les couloirs. La véranda ombragée de l'oasis de la grande ville offre un décor parfait pour un thé anglais à cinq heures.

Palmas reales se elevan hacia el cielo delante de los muros blancos del hotel y acentúan la arquitectura vertical de la grandiosa construcción art déco. Este hotel de larga tradición, construido por el arquitecto Sir Edwin Lutyens, en 1931, recibe a sus huéspedes en el atrio decorado con oro batido en medio de la zona comercial de Nueva Delhi. Las habitaciones y los pasillos están decorados con antigüedades, arañas de cristal y obras de arte pertenecientes a la colección del hotel. El escenario perfecto para el té inglés de las cinco de la tarde lo ofrece el porche sombreado de este oasis de la gran ciudad.

Palme regali si innalzano verso il cielo davanti alle mura bianche dell'hotel e ne sottolineano l'architettura verticale in art déco. Lo storico hotel, eretto nel 1931 dall'architetto sir Edwin Lutyens, nel centro del quartiere dello shopping e degli affari di Delhi, accoglie i suoi ospiti nell'atrio decorato in oro. Oggetti d'antiquariato, lampadari di cristallo e opere d'arte abbelliscono camere e corridoi. Lo spunto perfetto per un tè delle cinque in vero stile inglese è offerto dall'ombrosa veranda dell'oasi cittadina.

The inner courtyard of this bounteous Art Deco building is flooded with light. The lobby and soothingly cool spring fountain are located here.

Der großzügige Art déco-Bau verfügt über einen lichtdurchfluteten Innenhof. Hier befinden sich die Lobby und ein Kühle spendender Springbrunnen.

La spacieuse bâtisse du style art déco dispose d'une cour intérieure lumineuse. Elle comprend le lobby et une fontaine qui apporte de la fraîcheur.

El amplio edificio de tendencia art déco posee un patio exterior luminoso, donde se encuentran el lobby y una fuente refrescante.

La ricca costruzione art déco ha un cortile interno illuminato dalla luce esterna. Vi si trovano la lobby ed una fontana rinfrescante.

Gleaming marble floors, antique paintings and an English club atmosphere await the guests.

Schimmernde Marmorböden, antike Gemälde und englische Club-Atmosphäre erwarten die Gäste.

Des sols en marbre brillant, des tableaux anciens et une ambiance de club anglais accueillent les hôtes.

Los huéspedes disfrutarán de los suelos de mármol resplandecientes, las pinturas antiguas y el ambiente de club inglés.

Pavimenti in marmo, scintillanti dipinti antichi e atmosfera da club inglese attendono gli ospiti.

The Taj Mahal Palace & Tower

Mumbai, India

When the English architect W. A. Stevens built the hotel in 1903, it had not rival in the entire Orient. The palace still conveys its original charm today—a mixture of English hospitality and Indian opulence: concierges in turbans greet guests in the lobby and the suites in the old building are decorated with antiques, while the halls are reminiscent of art galleries. Traditional flair teams up with modern urbanity, for example in the restaurant Souk or in the Insomnia, Mumbai's largest nightclub.

Als der englische Architekt W. A. Stevens das Hotel 1903 erbaute, gab es im gesamten Orient nichts Vergleichbares. Noch heute versprüht der Palast seinen ursprünglichen Charme, einen Mix aus englischer Gastlichkeit und indischer Opulenz: In der Lobby empfangen Portiers mit Turbanen den Gast, die Suiten im alten Gebäude sind mit Antiquitäten ausgestattet, die Flure gleichen Kunstgalerien. Zum traditionellen Flair gesellt sich moderne Urbanität, wie in dem Restaurant Souk oder im Insomnia, Mumbais größtem Nachtclub.

Lorsque l'architecte anglais W. A. Stevens a construit cet hôtel en 1903, il n'existait rien de comparable dans tout l'orient. Aujourd'hui encore, le palace répand son charme original, un mélange d'hospitalité anglaise et d'opulence indienne : dans le lobby, des portiers en turban accueillent les hôtes, les suites dans le bâtiment ancien sont aménagées avec des antiquités, les couloirs s'apparentent à des galeries d'art. L'ambiance traditionnelle se marie à l'urbanisme moderne, comme dans le restaurant Souk ou dans l'Insomnia, le plus grand night-club de Mumbai.

Cuando el arquitecto inglés, W. A. Stevens, construyó el hotel en 1903, no había en todo oriente nada comparable. Aún hoy, transmite el palacio su encanto original, una mezcla de hospitalidad inglesa y opulencia india. Los porteros con turbante reciben al huésped en el vestíbulo, las suites del edificio antiguo están decoradas con antigüedades y los pasillos se asemejan a las galerías de arte. Al ambiente típico se une la urbanidad moderna, como en el restaurante Souk o en Insomnia, el club nocturno más grande de Mumbai.

Quando l'architetto inglese W. A. Stevens costruì l'hotel nel 1903, in tutto l'Oriente non c'era nulla di simile. Ancora oggi il palazzo trasmette il suo charme originale, un miscuglio tra ospitalità inglese ed opulenza indiana: nella lobby i portieri danno il benvenuto avvolti in turbanti, le suite del vecchio edificio sono arredate con mobili antichi, i corridoi sembrano delle gallerie d'arte. L'urbanità moderna si sposa con lo charme tradizionale, come al ristorante Souk oppure all'Insomnia, il più grande night club di Mombai.

Even the stairway alone in the stately Victorian building represents a worthy attraction. The swimming pool is located in the inner courtyard.

Allein das Treppenhaus des viktorianischen Prachtbaus ist eine Sehenswürdigkeit, im Innenhof des Hotels befindet sich das Schwimmbad.

A elle seule, la cage d'escalier du superbe bâtiment victorien est une curiosité, la piscine se trouve dans la cour intérieure.

La escalera de la magnífica construcción victoriana ya es de por sí un monumento. En el patio interior se encuentra la piscina.

La scalinata del sontuoso edificio vittoriano è splendida, nel patio dell'hotel si trova la piscina.

A walk around the hotel is like a voyage through time from the British colonial era into modern-day India. All in all, there are 565 rooms including 46 suites.

Ein Rundgang durch das Hotel gleicht einer Zeitreise von der britischen Kolonialzeit bis in die indische Gegenwart. Insgesamt gibt es 565 Zimmer inklusive 46 Suiten.

Une visite de l'hôtel ressemble à un voyage dans le temps, de l'époque coloniale britannique jusque dans l'Inde contemporaine. L'hôtel dispose en tout de 565 chambres et de 46 suites.

Dar una vuelta por el hotel es igual que un hacer un viaje en el tiempo desde la época colonial inglesa hasta la India actual. En total hay 565 habitaciones, de las cuales 46 son suites.

Un passaggio attraverso l'hotel assomiglia ad un viaggio nel tempo con partenza nel periodo coloniale britannico e con destinazione l'attuale realtà indiana. In totale l'hotel dispone di 565 camere, 46 suite incluse.

The Oberoi Rajvilas

Jaipur, India

An opulent resort with traditional Rajasthani architecture set amidst 32 acres of lush lawns and orchids, turquoise reflection pools, decorative fountains that play watery music, pavilions and tiled courtyards. Villas are clustered around shady gardens. Attentive staff enables each guest to live in the lifestyle of Rajasthani royalty. The world-class spa incorporates the use of Ayurvedic principles of holistic health maintenance.

Ein riesiges Resort mit traditioneller Rajasthani-Architektur inmitten von 13 Hektar üppigen Wiesen und Orchideen, türkischen Reflection Pools, dekorativen Spring-brunnen, die Wassermusik spielen, Pavillons und gekachelten Innenhöfen. Die Villen stehen dicht zusammen um schattige Gärten herum. Aufmerksame Mitarbeiter machen es jedem Gast möglich, den Lebensstil der königlichen Rajasthani zu leben. Das erstklassige Wellness-Center schließt auch die Anwendung ayurvedischer Prinzipien der Ganzheitsmedizin mit ein.

Un lieu de villégiature opulent dans l'architecture traditionnelle du Rajastan, situé sur plus de 13 hectares de pelouses luxuriantes et d'orchidées, de bassins aux reflets turquoise, de fontaines décoratives dont émane le bruit frais et joyeux de l'eau qui coule, de pavillons et de cours pavées de terres cuites. Les villas sont regroupées autour de jardins ombragés. Un personnel attentif permet à chaque hôte de vivre dans le style de vie des rois du Rajastan. L'espace balnéo de première catégorie comprend l'application des principes de préservation de la santé de l'Ayurveda.

Un resort enorme de arquitectura rajasthani tradicional ubicado en medio de 13 hectáreas de praderas exuberantes, orquídeas, piscinas reflectantes turcas, fuentes decorativas cuya agua tintinea al caer, pabellones y patios internos de loseta. Las villas están muy juntas alrededor de los jardines sombríos. Los amables empleados hacen posible que cada huésped viva según el estilo de vida de la majestuosa Rajasthani. El centro de wellness es de primera clase e incluye también el empleo de los principios ayurvédicos de la medicina holística.

Un resort opulento dalla tradizionale architettura Rajasthani sito tra quasi 13 ettari di siepi e orchidee, piscine azzurre, fontane decorative che suonano musica acquatica, padiglioni e cortili pavimentati. Le ville sono ordinate attorno a giardini ombreggiati. Uno staff attento dà ad ogni ospite la possibilità di vivere lo stile di vita di un reale del Rajasthan. Il centro benessere contempla l'utilizzo di principi dell'ayurvedica per il completo mantenimento della salute.

Moghal and Persian styles are evident in all 71 suites and communal areas.

Moghalischer und persischer Stil sind in allen 71 Suiten und Gemein-schaftsbereichen zu sehen.

Les styles mogol et perse sont évidents dans l'ensemble des 71 suites et dans les espaces publics.

En las 71 suites y en las salas comunes se aprecia el estilo mongol y persa.

Stili moghal e persiano emergono nelle 71 suite ed aree comuni.

Sculptured gardens are landscaped around a 250-year-old temple floating in a lotus pond, and a traditional mansion which now houses a luxurious Ayurvedic spa.

Gärten mit Skulpturen sind landschaftlich um einen 250 Jahre alten Tempel, der in einem Lotussee schwimmt, und ein traditionelles Landhaus herum gestaltet, das jetzt ein luxuriöses Ayurveda-Wellness-Center beherbergt.

Les jardins sculptés sont paysagés autour d'un temple vieux de 250 ans flottant sur un bassin de lotus et d'une demeure traditionnelle qui abrite aujourd'hui un espace balnéaire luxueux appliquant les principes de l'Ayurveda.

Los jardines con esculturas forman el paisaje que rodea un templo de 250 años, situado sobre un lago de lotos. Una casa de campo tradicional rodea el lago y aloja un lujoso centro de terapia ayurveda.

Giardini scultorei sono presenti attorno ad un tempio vecchio di 250 anni che sembra galleggiare in uno stagno di fior di loto, ed una villa tradizionale ospita attualmente il lussuoso centro benessere ayurvedico.

The Peninsula Hong Kong

Hong Kong, China

The Peninsula has opened its gates to the golden twenties. The furnishing conjures up times gone by, such as the indoor pool with an atmosphere of a Roman bath. At the same time, the swimmers can also cast a glance at the modern life of the city. Not only does is the hotel alleged to have the most spacious rooms in the city, but it also offers exceptional service: If desired, the guest can even be transported from the airport directly to the roof of the building by helicopter.

Das Peninsula hat seine Pforten in den Goldenen Zwanzigern eröffnet. Die Ausstattung beschwört vergangene Zeiten herauf, etwa im Hallenbad, das die Atmosphäre einer römischen Therme verbreitet. Gleichzeitig können die Schwimmer vom Becken aus aber auch einen Blick auf das moderne Leben der Metropole werfen. Das Hotel soll nicht nur über die geräumigsten Zimmer der Stadt verfügen, sondern auch ausgefallenen Service bieten: Auf Wunsch transportiert sogar ein Helikopter den Gast vom Flughafen direkt auf das Dach des Hauses.

Le Peninsula a ouvert ses portes dans les fastueuses années 1920. L'aménagement évoque les époques passées, comme par exemple dans la piscine couverte qui rend l'ambiance des thermes romains. En même temps, les nageurs peuvent, du bassin, jeter un oeil sur la vie moderne de la métropole. L'hôtel dispose non seulement des chambres les plus spacieuses de la ville, mais offre également des services originaux : sur demande, un hélicoptère transporte même les hôtes de l'aéroport directement sur le toit de l'établissement.

El Peninsula abrió sus puertas en los dorados años veinte. La decoración evoca tiempos pasados, como por ejemplo la piscina cubierta que emana una atmósfera de terma romana. A la vez, desde la piscina los bañistas pueden echar un vistazo a la vida moderna de la metrópoli. El hotel no sólo dispone de las habitaciones más grandes de la ciudad, según se dice, sino que, además, ofrece servicios extraordinarios: A petición, el huésped puede incluso ser trasladado en helicóptero desde el aeropuerto directamente a la azotea del hotel.

Il Peninsula ha aperto le sue porte nei magnifici anni venti. L'arredamento evoca tempi passati, per esempio la piscina coperta crea l'atmosfera delle terme dell'antica Roma. Nuotando è possibile osservare la vita moderna della metropoli. L'hotel non solo dispone delle camere più spaziose della città, ma offre anche un servizio insolito: un elicottero può, su richiesta, trasferire il cliente dall'aereoporto al tetto dell'hotel.

A genuine surprise awaits guest on the top floor. The Felix, designed by Philippe Starck, exhibits what may indeed represent his most successful restaurant design. At any rate, it offers the most fascinating view a restaurant can have.

Im obersten Stockwerk wartet eine echte Überraschung. Das von Philippe Starck entworfene Felix zeigt sein vielleicht bestes Restaurantdesign. Auf jeden Fall bietet es den faszinierendsten Ausblick, den ein Restaurant überhaupt haben kann.

Une vraie surprise vous attend à l'étage supérieur. Le Felix, un restaurant conçu par Philippe Starck, constitue peut-être son meilleur design. En tout cas, il offre la vue la plus fascinante qu'un restaurant puisse avoir.

En el último piso hay una verdadera sorpresa: Tal vez el mejor diseño de restaurante del diseñador Philippe Starck: El Felix ofrece la vista más fascinante que cualquier restaurante alguno pueda tener.

All'ultimo piano non manca una vera sorpresa. Il Felix progettato da Philippe Starck ha forse il suo miglior design per ristorante. In ogni caso offre la più affascinate vista che un ristorante possa assolutamente avere.

As the oldest and most historic luxury hotel in the former British crown colony, the Peninsula boasts furnishings that testify to the splendor of its time.

Als ältestes und traditionsreichstes Luxushotel der ehemaligen britischen Kronkolonie verfügt das Peninsula über eine Ausstattung, die vom Prunk seiner Entstehungszeit zeugt.

En tant qu'hôtel de de luxe le plus ancien et le plus riche en traditions de l'ancienne colonie britannique, le Peninsula dispose d'un équipement qui témoigne du faste de son époque de création.

Siendo el hotel de lujo más antiguo y tradicional de la ex colonia británica, el Peninsula posee un decorado que da testimonio de la suntuosidad de la época de su creación.

Essendo l'hotel di lusso più antico e ricco di tradizioni dell'ex colonia britannica, il Peninsula ha un arredamento che testimonia la sontuosità dell'epoca in cui è sorto.

The Landmark Mandarin Oriental Hong Kong

Hong Kong, China

A novelty of Hong Kong's hotel scene. In commissioning the designer duo Adam T. Tihany and Peter Remedios, working together here as a team for the first time, the traditional company Mandarin Oriental entirely focused on contemporary architecture. The fact that the hotel's 113 rooms boast an average size of nearly 550 square feet represents a genuine luxury in a metropolis, where space is in short supply. The themes of modern elegance and wellness permeate the entire hotel from the bathrooms to spa. Since their opening, the gourmet restaurant Amber on the 7th floor and the hotel bar MO Bar are among the city's most popular gastronomic addresses.

Eine Novität in Hongkongs Hotellerie. Mit der Beauftragung des Designerduos Adam T. Tihany und Peter Remedios, die hier erstmals im Team zusammenarbeiteten, setzte das Traditionsunternehmen Mandarin Oriental ganz auf zeitgenössische Architektur. Zu bewohnen ist sie in 113, durchschnittlich 50 m² großen Zimmern. Wahrer Luxus in einer Metropole, in der Platz Mangelware ist. Moderne Eleganz und Wellness sind die Themen, die sich durch das gesamte Haus ziehen, von den Badezimmern bis ins Spa. Das Gourmet-Restaurant Amber im 7. Stock sowie die Hotelbar MO Bar gehören seit ihrer Eröffnung zu den gefragtesten Gastronomie-Adressen in der Stadt.

Une nouveauté dans l'hôtellerie de Hong Kong. En confiant l'agencement de l'hôtel au duo de designers Adam T. Tihany et Peter Remedios, qui ont travaillé ici pour la première fois en équipe, la société traditionnelle Mandarin Oriental a misé entièrement sur l'architecture contemporaine. Cet hôtel dispose de 113 chambres d'une surface minimum de 50 m² : un véritable luxe dans une métropole où la place constitue une denrée rare. L'élégance moderne et le wellness sont des themes récurrents dans tout l'ensemble, des salles de bain au spa. Le restaurant gastronomique Amber installé au 7ème étage, ainsi que le MO Bar, comptent depuis leur ouverture parmi les adresses gastronomiques les plus demandées de la ville.

Una novedad en la hostelería de Hong Kong. Al ofrecer el proyecto a la pareja de diseñadores Adam T. Tihany y Peter Remedios, en su primer trabajo en común, la casa de tradición del Mandarin Oriental apostó por una arquitectura absolutamente contemporánea. El edificio dispone de 113 habitaciones, las más pequeñas de 50 m². Todo un lujo en una ciudad que sufre la carencia de espacio. Elegancia moderna y wellness son los temas presentes en toda la casa, desde los baños hasta el spa. En el piso 7, el restaurante para gourmets Amber y el MO Bar se han convertido en dos de las direcciones gastronómicas más solicitadas de la ciudad.

Una novità tra gli hotel di Hong Kong. Incaricando del progetto i designer Adam T. Tihany e Peter Remedios, che hanno lavorato insieme per la prima volta, la tradizionale impresa Mandarin Oriental ha puntato su uno stile architettonico assolutamente contemporaneo, composto da 113 camere, dalle dimensioni minime di 50 m². Un vero lusso in una metropoli in cui lo spazio è raro. Moderna eleganza e wellness sono i temi che si snodano per l'intero complesso, dai bagni alla spa. Il prelibato ristorante Amber al 7° piano ed il MO Bar sono stati, sin dalla loro apertura, tra gli indirizzi gastronomici più richiesti in città.

The hotel is connected to a new commercial and shopping center by a network of canopied pedestrian bridges.

Durch ein Netz aus überdachten Fußgängerbrücken ist das Hotel mit einem neuen Geschäfts- und Einkaufszentrum verbunden.

L'hôtel est relié au nouveau centre commercial et d'affaires par un réseau de passerelles couvertes pour piétons.

El hotel se comunica con un nuevo centro comercial a través de una red de puentes cubiertos para peatones.

L'hotel è collegato al nuovo centro commerciale da una rete di ponti pedonali coperti.

Amethyst crystal steam baths, revitalizing swimming pools, rainforest showers as well as Asia's first rhassoul bath are included in treatments offered by the oriental spa centre located on two floors.

Zu den Angeboten des Oriental Spa Centre, das sich über zwei Stockwerke erstreckt, gehören Amethyst-Kristall-Dampfbäder, vitalisierende Swimmingpools, Erlebnis-Duschen sowie Asiens erstes Rasulbad.

Installé sur deux étages, The Oriental Spa propose entre autres des bains de vapeur d'améthyste et de cristal, des piscines revigorantes, des douches originales ainsi que le premier bain Rasul d'Asie.

Entre las propuestas de The Oriental Spa de dos plantas, figuran baños de cristal y amatista, piscinas revitalizantes, duchas de relax, sin olvidar el primer baño Rasul de Asia.

Tra le attrattive della The Oriental Spa, distribuita su due piani, fanno parte i bagni turchi ai cristalli d'ametista, le piscine rivitalizzanti, le docce emozionali ed il primo bagno Rasul di tutta l'Asia.

Grand Hyatt Shanghai

Shanghai, China

The Grand Hyatt Shanghai describes itself as the world's tallest hotel as it occupies the 53rd to 87th floors in the Jin Mao Tower. Yet another superlative: it is alleged to have cities most spacious rooms. The 555 accommodations offer a view of the Huang Pu River or the city and offer a special feature in the bathrooms: a heated mirror in the shower always ensures a clear view. The hotel's location in the financial district Pudong makes it an ideal domicile for business travelers.

Als höchstes Hotel der Welt bezeichnet sich das Grand Hyatt Shanghai, denn es nimmt das 53. bis 87. Stockwerk des Jin Mao Towers ein. Eine weitere Superlative: Es soll über die größten Zimmer der Stadt verfügen. Die 555 Unterkünfte bieten einen Blick über den Fluss Huang Pu oder die Stadt und warten mit einer Besonderheit im Badezimmer auf: Ein beheizter Spiegel in der Dusche sorgt stets für einen klaren Blick. Die Lage des Hotels im Bankenviertel Pudong ist ideal als Domizil für Geschäftsreisende.

Le Grand Hyatt Shanghai se prétend l'hôtel le plus haut du monde car il occupe les étages 53 à 87 de la Jin Mao Tower. Un autre plus : il paraît qu'il dispose des plus grandes chambres de la ville. Les 555 logements ont vue sur le fleuve Huang Pu ou sur la ville et comportent une particularité dans la salle de bains : un miroir chauffé dans la douche garantit une vue toujours nette. La situation de l'hôtel dans le quartier des banques Pudong en fait un lieu de résidence idéal pour les voyages d'affaires.

El Grand Hyatt Shanghai se considera el hotel más alto del mundo pues ocupa los pisos 53 al 87 de la torre Jin Mao. Algo más impresionante: Se dice que tiene las habitaciones más grandes de la ciudad. Las 555 habitaciones tienen vistas al río Huang Pu o a la ciudad y ofrecen algo especial en el baño: Un espejo con calefacción en la ducha proporciona siempre una imagen despejada. La ubicación en el centro financiero Pudong lo hace el domicilio ideal para hombres y mujeres en viaje de negocios.

Il più alto hotel al mondo. Così si definisce il Grand Hyatt Shanghai, che occupa i piani tra il 53° e l'87° della Jin Mao Tower. Ancora un superlativo: si dice che disponga delle più grandi camere della città. Le 555 sistemazioni offrono una vista sul fiume Huang Pu o sulla città e presentano una particolarità nel bagno: uno specchio riscaldato nella doccia fa sì che ci si possa sempre vedere nitidamente. La posizione dell'hotel nel quartiere delle banche Pudong lo rende il domicilio ideale per chi viaggia per affari.

The guest rooms are part of a spectacular atrium, which spans over 33 floors.

Ein spektakuläres Atrium, das über 33 Geschosse reicht, erschließt die Gästezimmer.

Un atrium spectaculaire s'élevant sur 33 étages donne accès aux chambres.

Un atrio espectacular, que abarca más de 33 plantas, alumbra las habitaciones de los huéspedes.

Un atrio spettacolare su più di 33 piani dà accesso alle camere degli ospiti.

The public rooms *are designed elaborately and exclusively. The rooms offer, above all, exceptional comfort.*

Die öffentlichen Räume *sind aufwändig und exklusiv gestaltet. Die Zimmer bieten vor allem gemütlichen Komfort.*

Les espaces publics *sont aménagés avec soin et exclusivité. Les chambres offrent surtout un confort douillet.*

Los espacios públicos *están decorados exclusiva y minuciosamente. Las habitaciones ofrecen, sobre todo, una comodidad apacible.*

Le sale pubbliche *sono arredate in maniera elaborata ed esclusiva. Le camere offrono soprattutto comodità.*

Grand Hyatt Shanghai *Shanghai, China*   369

The Peninsula Palace Beijing

Beijing, China

An American travel magazine recently ennobled the Peninsula Palace as the best hotel in China. Its 468 rooms and 57 suites offer several technical specialties such as a television in the bathroom and a thermostat next to the door that states the outside temperature and humidity. The suites in the upper section cover two floors. Hungry guests can choose between two restaurants, among which the Huang Ting awaits with Cantonese cuisine.

Ein amerikanisches Reisemagazin adelte den Peninsula Palace unlängst zum besten Hotel Chinas. Seine 468 Zimmer und 57 Suiten bieten einige technische Besonderheiten, etwa einen Fernseher im Badezimmer oder ein Thermostat neben der Tür, das Außentemperatur und Luftfeuchtigkeit angibt. Die Suiten in den oberen Geschossen erstrecken sich über zwei Stockwerke. Hungrige Gäste haben die Wahl zwischen zwei Restaurants, von denen das Huang Ting mit kantonesischer Küche aufwartet.

Un magazine de voyage américain a récemment fait honneur au Peninsula Palace en le nommant meilleur hôtel de Chine. Ses 468 chambres et 57 suites offrent certaines particularités techniques, par exemple un téléviseur dans la salle de bains ou un thermostat près de la porte qui indique la température extérieure et l'humidité dans l'air. Les suites des étages supérieurs s'étendent sur deux niveaux. Les hôtes affamés ont le choix entre deux restaurants, parmi lesquels le Huang Ting qui propose de la cuisine cantonaise.

Una revista de turismo americana estadounidense catalogó recientemente al Peninsula Palace como el mejor hotel de China. Sus 468 habitaciones y 57 suites ofrecen algunas especialidades técnicas, como un televisor en el baño o un termostato al lado de la puerta que indica la temperatura exterior y la humedad. Las suites en los pisos superiores son dúplex. El huésped que tengan hambre pueden elegir entre dos restaurantes, uno de los cuales, el Huang Ting, ofrece cocina cantonesa.

Una rivista di viaggi americana di recente ha conferito al Peninsula Palace il titolo di migliore hotel della Cina. Le sue 468 stanze e 57 suite offrono alcune singolarità tecniche, per esempio un televisore nella stanza da bagno o, accanto alla porta, un termostato che indica la temperatura esterna e l'umidità dell'aria. Le suite superiori si distribuiscono su due piani. Gli ospiti affamati possono scegliere fra due ristoranti, tra cui lo Huang Ting che serve cucina cantonese.

The historical gate resembles the entrance to the Forbidden City. Yet, those who enter the Peninsula Palace enter a world modeled entirely based on western standards.

Die historische Pforte gleicht dem Zugang zur verboten Stadt. Doch im Peninsula Palace eröffnet sich eine Welt ganz nach westlichem Standard.

Le portail historique s'apparente à l'entrée de la cité interdite. Mais dans le Peninsula Palace, le monde s'ouvre sur un monde dominé par les standards occidentaux.

La puerta histórica iguala a la entrada a la ciudad prohibida. Sin embargo, en el Peninsula Palace se abre un mundo que sigue completamente los estándares de occidente.

Lo storico cancello è simile a quello che permette l'accesso alla città proibita. Ma al Peninsula Palace tutto il mondo è spalancato agli standard occidentali.

Modern furnishings dominate in the duplex suites; in the Jing Restaurant, transparent curtains screen the tables from each other.

In den Duplex-Suiten herrscht eine moderne Einrichtung vor, im Restaurant Jing schirmen transparente Vorhänge die Tische voneinander ab.

Dans les suites Duplex domine un aménagement moderne, des rideaux transparents séparent les tables l'une des autres dans le restaurant Jing.

En las suites dúplex predomina una decoración moderna, en el restaurante Jing las mesas se separan unas de otras por cortinas transparentes.

Nelle suite doppie domina l'arredamento moderno, nel ristorante Jing tende trasparenti separano i tavoli.

The Dharmawangsa

Jakarta, Indonesia

Peace and space represent true luxury in Jakarta, a city of millions. In one of the posh residential areas in front of the city gates, one finds what one seeks: an elegant hotel, furnished with princely four-poster beds made from rosewood, antique inlaid-work furniture and silk pillows is hidden in a secluded garden. The rooms and penthouse suites are based on the styles of Java, Bali, East-Indonesia and South-Sumatra. And if one still wishes to explore the city: the Kemang nightclub district is not far off.

Ruhe und Platz sind wahrer Luxus in der Millionenmetropole Jakarta. In einem vornehmen Villenviertel vor den Toren der Metropole findet man das Gesuchte: Hier versteckt sich in einem lauschigen Garten ein elegantes Hotel, ausgestattet mit fürstlichen Himmelbetten aus Rosenholz, antikem Intarsien-Mobiliar und Seidenkissen. Die Zimmer und Penthouse-Suiten sind den Stilen der Regionen Java, Bali, Ost-Indonesien und Süd-Sumatra nachempfunden. Und wen es doch in die Stadt zieht: das Amüsierviertel Kemang ist nicht weit.

Le calme et l'espace constituent un réel luxe à Jakarta, métropole comptant plusieurs millions d'habitants. C'est dans un quartier résidentiel chic aux portes de la métropole que l'on trouve ce que l'on cherchait : un élégant hôtel se cache ici, dans un jardin où se sent vraiment bien, aménagé avec des lits à baldaquin princiers en bois de rose, du mobilier antique en marqueterie et des coussins de soie. Les chambres et suites penthouse sont inspirées des styles des régions de Java, de Bali, de l'est de l'Indonésie et du sud de Sumatra. Et si le besoin d'aller en ville se fait quand même sentir : le quartier chaud Kemang n'est pas loin.

Tranquilidad y espacio son verdaderos lujos en una metrópoli tan densamente poblada como Jakarta. En un elegante barrio residencial a las puertas de la ciudad se encuentra lo que buscan: Aquí se esconde en medio de un acogedor jardín un elegante hotel, dotado de fantásticas camas con dosel hechas de palo de rosa, antiguo mobiliario con incrustaciones y cojines de seda. Las habitaciones y las suites del penthouse están decoradas en los estilos de las regiones de Java, Bali, Indonesia oriental y el Sur de Sumatra. Y si aún busca más de la ciudad : La zona de diversión Kemang no se encuentra muy lejos.

Tranquillità e spazio nella grande metropoli di Giacarta sono un vero lusso. In un quartiere residenziale signorile ed esclusivo alle porte della metropoli si trova quello che si cerca: qui in un giardino appartato si nasconde un hotel elegante, arredato con principeschi letti a baldacchino in legno di rosa, antica mobilia intarsiata e cuscini di seta. Le camere e le penthouse suite si rifanno agli stili di Giava, di Bali, dell'Indonesia Orientale e di Sumatra. E per chi si sente attratto dalla città? Il quartiere dei locali notturni, Kemang, non è lontano.

Park and pool as well as the largest of the suites with their exceedingly spacious bathrooms impart the guests with the feeling of being on a country estate.

Park und Pool sowie die größeren unter den Suiten mit ihren überaus geräumigen Badezimmern vermitteln den Gästen das Gefühl, sich auf einem Landgut zu befinden.

Le parc et la piscine, ainsi que les plus grandes des suites avec leurs salles de bains extrêmement spacieuses, donnent aux hôtes la sensation de se trouver dans une propriété rurale.

El parque y la piscina, así como las suites más grandes con sus amplísimos baños, proporcionan al huésped la sensación de estar en una hacienda.

Parco e piscina, ma anche le suite più grandi, con i loro bagni estremamente spaziosi, trasmettono agli ospiti la sensazione di trovarsi in una tenuta.

The intelligently layout permeates the rooms with cozy atmosphere, for example in the library. The traditional Sumatra architecture is easily recognizable.

Durch intelligent angeordnete Räume entsteht überall eine private Wohnatmosphäre, wie etwa in der Bibliothek. Gut erkennbar ist die traditionelle Sumatra-Architektur.

Grâce à la disposition réussie des chambres, une ambiance d'habitation privée règne partout, comme par exemple dans la bibliothèque. L'architecture traditionnelle de Sumatra est aisément décelable.

Gracias a los espacios, que están ordenados inteligentemente, el huésped disfruta, en general, de una atmósfera de privacidad durante su estancia, casi como en la biblioteca. La arquitectura sumatra es fácilmente reconocible.

Grazie agli spazi ordinati in maniera intelligente si crea dappertutto un ambiente intimo, come in biblioteca. Facilmente riconoscibile è la tradizionale architettura sumatrese.

The Ritz-Carlton, Bali Resort & Spa

Bali, Indonesia

Set along the cliffs of Jimbaran peninsula is the location for the luxurious resort with private beach and 18-hole putting course away from the bustle of the tourists. The 375 rooms, suites and villas are scattered about the tropical parkland site, many of them offer a panoramic view across the Indian Ocean. A highlight in terms of contemporary design is the new complex with 38 cliff villas, the restaurants Dava, Martini Bar, pool area and wedding chapel. For their culinary delights guests can choose among four restaurants and three bars.

Entlang der Klippen der Halbinsel Jimbaran gebaut, liegt das luxuriöse Resort mit Privatstrand und 18-Loch Putting Course abseits des touristischen Trubels. Die 375 Zimmer, Suiten und Villen sind verstreut über die tropische Parkanlage, viele von ihnen bieten eine Panoramaaussicht über den Indischen Ozean. In Sachen Design besonders attraktiv ist der neue Komplex der 38 Cliff-Villen mit dem Restaurant Dava und Martini Bar sowie eigener Poollandschaft und Hochzeitskapelle. Kulinarisch haben die Gäste die Auswahl zwischen vier Restaurants und drei Bars.

C'est le long des rochers de la presqu'île de Jimbaran, loin de l'effervescence touristique, qu'a été aménagé cet ensemble luxueux, avec plage privée et terrain de golf à 18 trous. Les 375 chambres, suites et villas sont éparpillées dans le parc tropical, certaines d'entre elles offrant même une vue panoramique sur l'Océan Indien. Avec le restaurant Dava et le Martini Bar, ainsi que l'agencement superbe de son ensemble de piscines et sa chapelle de mariage, le nouveau complexe de villas aux 38 rochers est particulièrement attractif en matière de design. Pour les repas, les visiteurs ont le choix entre quatre restaurants et trois bars.

Situado en los acantilados de la península de Jimbaran se encuentra el lujoso resort con playa propia y campo de golf de 18 hoyos, completamente al margen del ajetreo turístico. Las 375 habitaciones, villas y suites se dispersan por el parque tropical y muchas de ellas cuentan con vistas panorámicas al Océano Índico. En cuanto al diseño, lo que más destacan son las nuevas 38 villas del acantilado, el restaurante Dava, Martini Bar, el area de la piscina y la capilla de bodas. Para la delicia culinaria los huéspedes pueden escoger entre los cuatro restaurantes y tres bares.

Costruito lungo la scogliera della penisola di Jimbaran, questo lussuoso resort, dotato di spiaggia privata e putting course con 18 buche, sorge lontano dal trambusto turistico. Le 375 camere, suite e ville, molte delle quali con vista panoramica sull'Oceano Indiano, sono sparse nel parco tropicale. Particolarmente attraente dal punto di vista del design è il nuovo complesso che comprende 38 Cliff Ville, il ristorante Dava, il Martini bar, un proprio parco piscina ed una cappella matrimoniale. Per quel che riguarda l'aspetto gastronomico, gli ospiti possono scegliere tra quattro ristoranti e tre bar.

A signature feature of the 95,000-square foot spa is its thalassic treatment, a 7,000-square foot saltwater pool, the largest of its kind in the entire world.

Eine Besonderheit des 9000 m² großen Spa ist die Thalassotherapie mit einem 650 m² großen Salzwasserpool, dem weltweit größten seiner Art.

La particularité du spa de 9000 m² est le centre de thalassothérapie avec sa piscine d'eau salée de 650 m², la plus grande au monde dans son genre.

Una de las exclusividades del spa de 9000 m² es la talasoterapia, con piscina de agua salada de 650 m², la más grande de su categoría.

Una particolarità del centro benessere di 9000 m² è la talassoterapia, con una piscina d'acqua salata di 650 m², la più grande al mondo di questo tipo.

In architectural terms, the resort fluctuates between neo-Baroque Ritz-Carlton tradition and minimalist Bali-modern.

In der Architektur bewegt sich die Anlage zwischen neobarocker Ritz-Carlton-Tradition und minimalistischem Bali-Modern.

Au niveau architectural, le complexe évolue entre la tradition néo-baroque du Ritz-Carlton et la modernité minimaliste de Bali.

En el plano arquitectónico, el lugar combina la tradición neobarroca del Ritz-Carlton y las líneas modernas y minimalistas balinesas.

Architettonicamente la struttura si colloca tra la tradizione neobarocca propria del Ritz-Carlton e lo stile moderno minimalista di Bali.

Raffles Hotel Singapore

Singapore, Singapore

The Raffles Hotel was established in 1887. After several expansions, it attained its present design in neo-renaissance style. The 103 suites feature furniture dating back to the hotel's origin and two roughly hundred year old original tables invite one play a round in the billiard room. Even an in-house museum depicting the hotel's long history as a legend adds to the atmosphere of the hotel temple.

Bereits 1887 wurde das Raffles Hotel gegründet, nach mehreren Erweiterungen erhielt es seine heutige Gestalt im Neorenaissance-Stil. Die 103 Suiten sind mit Möbeln aus der Entstehungszeit des Hotels eingerichtet, und im Billardraum laden zwei etwa hundert Jahre alte Originaltische zum Versenken der Kugeln ein. Zur Atmosphäre des längst zur Legende gewordenen Hoteltempels trägt auch ein eigenes Museum bei, das seine Geschichte veranschaulicht.

Le Raffles Hotel a été créé dès 1887, il obtint sa forme actuelle en style néorenaissance après plusieurs agrandissements. Les 103 suites sont aménagées avec des meubles datant de l'époque de la création de l'hôtel, et dans la salle de billard, deux tables d'origine vieilles d'environ cent ans invitent à faire disparaître les boules. Un musée de l'hôtel retraçant son histoire contribue à l'ambiance de temple-hôtel entré depuis longtemps dans la légende.

El Raffles Hotel fue fundado ya en 1887; tras muchas ampliaciones alcanzó su aspecto actual de estilo neorrenacentista. Las 103 suites están decoradas con muebles de la época de su inauguración y en el salón de billar dos mesas originales de aproximadamente 100 años de antigüedad invitan al juego. Al ambiente de este hotel-templo, convertido en leyenda desde hace ya tiempo, contribuye un museo propio que ilustra su historia.

Il Raffles Hotel fu fondato nel 1887; dopo diversi ampliamenti è giunto alla struttura odierna in stile neorinascimentale. Le 103 suite sono arredate con mobili dell'epoca in cui sorse l'hotel, e nella sala da biliardo due originali tavoli, vecchi di quasi cento anni, invitano a buttare le biglie in buca. All'ambiente dell' hotel, da molto tempo ormai una leggenda, contribuisce anche un museo proprio, che ne illustra la storia.

In the midst of the booming Singapore skyscraper metropolis, the Raffles remains true to its roots. In 1987, it was declared a national monument.

Inmitten der boomenden Hochhausmetropole Singapur bleibt das Raffles seinen Traditionen treu. 1987 wurde es zum nationalen Monument erklärt.

Situé au centre de Singapour, la métropole bouillonnante des gratte-ciels, le Raffles reste fidèle à ses traditions. Il a été nommé Monument National en 1987.

En medio de esta próspera metrópoli de rascacielos, el Raffles sigue fiel a sus tradiciones. En 1987 fue declarado Monumento Nacional.

Il Raffles resta fedele alle sue tradizioni pur trovandosi nel centro di Singapore, una metropoli di grattacieli in piena crescita. Nel 1987 è stato dichiarato monumento nazionale.

The lobby, 13 restaurants and five bars radiate bright generosity.

Die Lobby, 13 Restaurants und fünf Bars verbreiten helle Großzügigkeit.

Le lobby, 13 restaurants et cinq bars répandent un luxe lumineux.

El vestíbulo, los 13 restaurantes y las cinco barras irradian una generosidad clara.

La Lobby, 13 ristoranti e cinque bar diffondono una chiara generosità.

The Fullerton Hotel Singapore

Singapore, Singapore

In 1928, the Fullerton was erected in neoclassicist style and housed, in sequential order, the main post office, the chamber of commerce and the stock exchange before finally being opened as one of the most beautiful new hotels in Singapore in 2001. Situated between the Singapore River and the Marina Bay, over half of the rooms offer a multifarious view of the water and skyline. In addition, almost the entire downtown can be reached by foot.

1928 wurde das Fullerton im neoklassizistischen Stil errichtet und beherbergte nacheinander das Hauptpostamt, die Handelskammer und die Börse, bevor es 2001 schließlich als eines der schönsten neuen Hotels in Singapur eröffnet wurde. Zwischen dem Singapur River und der Marina-Bucht gelegen, bieten über die Hälfte der Räume eine abwechslungsreiche Aussicht auf Wasser und Skyline. Zudem ist von hier aus nahezu das gesamte Stadtzentrum zu Fuß erreichbar.

Le Fullerton a été fondé en 1928 dans le style néoclassique et hébergea tour à tour la poste principale, la chambre du commerce et la bourse, avant que l'un des plus beaux hôtels récents de Singapour ne soit finalement ouvert en 2001. Situées entre la Singapour River et la baie de Marina, plus de la moitié des pièces offrent une vue diversifiée sur l'eau et les gratte-ciels. De plus, d'ici, quasiment la totalité du centre-ville est accessible à pied.

El Fullerton fue construido en 1928 en estilo neoclásico y albergó sucesivamente la oficina de correos, la cámara de comercio y la bolsa, antes de ser inaugurado en 2001 como uno de los más hermosos hoteles de Singapur. Ubicado entre el río Singapur y Marina Bay, más de la mitad de las habitaciones ofrecen una variada vista hacia el río y el horizonte de la ciudad. Además, se puede ir andando a casi todas las zonas del centro.

Il Fullerton fu eretto nel 1928 in stile neoclassico e ha ospitato, prima della sua riapertura nel 2001, vari edifice tra cui la Posta Centrale, la Camera di Commercio e la Bors Attualmente è, uno dei migliori e nuovi hotel di Singapore. Situato tra il Singapore River e la baia Marina, più della metà delle camere offre viste sull'acqua e sulla città. Inoltre da qui è raggiungibile a piedi il centro cittadino.

The location on the water, now very picturesque, used to have concrete advantages when the building still housed the post office as letters and packages were distributed by boat.

Die Lage am Wasser, heute sehr malerisch, hatte früher, als das Gebäude noch die Post beherbergte, handfeste Vorteile: Briefe und Pakete wurden mit dem Boot verteilt.

Sa situation au bord de l'eau, aujourd'hui très pittoresque, comportait autrefois, lorsque le bâtiment hébergeait la poste, de grands avantages : les lettres et les colis étaient distribuées par bateau.

La situación a orillas del río, actualmente tan pintoresca, tenía, en la época en que albergaba la oficina de correos, una ventaja contundente: Las cartas y los paquetes se repartían con el bote.

La posizione sull'acqua, oggi molto pittoresca, era un tempo, quando l'edificio ospitava ancora la Posta, un grande vantaggio: lettere e pacchetti venivano distribuiti con la barca.

Part of the hotel rooms is oriented inwards to the imposing glass covered atrium.

Ein Teil der Hotelzimmer orientiert sich nach innen zu dem imposanten glasüberdeckten Atrium.

Une partie des chambres de l'hôtel est orientée vers l'intérieur, en direction de l'imposant atrium au plafond de verre.

Parte de las habitaciones se orientan hacia el interior, hacia el imponente atrio cubierto con techo de cristal.

Una parte delle camere dell'hotel dà sull'interno verso l'imponente atrio rivestito in vetro.

The Oriental
Bangkok, Thailand

Above the Chao Phrya, the river that winds through the metropolis like a snake, looms The Oriental. For over a century, literary figures from around the world have drawn their inspiration from its atmosphere. The suites in the Authors Wing both pay homage to famous authors as well as being attuned to them: wooden wainscoting and a nautical flair for Captain Anderson, colonial style with teak and silk for the novelist Wilbur Smith, pink damask for the romancière Barbara Cartland.

Am Chao Phrya, dem Fluss, der sich wie eine Schlange durch die Metropole windet, ragt The Oriental auf. Über ein Jahrhundert lang haben sich Literaten aus aller Welt von der Atmosphäre des Hotels inspirieren lassen. Die Suiten im Authors Wing sind eine Hommage an berühmte Schriftsteller und auf sie abgestimmt: Holzvertäfelung und nautisches Flair für Kapitän Anderson, Kolonialstil mit Teak und Seide für Novellist Wilbur Smith, rosa Damast für Romancière Barbara Cartland.

The Oriental se dresse le long du Chao Phrya, le fleuve qui se contorsionne tel un serpent à travers la métropole. Pendant plus d'un siècle, les gens de lettres du monde entier se sont laissés inspirer par l'atmosphère de l'hôtel. Les suites situées dans l'Aile des Auteurs (Authors Wing) rendent hommage aux écrivains célèbres et sont réalisées à leur mesure : boiseries et ambiance nautique pour le capitaine Anderson, style colonial en teck et soie pour le romancier Wilbur Smith, damas rose pour la romancière Barbara Cartland.

A orillas del Chao Phrya, el río que se desliza como una serpiente por la metrópoli, sobresale The Oriental. Por más de un siglo escritores de todo el mundovse inspiraron en el ambiente del hotel. Las suites en el ala de los autores (Authors Wing) son un homenaje a escritores famosos y de acuerdo a ellos están decoradas: Revestimiento de madera y aire naútico, para el Capitán Anderson; estilo colonial con madera de teca y seda, para el novelista Wilbur Smith; damasco rosado, para la novelista Barbara Cartland.

Sul Chao Phrya, il fiume che si snoda come un serpente nella metropoli, si erge The Oriental. Per più di un secolo letterati di tutto il mondo si sono lasciati ispirare dalle atmosfere dell'hotel. Le suite nell'ala degli autori (Authors Wing) sono un omaggio a famosi scrittori: rivestimenti in legno e aria nautica per il capitano Anderson, stile coloniale in tek e seta per il novellista Wilbur Smith, damasco rosa per la scrittrice Barbara Cartland.

Thanks to the mild climate in Thailand, hotel life often takes place outdoors—at the pool for example or on the large terraces of the building.

Dank des milden Klimas in Thailand spielt sich das Hotelleben oft auch draußen ab — etwa am Pool oder auf den großen Terrassen des Gebäudes.

Grâce au climat doux thaïlandais, la vie de l'hôtel se déroule souvent à l'extérieur — par exemple sur le bord de la piscine ou sur les grandes terrasses du bâtiment.

Gracias al clima templado de Tailandia, la vida del hotel transcurre a menudo en el exterior, en la piscina o en la gran terraza del edificio.

Grazie al clima mite della Tailandia, la vita dell'hotel si svolge spesso all'aperto, ad es. in piscina oppure sulle grandi terrazze dell'edificio.

Select collector's pieces, noble period furniture and a historic atmosphere: a walk through the hotel resembles a visit to an antique dealer.

Ausgesuchte Sammlerstücke, edle Stilmöbel und historische Atmosphäre: Der Gang durch das Hotel gleicht dem Besuch eines Antiquitätengeschäfts.

Des pièces de collection choisies, de beaux meubles stylés et une atmosphère historique : faire le tour de l'hôtel équivaut à visiter un magasin d'antiquités.

Piezas de colección exclusivas, finos muebles de época y un ambiente histórico: Un recorrido por el hotel parece la visita a una tienda de antigüedades.

Pezzi scelti da collezione, preziosi mobili in stile e aria storica: passeggiare per l'hotel è come entrare in un negozio di antiquariato.

Mandarin Oriental Dhara Dhevi

Chiang Mai, Thailand

60 villas, 84 suites and dual theme residences combine to become a luxurious oasis on the edge of the cultural destination Chiang Mai in northern Thailand. In terms of architectural style, the resort draws on traditional Lanna architecture, which is well known for its pitched roofs with carvings. Century-old Asian healing methods are applied in "The Dheva Spa" covering nearly 33,000-square feet. The construction is modeled after the Mandalay Palace in Myanmar and very deliberately radiates a fairytale-like atmosphere.

60 Villen, 84 Suiten und zwei Themen-Residenzen formen sich am Rande der nordthailändischen Kulturdestination Chiang Mai zu einer luxuriösen Oase. In ihrem Baustil folgt das Resort der traditionellen Lanna-Architektur, die für ihre mit Schnitzereien versehenen Spitzdächer bekannt ist. Im über 3000 m² großen „The Dheva Spa" werden jahrhundertealte Heilmethoden Asiens angewandt. Die Anlage ist dem Mandalay Palast in Myanmar nachempfunden und strahlt ganz bewusst märchenhafte Atmosphäre aus.

60 villas, 84 suites et deux résidences à thèmes forment un oasis luxueux en périphérie de la destination culturelle Chiang Mai dans le nord de la Thaïlande. Le style de construction de l'hôtel ressemble à l'architecture traditionnelle Lanna, connue pour ses toits pointus sculptés. Des méthodes de guérison asiatiques vieilles de plusieurs siècles sont administrées dans « The Dheva Spa » de plus de 3000 m². L'ensemble prend exemple sur le palais Mandalay à Myanmar et reflète une ambiance voulue de conte de fées.

60 villas, 84 suites y dos residencias temáticas forman un oasis de lujo en la periferia de Chiang Mai, destino cultural al norte de Tailandia. En su estilo arquitectónico, el resort sigue la línea de la tradicional arquitectura lanna, conocida por sus tejados a dos aguas adornados con tallas. En los más de 3000 m² del gran "The Dheva Spa" se aplican métodos de sanación asiáticos que tienen siglos de antigüedad. El complejo se compenetra con el Mandalay Palast en Myanmar e irradia un ambiente fabuloso.

60 ville, 84 suite e due residenze a tema compongono nella destinazione culturale di Chiang Mai, a nord della Tailandia, un'oasi di lusso. Lo stile costruttivo del Resort persegue la tradizionale architettura Lanna, conosciuta per i suoi tetti spioventi intagliati nel legno. Nel centro benessere "The Dheva Spa", grande più di 3000 m², vengono utilizzati rimedi antichi. La struttura è stata concepita sull'esempio del Mandalay Palast a Myanmar e risplende consapevolmente un'aurea fiabesca.

Most suites boast a partially covered wooden terrace. Some even feature their own pool.

Die meisten Suiten haben eine teilweise überdachte Holzterrasse. Einige besitzen sogar ihren eigenen Pool.

La majeure partie des suites dispose d'une terrasse en bois partiellement couverte. Certaines possèdent même une piscine privée.

La mayoría de las suites tienen una terraza de madera techada parcialmente y algunas tienen incluso su propia piscina.

La maggior parte delle suite ha una terrazza in legno parzialmente coperta. Alcune hanno addirittura una piscina privata.

Between rice fields and tropical vegetation, the wooden footbridges connect the living quarters with the spa, lobby, library as well as six restaurants and cafés.

Zwischen Reisfeldern und tropischer Vegetation verbinden Holzstege die Wohngebäude mit Spa, Lobby, Bibliothek sowie sechs Restaurants und Cafés.

Entre les champs de riz et la végétation tropicale, des passerelles en bois relient les bâtiments d'habitation avec le Spa, le lobby, la bibliothèque, ainsi que les six restaurants et cafés.

Entre campos de arroz y vegetación tropical, las pasarelas de madera unen los edificios de viviendas con el spa, el lobby y la biblioteca, así como con seis restaurantes y cafés.

Tra le risaie e la vegetazione tropicale gli edifici sono collegati tramite dei pontili di legno al centro benessere, alla reception, alla biblioteca e ai sei ristoranti e al bar.

Aleenta Resort and Spa Phuket - Phangnga

Phuket, Thailand

And the endless horizon of the sea represents an eternal attraction. In this respect alone, the isolated complex of the Aleenta offers luxurious conditions. A whole area comprised of individual villas, suites and penthouses awaits the guest—all featuring an open view of the colorful reflexes of the Andaman Lake. In addition to the impressive accommodations, other highlights of the resort lies in the exclusive wellness activities directly at the pool.

Und ewig lockt der endlose Horizont des Meeres. Allein schon in dieser Hinsicht bietet die abgeschiedene Anlage von Aleenta luxuriöse Bedingungen. Ein ganzes Areal von einzelnen Villen, Suiten und Penthäusern steht bereit – allesamt mit freiem Blick auf die farbenfrohen Reflexe des Andamansees. Neben den eindrucksvollen Unterkünften setzt das Resort mit exklusiven Wellness-Anwendungen direkt am Pool weitere Glanzpunkte.

L'appel incessant de l'horizon infini de la mer. Déjà, vu sous cet aspect, le site isolé d'Aleenta offre des conditions luxueuses. Tout un ensemble de villas individuelles, de suites et d'appartements terrasses sont à la disposition des hôtes – toutes et tous avec une vue libre sur les reflets colorés du lac Andaman. Outre les logements impressionnants, l'hôtel dispose d'une autre particularité sous la forme de soins de bien-être administrés directement au bord de la piscine.

Y eternamente nos seduce el horizonte infinito del mar. Tan sólo en este aspecto, el complejo periférico de Aleenta ya nos ofrece condiciones lujosas. Un área completa de villas individuales y penthouses que están preparadas para los huéspedes y desde las que se puede disfrutar de los reflejos coloridos del mar de Andaman. Además del impresionante alojamiento, el resort tiene como punto fuerte los tratamientos exclusivos de wellness directamente en la piscina.

L'orizzonte infinito del mare è un'attrazione senza tempo. Solo per questo l'appartata costruzione dell' Aleenta offre condizioni lussuose. Un intero areale composto da singole ville, suite e penthouse è già pronto: tutte con vista diretta sui riflessi colorati del lago di Andaman. Oltre agli alloggi impressionanti, il Resort ha altri punti di forta dati da servizi wellness esclusivi direttamente in piscina.

The architecture in Aleenta is marked by open space areas—both in the villas as well as on the premises.

Open Space Areas bestimmen die Architektur in Aleenta – in den Villen wie in der Anlage.

Les espaces ouverts prédominent dans l'architecture d'Aleenta – dans les villas autant que dans l'ensemble des installations.

Las áreas abiertas determinan la arquitectura en Aleenta, tanto en las villas como en el resto de las instalaciones.

Aree di spazio all'aperto determinano l'architettura ad Aleenta – sia nelle ville sia all'interno dell'impianto.

Those staying here are always but a few paces away from the pool and sea.

Wer hier erwacht, hat immer einen Pool und das Meer zum Greifen nahe.

Celui qui se réveille ici, a toujours une piscine ou la mer à portée de main.

Quien se despierta aquí tiene siempre la piscina y el mar al lado.

Chi lo desidera può sempre rifugiarsi vicino alla piscina ed al mare.

Amanpuri
Phuket, Thailand

The philosophy of the worldwide Aman resorts lies in arousing the joy of experiencing foreign cultures. They combine the desire to indulge with a sense for the extraordinary. Amanpuri doubtlessly ranks among this class of exquisite travel destinations. Entwined by a grove of palm trees, the complex impresses its guests with its far-eastern grace, which is visible in its focus on the essentials. Nonetheless, the resort focuses on western generosity—sheer luxury for body and soul.

Die Freude am Erleben fremder Kulturen zu wecken, prägt die Philosophie der weltweiten Aman-Resorts. Sie vereinen die Lust zum Verwöhnen mit dem Sinn für das Außergewöhnliche. Amanpuri gehört ohne Frage in diese Riege erlesener Reiseziele. Umrankt von einem Palmenhain beeindruckt die Anlage durch ihre fernöstliche Anmut, spürbar an der Konzentration auf das Wesentliche. Gleichwohl setzt das Resort auf westliche Großzügigkeit – schierer Luxus für Seele und Körper.

Initier aux plaisirs de la découverte de cultures différentes, telle est la philosophie de la chaîne hôtelière mondiale Aman. Elle combine le désir de choyer avec un sens aigu de l'exceptionnel. L'Amanpuri fait sans aucun doute partie de cette ligue de lieux de villégiature exclusifs. Entourés d'une palmeraie, les installations impressionnent par leur grâce Est-Asiatique, qui se reflète dans la concentration sur l'essentiel. L'hôtel table par contre sur la grandeur occidentale – le luxe pur pour le corps et l'âme.

El placer de despertar el interés por conocer otras culturas impregna la filosofía del resort universal Aman. Se combinan el deseo de colmar de atenciones con el sentido de lo extraordinario. Amanpuri es sin duda uno de los destinos selectos. Rodeado por un bosque de palmeras, el complejo impresiona por su encanto típico del lejano oriente, que se hace palpable por la concentración en lo esencial. No obstante, el resort apuesta por la generosidad occidental, lujo puro para el alma y el cuerpo.

Risvegliare la gioia dell'esperienza di culture straniere influenza la filosofia dei Resort-Aman in tutto il mondo. Riuniscono la voglia di essere viziati al senso per le cose particolari. Amanpuri appartiene, senza dubbio, a questi nobili luoghi di vacanza. Circondato da palme, la struttura colpisce per la sua grazia tipica del lontano Oriente, dove l'importante è l'essenziale. Contemporaneamente il Resort punta alla generosità occidentale – puro lusso per anima e corpo.

Clear forms and isolated angles set the architectural tone.

Klare Formen und abgeschiedene Winkel geben architektonisch den Ton an.

Des formes claires et des recoins discrets sont les points forts de l'architecture.

El tono arquitectónico lo ponen las formas claras y los ángulos ocultos.

L'accento architettonico è creato da forme chiare e angoli isolati.

Idyllic, wherever the eye may wander. A successful composition of tradition and contemporary elegance.

Idylle, wohin das Auge schaut. Ein gelungener Mix aus Tradition und zeitgemäßer Eleganz.

L'idylle est partout. Un mélange réussi entre la tradition et l'élégance contemporaine.

Una vista idílica por donde quiera que se mire. Una mezcla lograda de tradición y elegancia moderna.

Un idillio per gli occhi. Un mix di successo tra tradizione ed eleganza contemporanea.

Trisara

Phuket, Thailand

The name Trisara is Sanskrit and means "the third garden in heaven". In this manner, the resort promises its guest the final pre-stages of enlightenment on earth. It includes a series of individual pool villas, which with their rooms each encompassing nearly 2,600-square feet offer downright luxurious dimensions and furnishings. Only the pool suites are somewhat smaller and more modest. The location itself is just as unique—white constructions with their quaint pagoda roofs amidst a primeval forest.

Der Name Trisara entstammt dem Sanskrit und bedeutet „Der dritte Garten im Himmel". Auf diese Weise verspricht das Resort dem Gast, die letzten Vorstufen der Erleuchtung auf Erden. Dazu gehört eine ganze Reihe von einzeln stehenden Poolvillen, die mit ihren 240 m² großen Räumen geradezu luxuriöse Ausmaße und Ausstattungen bieten. Nur etwas kleiner und bescheidener präsentieren sich die Poolsuiten. Ebenso einzigartig ist die Lage, der inmitten von Urwald platzierten weißen Bauten mit ihren putzigen Pagodendächern.

Le nom Trisara vient du sanskrit et signifie « le troisième jardin du ciel ». C'est ainsi que l'hôtel promet à ses hôtes les dernières étapes préalables à l'illumination sur terre. Un certain nombre de villas individuelles avec piscine, auxquelles les superficies de 240 m² et les aménagements confèrent des dimensions tout à fait luxueuses. Les suites avec piscines sont un peu plus petites et modestes. La situation des bâtiments avec leurs sympathiques toits de pagodes disséminés dans la jungle est également unique.

El nombre Trisara proviene del sánscrito y significa "el tercer jardín del cielo". De esta manera, el resort promete al huésped el último paso hacia la iluminación en la tierra. Parte de este propósito es una serie completa de villas con piscinas individuales que, con sus grandes espacios de 240 m², ofrecen un tamaño y un equipamiento casi lujosos. Sólo las suites con piscina parecen algo más pequeñas y modestas. Igualmente única es la ubicación de los edificios blancos con sus techos tipo pagoda, que se encuentran en medio de la selva.

Il nome Trisara deriva dal sanscrito e significa "Il terzo giardino in Cielo". Così il Resort promette all'ospite di vivere sulla terra. Fanno del complesso un'intera fila di singole ville con piscina che, con le loro camere grandi 240 m², offrono dimensioni e arredi di lusso. Solo leggermente più piccole e modeste sono le suite sulla piscina. Unica è anche la posizione delle casette bianche con i loro tetti a pagoda, situate al centro della foresta vergine.

Architectural spots of light at the night—surrounded by nature and the sea.

Architektonische Lichtpunkte in der Nacht — umschlossen von Natur und Meer.

Points de lumière d'architecture dans la nuit — entourés par la nature et la mer.

Son puntos de luz arquitectónicos en la noche que están rodeados por la naturaleza y el mar.

Punti architettonici luminosi notturni circondati dalla natura e dal mare.

The suites of the hotel are generous in terms of surface and comfort, while the paths meander through the intimate hotel premises.

Großzügig an Fläche und Komfort präsentieren sich die Suiten des Hotels, verschlungen dagegen die Pfade der intimen Anlage.

Les suites de l'hôtel présentent des dimensions et un confort luxueux, tandis que les sentiers qui traversent l'ensemble préservent l'intimité.

Las suites del hotel son amplias y confortables, mientras que las veredas de estas íntimas instalaciones se entrelazan.

Le suite degli hotel sono ampie e ricche di comfort, e di intimità.

Sala Samui Resort and Spa

Koh Samui, Thailand

Set on the previously almost untouched Choeng Mon Beach on the northeast end of the island, this boutique resort with 69 luxury villas is characterized by a unique style of traditional architecture and contemporary ambiance. White walls, cushions, linen covers and fabric tracks compliment each other together with the selectively applied dark wood on the walls, flooring and furniture items. Many wish for this kind interior in a holiday home. Here, you have the chance to live your dream, including a private pool and Mandara spa.

Am bisher noch kaum berührten Choeng-Mon-Strand im Nordosten der Insel prägt dieses Boutique-Resort mit 69 Luxusvillen einen eigenen Stil aus traditioneller Architektur und zeitgenössischem Ambiente. Weiße Wände, Polster, Leinenbezüge und Stoffbahnen ergänzen sich mit den behutsam eingesetzten dunklen Hölzern an Wänden, Böden und Möbelstücken. Eine Einrichtung, wie sie sich viele für ein Ferienhaus erträumen. Hier kann man den Traum Probe wohnen, inklusive privatem Pool und Mandara-Spa.

Au Nord-Est de l'île, le long de la plage de Choeng Mon encore quasiment intacte jusqu'ici, cet hôtel-boutique présente son propre style d'architecture traditionnelle et d'ambiance contemporaine avec 69 villas de luxe. Murs blancs, rembourrage, revêtements en lin et bandes de tissu sont complétés par le bois sombre soigneusement apposé aux murs, aux sols et aux meubles. Nombreuses sont les personnes qui rêveraient d'une telle installation pour leur maison de vacances. Elles peuvent ici obtenir un échantillon de leur rêve, piscine privée et spa Mandara inclus.

En la apenas explotada playa de Choeng Mon, al norte de la isla, se ubica un Boutique-Resort con 69 villas de lujo y un estilo propio que intercala arquitectura tradicional y ambiente contemporáneo. Paredes blancas, tapicería, fundas de lino y tiras de tela se complementan con las maderas oscuras cuidadosamente integradas en las paredes, suelos y mobiliario. La decoración ideal para una casa de vacaciones; un sueño que se puede probar con piscina y spa Mandara incluidos.

Sulla spiaggia di Choeng Mon, nella parte nordorientale dell'isola, ancora intatta, questa residenza esclusiva con 69 lussuose ville si distingue per il caratteristico stile architettonico tradizionale e contemporaneo. Pareti bianche, mobili imbottiti, fodere di lino e passerelle di stoffa si integrano magnificamente con il legno scuro – utilizzato con la dovuta parsimonia – delle pareti, dei pavimenti e dell'arredo. Arredo da sogno per una residenza di villeggiatura. Ma il sogno è qui realtà, con la piscina privata e il centro benessere Mandara Spa.

Choose from villas with one or two bedrooms. All of them have a spacious, semi-open bath and terrace. 53 of them feature their own mini-swimming pool.

Zur Auswahl stehen Villen mit einem oder zwei Schlafzimmern. Alle verfügen sie über ein geräumiges, halboffenes Bad und Terrasse. 53 von ihnen haben ihr eigenes Mini-Schwimmbad.

Au choix, des villas comprenant une ou deux chambres à coucher. Toutes disposent d'une salle de bain spacieuse semi-ouverte et d'une terrasse. Parmi elles, 53 possèdent leur propre mini-piscine.

La elección está entre villas con una o dos habitaciones. Todas cuentan con un amplio baño semiabierto además de terraza y 53 de ellas disfrutan de mini piscina.

È possibile scegliere ville con una o due camere da letto, tutte dotate di uno spazioso bagno semiaperto e di una terrazza. 53 dispongono anche di una mini-piscina privata.

Spa activities can be enjoyed either in the spa rooms provided, in one's own villa, or at the pool near the beach.

Spa-Anwendungen werden entweder in den dafür vorgesehenen Räumen, in der eigenen Villa oder am Pool in der Nähe des Strandes durchgeführt.

Les soins balnéaires sont administrés soit dans les espaces prévus à cet effet, soit dans les villas ou au bord de la piscine située à proximité de la plage.

Los tratamientos en el spa se llevarán a cabo o en los espacios preparados para este fin, en los de la propia villa o en la piscina cercana a la playa.

I trattamenti del centro benessere vengono effettuati nelle sale stabilite, oppure presso la propria villa, o, ancora sulla piscina vicino alla spiaggia.

Raffles Hotel Le Royal

Phnom Penh, Cambodia

With its mixture of Khmer architecture and French colonialism, the hotel built in 1929 is one of the legends of Indochina. The original building and an add-on modeled after the original surround both pools in a tropical garden. They not only house 170 rooms and suites, but also three restaurants, a café and the Elephant Bar, once again a true institution in Phnom Penh.

Mit seiner Mischung aus Khmer-Architektur und französischem Kolonialismus zählt das 1929 erbaute Hotel zu den Legenden Indochinas. Um die beiden Pools in einem tropischen Garten gruppieren sich das ursprüngliche Gebäude und eine dem Original nachempfundene Erweiterung. Darin befinden sich neben 170 Zimmern und Suiten insgesamt auch drei Restaurants, ein Café und die Elephant Bar, in Phnom Penh heute wieder eine echte Institution.

Avec son mélange d'architecture Khmer et de colonialisme français, cet hôtel construit en 1929 compte parmi les légendes de l'Indochine. Autour des deux piscines dans le jardin tropical se regroupent le bâtiment ancien et une extension dans le même style que l'original. L'hôtel comporte 170 chambres et suites, trois restaurants, un café et l'Elephant Bar, qui est de nos jours à nouveau une vraie institution à Phnom Penh.

Con su mezcla de arquitectura khmer y estilo colonialista francés, el hotel, construido en 1929, es parte de las leyendas de Indochina. Alrededor de las dos piscinas, en el jardín tropical, se agrupan el edificio original y una ampliación que se compenetra con el mismo. Ahí se encuentran las 170 habitaciones y suites, tres restaurantes, un Café y el Elephant Bar, que vuelve a ser hoy en día una verdadera institución en Phnom Penh.

Con il suo miscuglio tra architettura cambogiana e tracce del colonialismo francese, questo hotel, costruito nel 1929, è una delle leggende dell'Indocina. Attorno alle due piscine, in un giardino tropicale, si trovano l'edificio originale ed il suo ampliamento ad imitazione dell'originale. All'interno si trovano, oltre alle 170 camere e suite, tre ristoranti, un bar e l'Elephant Bar, che a Phnom Penh rappresenta di nuovo una vera istituzione.

The hotel, which resembles a palace, is located in the center of Phnom Penh.

Das an einen Palast erinnernde Hotel liegt im Zentrum von Phnom Penh.

Cet hôtel bâti dans le style d'un palais se trouve dans le centre de la ville de Phnom Penh.

El hotel, que recuerda a un palacio, se ubica en el centro de Phnom Penh.

L'hotel, che ricorda un palazzo, si trova nel centro di Phnom Penh.

While furnishing it, the operators focused on nostalgia and conserved traditional elements, such as the free-standing bathtub.

Bei der Einrichtung haben die Betreiber auf Nostalgie gesetzt und traditionelle Elemente, wie die freistehende Badewanne, erhalten.

Lors de sa construction, les gérants ont misé sur la nostalgie et ont conservé au mieux les éléments traditionnels tels les baignoires non encastrées.

Los propietarios han apostado en la decoración y el mobiliario por un estilo nostálgico y han mantenido elementos tradicionales como las bañeras con patas.

Per le scelte negli arredi, i gestori hanno puntato sullo stile nostalgico mantenendo intatti elementi tradizionali, come ad es. la vasca da bagno fuori terra.

416   Raffles Hotel Le Royal *Phnom Penh, Cambodia*

Park Hyatt Tokyo

Tokyo, Japan

"Lost in Translation", this film made the hotel world-famous in 2003. The bar, pool, and suites served as backdrops for the most important scenes in the subtle love story. The Park Hyatt Tokyo lies in the fourteen upper floors of a skyscraper designed by Kenzo Tange. Along with the spectacular views of the largest city in the world, the 177 hotel rooms offer pure luxury and an abundance of space in a metropolis that is bursting at the seams. They are alleged to be the most spacious in the whole city.

„Lost in Translation" – dieser Film machte das Hotel im Jahr 2003 weltberühmt. Für die wichtigsten Szenen der subtilen Liebesgeschichte dienten die Bar, der Pool und die Suiten als Kulisse. Das Park Hyatt Tokyo liegt in den vierzehn obersten Stockwerken eines Wolkenkratzers, den Kenzo Tange entwarf. Neben den spektakulären Ausblicken auf die größte Stadt der Welt bieten die 177 Hotelzimmer etwas, das in der engen, aus allen Nähten platzenden Metropole wahrer Luxus ist: viel Platz. Sie sollen die größten der Stadt sein.

« Lost in Translation » – ce film a rendu l'hôtel célèbre en 2003. Le bar, la piscine et les suites ont servi de décors aux scènes les plus importantes de cette subtile histoire d'amour. Le Park Hyatt Tokyo se trouve dans les quatorze étages supérieurs d'un gratte-ciel conçu par Kenzo Tange. Outre les vues spectaculaires sur la plus grande ville du monde, les 177 chambres de l'hôtel offrent quelque chose qui est un vrai luxe dans la métropole étroite et qui explose littéralement : beaucoup de place. Elles seraient les plus grandes de la ville.

"Lost in Translation" está película hizo mundialmente famoso al hotel en el 2003. Para las escenas más importantes de esta sutil historia de amor se utilizaron como escenarios el bar, la piscina y suites. El Park Hyatt Tokyo se encuentra en los últimos catorce pisos de un rascacielos diseñado por Kenzo Tange. Junto a las espectaculares vistas de la ciudad más grande del mundo, las 177 habitaciones ofrecen algo que es un verdadero lujo en esta metrópoli densamente poblada, mucho espacio. Se dice que son las habitaciones más grandes del ciudad.

"Lost in Translation" é il film che nel 2003 ha reso l'hotel famoso nel mondo. Il bar, la piscina e le suite hanno fatto da scenografia alle più importanti scene della complessa storia d'amore. Il Park Hyatt Tokyo si trova al 14°piano di un grattacielo progettato da Kenzo Tange. Oltre alle spettacolari vedute sulla più grande città del mondo, le 177 camere dell'hotel offrono qualcosa che in questa angusta metropoli, ormai sul punto di scoppiare, è un vero lusso: lo spazio. Dovrebbero essere le camere più grandi della città.

The floor to ceiling windows in the indoor swimming pool and restaurant allow views of the bustling activities in the streets of Tokyo and of Mount Fuji when the sky is clear.

Die raumhohe Verglasung im Pool und in den Restaurants gestattet Ausblicke auf das quirlige Treiben in den Straßen Tokios und – bei gutem Wetter – auf den Berg Fuji.

Les vitrages aussi hauts que la pièce dans la piscine couverte et dans les restaurants offrent une vue sur la vie turbulente dans les rues de Tokyo et – par beau temps – sur le mont Fuji.

Los altos ventanales en la piscina cubierta y en los restaurantes permiten observar el vivo trajín de las calles de Tokio y con tiempo despejado el monte Fuji.

Le vetrate a tutt'altezza permettono di vedere, dalla piscina coperta e dai ristoranti, il vivacissimo viavai delle strade di Tokyo e tempo permettendo il monte Fuji.

The interior and materials are exquisitely selected. Thus, the design manages to convey a pleasant atmosphere.

Interieur und Materialien sind exquisit ausgewählt. So gelingt es dem Design, eine angenehme Atmosphäre zu verströmen.

L'aménagement intérieur et les matériaux sont d'un choix exquis. Ainsi le design réussit à répandre une ambiance agréable.

Los interiores y los materiales fueron seleccionados con exquisitez. De esta manera, el diseño consigue irradiar un ambiente grato.

Gli interni ed i materiali sono stati scelti in maniera squisita. In tal modo il design è in grado di trasmettere un'atmosfera piacevole.

The Westin Sydney

Sydney, Australia

Located in the downtown not far from the famous Sydney opera, the hotel overlooks the Martin Place. The guestrooms are partially located within a protected historical building from 1887, which used to accommodate the post office. The other rooms are located in a modern tower of 31 floors. One is distinguished by its high ceilings and historic furniture, while the other by its room-high glazing and a pleasant view. Stores that have settled thanks to the hotel's central location invite one to go shopping.

Unweit der berühmten Oper von Sydney in der Innenstadt gelegen, schaut das Hotel über Martin Place. Teilweise liegen die Gästezimmer in einem denkmalgeschützten Altbau aus dem Jahr 1887, der früher die Post beherbergte, teilweise aber auch in einem modernen Turm von 31 Stockwerken. Die einen zeichnen sich durch hohe Decken und eine historische Ausstattung aus, die anderen durch raumhohe Verglasungen und eine gute Aussicht. Läden, die dank der zentralen Lage das Atrium des Hotels besiedeln, laden zum Shopping ein.

Situé non loin du célèbre opéra de Sydney dans le centre ville, l'hôtel a vue sur Martin Place. Les chambres des hôtes se trouvent en partie dans un ancien bâtiment datant de 1887 et classé monument historique qui hébergeait autrefois la poste, mais pour une autre partie aussi, dans une tour moderne de 31 étages. Les unes se distinguent par des plafonds élevés et un aménagement historique, les autres par des vitrages aussi hauts que la pièce et une belle vue. Les magasins qui occupent l'atrium de l'hôtel grâce à sa position centrale invitent au shopping.

No lejos de la famosa Ópera de Sydney, en el centro de la ciudad, se encuentra el hotel mirando hacia la Martin Place. Las habitaciones están ubicadas, en parte, en una antigua construcción de 1887, declarada patrimonio nacional, que antaño albergaba la oficina de correos. Otras se encuentran en una moderna torre de 31 pisos. Las primeras se caracterizan por los techos altos y una decoración histórica, las últimas, por sus altos ventanales y una buena vista. Gracias a su ubicación central, el atrio acoge numerosas tiendas que invitan al shopping.

Non lontano dal famoso teatro dell'opera di Sidney del centro città, si trova l'hotel che si affaccia sulla Martin Place. Le camere trovano posto in due edifici. In parte in un edificio d'epoca del 1887 sottoposto alla tutela dei beni culturali e un tempo sede della posta, e in parte in una torre moderna di trentun piani. Le prime si distinguono per i soffitti alti e l'arredo antico, le altre per le vetrate a tutt'altezza e il magnifico panorama. I negozi che, grazie alla posizione centrale, occupano l'atrio dell'hotel, invitano allo shopping.

The restaurant Mosaic, located in the first upper storey, overlooks the glass-covered courtyard.

Vom Restaurant Mosaic, das im ersten Obergeschoss liegt, lässt sich der glasüberdachte Hof überblicken.

Du restaurant Mosaic, situé au premier étage, vous pouvez embrasser du regard la cour recouverte d'un toit en verre.

Desde el restaurante Mosaic, ubicado en el primer piso, se puede mirar hacia el patio con techo de cristal.

Dal ristorante Mosaic, che si trova al primo piano, è possibile vedere il cortile dalla vetrata.

Though tradition is rare in Australia, it can nonetheless be experienced in every corner of the Heritage Wing of the Westin Sydney.

Tradition ist selten in Australien, im Heritage Wing des Westin Sydney ist sie jedoch an jeder Ecke zu spüren.

La tradition est rare en Australie, on peut cependant la ressentir dans chaque recoin de l'Heritage Wing du Westin Sydney.

Lo tradicional no es muy común en Australia, sin embargo, en el Heritage Wing del Westin Sydney se respira tradición por todas partes.

Nonostante la scarsità della tradizione australiana, nel museo del Westin Sydney è possibile sentirla ovunque.

Index

Wyoming

Jackson Hole

Amangani
1535 North East Butte Road, Jackson, Wyoming 83001, USA
T +1 307 734 7333, F +1 307 734 7332
www.amanresorts.com

29 Suites, six Deluxe Suites, four Amangani Suites and the Grand Teton Suite, all featuring fireplaces, The Grill dining room with fireplace, bar with adjacent terrace, lounge. Library. health center, gym, 115-feet heated outdoor swimming pool and whirlpool. 20 minutes from Jackson Hole Airport by complimentary transfer. Less than 100 km from Yellowstone National Park.

California

Laguna Niguel

The Ritz-Carlton, Laguna Niguel
1 Ritz-Carlton Drive, Dana Point, California 92629, USA
T +1 949 240 2000, F +1 949 240 0829
www.ritzcarlton.com

393 rooms, including 30 suites and 38 Ritz-Carlton Club Level rooms. Restaurant 162' with ocean view nestled 162 feet above the ocean, club grill and bar, pool bar. Spa, tennis, swimming, surfing, boogie boarding, sailing, kayaking, sport fishing, and whale watching. 19 meeting rooms, pool terraces, oceanfront lawns. Two miles of sandy beach. 40 km from John Wayne International Airport, 100 km from Los Angeles International Airport.

Beverly Hills

The Beverly Hills Hotel
9641 Sunset Boulevard, Beverly Hills, California 90210, USA
T +1 310 276 2251, F +1 310 887 2887
www.beverlyhillshotel.com

204 guest rooms and suites, including 21 one-of-a-kind bungalows. Restaurant and bar. Three ballrooms, business services. 20 minutes from Los Angeles International Airport.

San Francisco

Four Seasons San Francisco
757 Market Street, San Francisco, California 94103, USA
T +1 415 633 3000, F +1 415 633 3001
www.fourseasons.com

277 guest rooms, including 46 suites. Restaurant, lounge and bar. Pool, spa and fitness facilities, sauna/steam rooms. Located in the Yerba Buena cultural district, two blocks from Union Square, the Financial District, the Moscone Convention Center and the Museum of Modern Art.

Big Sur

Post Ranch Inn
Highway 1, P.O. Box 219, Big Sur, California 93920, USA
T +1 831 667 2200, F +1 831 667 2824
www.postranchinn.com

30 non-smoking rooms, restaurant Sierra Mar overlooking the Ocean. Spa, massages, aromatherapy, crystal and gemstone treatment, shamanic consultation session. 30 minutes south of Carmel and two hours south of San José International Airport.

Florida

Miami

The Setai
2001 Collins Avenue, Miami, Florida 33139, USA
T +1 305 520 6000, F +1 305 520 6600
www.setai.com

125 suites with one, two, and three bedrooms, 929 m² penthouse with rooftop pool. Restaurant, lounge bar and beach bar. Three beachfront pools. Spa with ocean view. Fitness center with personal trainers, yoga, tai chi. Water sports, golf, tennis. Located on the beach of South Beach.

Miami Beach

Casa Casuarina
1116 Ocean Drive, Miami Beach, Florida 33139, USA
T +1 305 672 6604, F +1 305 672 5930
www.casacasuarina.com

10 suites. Private invitation-only membership club. Four Lounges, Polo bar, Observatory roof deck, overlooking the Atlantic and Ocean Drive. Luxury private beach cabanas. Spa with massage, reflexology, acupressure, gemstone therapy. Located near the Ocean Drive. 20 km from Miami International Airport, 37 km from Ft. Lauderdale International Airport.

Miami Beach

The Ritz-Carlton, South Beach
1 Lincoln Road, Miami Beach, Florida 33139, USA
T +1 786 276 4000, F +1 786 476 4100
www.ritzcarlton.com

376 guest rooms and suites. Original art collection featuring established and emerging artists. 3 restaurants, including David Bouley's Evolution, beach club, Lapidus Lounge featuring lounge music created especially for the hotel. Conference facilities. Spa with 14 treatment rooms. Children's program The Ritz Kids. Located directly on Miami Beach, 20 minutes from Miami International Airport.

Illinois

Chicago

The Peninsula Chicago
108 East Superior, Chicago, Illinois 60611, USA
T +1 312 337 2888, F +1 312 751 2888
www.chicago.peninsula.com

339 guest rooms and suites, four restaurants, and bar. 1,300 m² Peninsula Spa on the top two floors with natural light, half-Olympic-length indoor swimming pool, outdoor sundeck with health-conscious spa cuisine. Fitness center, ballroom and meeting facilities. Located in the heart of Chicago's "Magnificent Mile".

New York

New York

Four Seasons Hotel New York
57 East 57th Street, New York, New York 10022, USA
T +1 212 758 5700, F +1 212 758 5711
www.fourseasons.com

368 rooms, some with furnished terraces, including 63 suites. Restaurant L'Atelier de Joel Robuchon, 57 Restaurant and TY Lounge. Spa with whirlpool, sauna, and steam room. In Manhattan's premier business and shopping district. 30 minutes from LaGuardia Airport.

New York

Mandarin Oriental New York
80 Columbus Circle at 60th Street, New York, New York 10023, USA
T +1 212 805 8800, F +1 212 805 8888
www.mandarinoriental.com

202 rooms and 46 suites on floors 35 to 54 with floor-to-ceiling views. Restaurant and lobby lounge on the 35th floor. 1,350 m² spa, gym, swimming pool, fitness center. Located on the top of the Time Warner Center at the Southwest tip of Central Park, a ten-minute walk from Fifth Avenue.

New York

Hotel (The Mercer)
147 Mercer Street, New York, New York 10012, USA
T +1 212 966 6060, F +1 212 965 3838
www.mercerhotel.com

75 loft-like rooms and suites on six floors. Restaurant on two floors, comprising a 40-seats street-level café adjacent to the hotel lobby. Private trainers, yoga, massage therapists. Located in Soho.

New York

The Lowell New York
28 East 63rd Street, New York, New York 10021, USA
T +1 212 838 1400, F +1 212 319 4230
www.lowellhotel.com

47 individually decorated suites and 23 deluxe rooms. Many suites with fireplaces and terraces. Two restaurants, fitness center with Health Snack Station. Located on a quiet street between Madison Avenue and Park Avenue, in the heart of the exclusive and fashionable Upper East Side.

Caribbean

Mustique

Cotton House
St. Vincent, Mustique, The Grenadines
T +1 784 456 4777, F +1 784 456 5887
www.cottonhouse.net

19 suites and rooms in cottages, some with private plunge pools. Cotton Hill Residence with private pool. Beach restaurant, gastronomic restaurant, beach bars. Pool and spa. 45 minutes from Barbados International Airport.

St Barthélemy

Le Sereno
St. Barthélemy, French West Indies
T +1 5905 9029 8300
www.lesereno.com

37 suites. Gourmet restaurant, bar and lounge. Beachfront freshwater swimming pool, spa, fitness center. Private airport transportation. Resort located in the heart of the French West Indies, 25 km southeast of St. Maarten.

Mexico

Germany

Berlin

Adlon Kempinski
Unter den Linden 77, 10117 Berlin, Germany
T +49 30 2261 0, F +49 30 2261 2222
www.hotel-adlon.de

328 luxurious rooms and 66 suites, from which 128 are non-smoking, 2 are handi-capped-friendly and 6 for allergy sufferers. Lobby Lounge & Bar, international Restaurant Quarré, Gourmet Restaurant Lorenz Adlon, french cuisine, private dining rooms, Pool bar, Adlon catering. Meeting and banquet facilities, ballroom. Spa, fitness. Located in the center of Berlin, 150 m to the Brandenburg gate. Airport: Berlin-Tegel 9 km, Berlin-Schönefeld 21 km, Berlin-Tempelhof 5 km.

Berlin

Ritz Carlton Berlin
Potsdamer Platz 3, 10785 Berlin, Germany
T +49 3033 7777, F +49 3033 777 5555
www.ritzcarlton.com/hotels/berlin

302 rooms including 39 suites, 37 Club Level rooms and suites, and one Ritz-Carlton Suite. Gourmet restaurant Vitrum, Restaurant Desbrosses, an authentic French Brasserie, Lobby Lounge featuring classical afternoon tea time, The Curtain Club hotel bar. Meeting and event facilities, professional conference services, ballroom, library. Spa. Located at Potsdamer Platz, in the center of Berlin, 11 km from international Airport Tegel, 4 km from Berlin Tempelhof Airport.

Bellin

Jagdschloss Bellin
Am Schloss 3, 18292 Bellin/Mecklenburg-Vorpommern, Germany
T +49 384 580, F +49 384 5820
www.jagdschloss-bellin.de

3 rooms single and double and 9 apartments for 2, 4 and 6 persons. Business facilities. Sauna. Bicycle rent. Located in a large park 10 km from Güstrow and 200 km north of Berlin.

Frankfurt

Villa Kennedy
Kennedyallee 70, 60596 Frankfurt, Germany
T +49 69 71 7120, F +49 69 71 712 2430
www.villakennedy.com

163 rooms, including 28 suites and 1 presidential suite. Restaurant, bar, lounge. Nine daylight meeting rooms, ballroom. Spa, fitness. Inner courtyard garden. Located close to the center of Frankfurt. Frankfurt International Airport is 20 minutes by car.

Munich

Mandarin Oriental, Munich
Neuturmstraße 1, 80331 Munich, Germany
T +49 8929 0980, F +49 8922 2539
www.mandarinoriental.com

73 rooms including 20 suites and junior suites. Restaurant Mark's (Michelin star), Mandarin Bar. Business work station, 3 meeting rooms for up to 120 guests. Outdoor swimming pool on the roof terrace. In the historic city center within walking distance of the most attractions and elegant shops.

Austria

Vienna

Hotel Imperial
Kärntner Ring 16, 1015 Vienna, Austria
T +43 1 501 100, F +43 1 5011 0410
www.luxurycollection.com/imperial

138 rooms, 32 suites. MariaTheresia Bar, Imperial Restaurant, Café Imperial. 7 meeting rooms for up to 480 people. Near by Museum of Fine Arts, Spanish Riding School and Hofburg Convention Center.

Vienna

Palais Coburg
Coburgbastei 4, 1010 Vienna, Austria
T +43 1 51818 0, F +43 1 51818 100
www.palais-coburg.com

35 suites. Gourmet Restaurant Coburg, Coburg Wine Bistro (Gardenpavilion and Wine Bar). Nine function rooms providing meeting and event facilities, concert hall. Palais Coburg also houses The Institute for Strategic Capital Market, with the Coburg safe deposit facility. Located in the center of Vienna.

Switzerland

St. Moritz

Badrutt's Palace Hotel St. Moritz
Via Serlas 27, 7500 St. Moritz, Switzerland
T +41 81 837 1000, F +41 81 837 2999
www.badruttspalace.com

165 rooms, including 30 suites. 7 restaurants, 3 bars and a night club. Spa, private ice-rink, ski-school. Personal butler service. Children's activities. Located in the center of St. Moritz at the shore of the lake.

St. Moritz

Suvretta House
Via Chasellas 1, 7500 St. Moritz, Switzerland
T +41 81 836 3636, F +41 81 836 3737
www.suvrettahouse.ch

184 rooms, 6 suites. 2 Restaurants, two bars, lobby. Conference and event facilities, ballroom, theatre. Spa, fitness, beauty, sports. Children's restaurant and activities. Embedded in the fantastic alpine landscape of the Upper Engadine.

Zurich

Park Hyatt Zurich
Beethoven-Straße 21, 8002 Zürich, Switzerland
T +41 43 883 1234, F +41 43 883 1235
www.zurich.park.hyatt.ch

142 rooms, including 12 suites. Restaurant and bar. Business center, meeting and event facilities for up to 300 people, ballroom. Wedding planning. Health Club. Located in the center of Zurich, 20 minutes from Zurich Unique International Airport, Kloten.

France

Paris

Le Dokhan's
117, Rue Lauriston, 75016 Paris, France
T +33 1 5365 6699, F +33 1 5365 6688

45 rooms including 4 suites, restaurant, bar. Located in the city center, 10 minutes to Eiffel Tower, 30 km to Charles-de-Gaulle Airport.

Paris

Murano Urban Resort
13, Boulevard du Temple, 75003 Paris, France
T +33 1 4271 2000, F +33 1 4271 2101
www.muranoresort.com

52 rooms and suites. Restaurant with an open terrace and lounge-bar. Spa with hammam, 3 heated pools, Jacuzzi and fitness centre. 2 suites with heated swimming pools. Located in the Marais quarter.

Paris

Plaza Athénée
25, Avenue Montaigne, 75008 Paris, France
T +33 1 5367 6665, F +33 1 5367 6666
www.plaza-athenee-paris.com

106 rooms, 81 suites. 3 restaurants, Gourmet restaurant Plaza Athénée run by Alain Ducasse. Fitness center. Located in the city center, 10 minutes from Arc de Triomphe and Eiffel Tower, 30 km from Charles-de Gaulle Airport.

Paris

Le Meurice
228 rue de Rivoli, 75001 Paris, France
T +33 1 4458 1010, F +33 1 4458 1015
www.lemeurice.com

160 rooms including 23 suites and 16 junior suites. Two restaurants, one bar. Meeting and event facilities for 20 up to 450 people, ceremonial Salon Pompa-dour. Business center services. Spa, fitness. Hotel limousine on request, disabled access. Located in the heart of Paris between Place de la Concorde and the Louvre on rue de Rivoli, in the fashionable 1st arrondissement.

Paris

Hotel de Crillon
10, Place de la Concorde, 75008 Paris, France
T +33 1 4471 1500, F +33 1 4471 1502
www.crillon.com

147 rooms, including 44 suites. Two restaurants, lounge serving afternoon tea, bar. Banquets, business meetings. Fitness, flower arranging school. Located in the center of Paris, in walking distance to the Champs-Elysées.

Italy

Como

Villa d'Este
Via Regina, 40, 22012 Como, Italy
T +39 031 348 1, F +39 031 348 844
www.villadeste.com

154 rooms and suites. 4 reception rooms up to 250/300 guests, 9 meeting rooms. Indoor pool and 2 outdoor pools. Wellness facilities, squash courts. The sporting club is directly connected to the Cardinal Villa. 18 holes Golf Club Villa d'Este 11 km from the Hotel. The hotel is surrounded by ten hectar private park, direct access to the Lake of Como. On the shore of the Lake of Como, 67 km to Malpensa International Airport.

Gargnano

Grand Hotel a Villa Feltrinelli
Via Rimembranza 38-40, 25084 Gargnano, Italy
T +39 0365 798 000, F +39 0365 798 001
www.villafeltrinelli.com

21 rooms and suites, "Boat House" with private landing stage, swimming pool, library, open fireside, private dining room. Situated on the western shore of the Lake Garda.

Rome

St. Regis Grand Hotel, Rome
Via Vittorio E. Orlando 3, 00185 Rome, Italy
T +39 064 7091, F +39 06 474 7307
www.starwoodhotels.com/stregis

138 rooms and 38 suites. Le Grand Bar, Di Vino Private Wine Cellar and Vivendo Restaurant serving mediterranean, regional an international contemporary cuisine. Meeting and business service, ballroom. Private diplomatic entrance with, foyer and elevator. Health Club. Wedding service. Butler service. Located in the heart of Rome close to Via Veneto.

Milan

Bulgari Hotel, Milan
Via Privata Fratelli Gabba 7/b, 20121 Milan, Italy
T +39 02 805 805 1, F +39 02 805 805 222
www.bulgarihotels.com

58 rooms and suites, the majority of them overlook the 4,000 m² private garden. Gold mosaic swimming pool. ESPA: massages, shiatsu, stone therapy, steam room, pre/post natal treatment, jet-lag eliminator massages.

Milan

Four Seasons Hotel Milano
Via Gesù 6/8, 20121 Milan, Italy
T +39 02 7708 8, F +39 02 7708 5000
www.fourseasons.com/milan

118 rooms including 41 suites. 2 restaurants, foyer lounge. Business center, conference facilities for up to 300 guests. Fitness center. Located in the city center, within walking distance to Piazza al Duomo and La Scala Opera, 60 minutes from Malpensa International Airport.

Venice

Bauer Venezia
San Marco 1459, 30124 Venice, Italy
T +39 041 520 7022, F +39 041 520 7557
www.bauervenezia.com

96 rooms, 21 suites. 2 restaurants, meeting facilities for small meetings. Il Palazzo at the Bauer: 35 palatial rooms, 40 suites. Gourmet restaurant "De Pisis" with terrace on the Grand Canal, "Settimo Cielo" terrace and lounge on the 7th floor with view over the city. Located in the historical center.

Sardinia

Hotel Cala di Volpe
Costa Smeralda, 07020 Porto Cervo, Italy
T +39 0789 976 111, F +39 0789 976 617
www.costasmeraldaresort.com

The hotel provides 125 rooms, two restaurants (one main inside restaurant only for the dinner, second one is a barbecue restaurant) two bars. Meeting and event facilities. Fitness, water-skiing school, golf. Private harbor. Located at the Mediterranean, north-east part of Sardinia.

Spain

Barcelona

Hotel Arts Barcelona
Marina 19-21, 08005 Barcelona, Spain
F +34 93 221 10 00, F +34 93 221 10 70
www.ritzcarlton.com/hotels/barcelona

482 luxurious rooms with panoramic views of both the city and sea, including 56 suites. Breakfast room Café Veranda, three restaurants for informal dining, Enoteca with an extensive selection of over 500 Spanish and international wines. Fourteen meeting rooms including a grand ballroom that can accommodate more than 1,000 people for a reception. Spa with views of the Mediterranean. Wedding services. Located in the beachfront near Barcelona's finest shops and restaurants.

Madrid

Hotel Ritz
Plaza de la Lealtad 5, 28014 Madrid, Spain
T +34 91 701 6767, F +34 91 701 67 76
www.ritzmadrid.com

137 rooms and 30 suites. Restaurant and garden terrace, two bars, private dining rooms. Fitness center. Located in the heart of Madrid, close to the Prado and the Thyssen Museum.

Madrid

Santo Mauro
C/Zurbano, 36, 28010 Madrid, Spain
T +34 913 196 900, F +34 913 085 477
www.hotelacsantomauro.com

51 rooms and suites. Restaurant and lobby bar. Indoor swimming pool, garden. Fitness center. Butler service. Located in the center of Madrid close to Paseo de la Castellana.

Majorca

Mardavall Hotel & Spa
Arabella Parc, Calle Estornell, 07011 Palma de Mallorca, Spain
T +34 971 606 421, F +34 971 606 429
www.mallorca-resort.com

133 rooms viewing on the sea including 89 suites. Two restaurants. Conference facilities for up to 192 participants, foyer suitable for receptions. Spa, two golf courses. Wedding service. Kids Club. Located between the Tramuntana mountains and the Mediterranean.

Seville

Hotel Alfonso XIII
San Fernando 2, 41004 Sevilla, Spain
T +34 95 491 7000, F +34 95 491 7099
www.starwoodhotels.com/luxury/alfonsoxii

147 rooms including 19 suites. Sevillian inner courtyard with fountain, San Fernando Bar, poolside snack-bar (open in summer). 7 splendid function rooms. Located in the historical city center, near the banks of the Guadalquivir river and only few minutes away from the Cathedral, Plaza de España, the Toro del Oro and Reales Alcazares.

Greece

Athens

Hotel Grande Bretagne
Constitution Square, 105-63 Athens, Greece
T +30 210 333 0000, F +30 210 322 8034
www.grandebretagne.gr

290 rooms, 31 suites. GB Roof Garden roof-top restaurant, GB Corner brasserie, Winter Garden café-style restaurant, Alexander's bar. Banquet and meeting facilities, ballroom. GB Spa. Located in the center of Athens.

Turkey

Istanbul

Ciragan Palace Kempinski
Ciragan Caddesi 32, Besiktas, 34349 Istanbul, Turkey
T +90 212 326 4646, F +90 212 259 6687
www.ciragan-palace.com

284 rooms and 31 suites. Three restaurants serving Turkish and international cuisine, Ciragan Barbecue during summer season, Sultan's Brunch, bar, wine bar. Banqueting and wedding service, business center. Health Club, fitness, Turkish bath, beauty. Located at the Bosphorus, 45 minutes from Istanbul Atatürk Airport.

Morocco

Marrakech

Amanjena
Route de Quarzazate, Km 12, 40000 Marrakech, Morocco
T +212 4 440 3353, F +212 4 440 3477
www.amanjena.com

32 pavilions with fireplace, private pool and garden. 6 Maisons. Al-Hamra Suite, 180 m² pavilion, 2 minzahs and its own 40 m² pool. Spa: Heated swimming pool. With 2 hamams, steam bath, massages, manicures, pedicures and facials. 8 km south of the center of Marrakech.

Skoura

Dar Ahlam
Douar Oulad Cheik Ali, Skoura (Province d'Quarzazate), Morocco
T + 212 24 852 239, F + 212 24 852 090
www.darahlam.com

12 rooms. Restaurant. Meeting facilities from five to 30 people. Beauty center, hamam, jacuzzi, heated pool. Direction: On the road to Ouarzazate towards Olerzouga (Dades valley). At the entry of Skoura, call the Dar Ahlam and they will send you a guide.

United Arab Emirates

Dubai

Madinat Jumeirah
P.O. Box 75157, Dubai, United Arab Emirates
T +971 4 366 8888, F +971 4 366 7788
www.jumeirah.com

Resort: Arabian village style, comprises 867 rooms and suites including 2 Grand Boutique Hotels and 28 Traditional Courtyard Summer Houses. 45 restaurants, cafés and bars. Amphitheatre, conference facilities. Six Senses Spa, healthclub. 25 minutes from Dubai International Airport.

Dubai

One&Only Royal Mirage
P.O. Box 37252, Dubai, United Arab Emirates
T +971 4 399 9999, F +971 4 399 9998
www.oneandonlyresorts.com

The resort comprises 3 properties: The Palace (226 rooms and 20 suites with balcony or terrace), Arabian Court (162 rooms and 10 suites with balcony or terrace), Residence & Spa (3 Royal Villas, 18 suites and 32 deluxe rooms). 7 restaurants, beach bar, grill, rooftop bar, lounge. Health club, spa, hamam. 20 minutes from Dubai International Airport.

Abu Dhabi

Emirates Palace Abu Dhabi
Abu Dhabi West Corniche, P.O. Box 39999, Abu Dhabi, United Arab Emirates
T +971 2 690 9000, F +971 2 690 9999
www.emiratespalace.com

302 rooms, 92 suites including 4 Presidential suites. 4 restaurants, 3 bars. Auditorium, ballroom for 2,800 guests, 48 meeting rooms, business center. Private beach, 2 pools, spa. 30 km from Abu Dhabi International Airport.

Mauritius

Turtle Bay

The Oberoi Mauritius
Turtle Bay, Pointe aux Piments, Mauritius
T +230 204 3600, F +230 204 3625
www.oberoihotels.com

72 villas in total including 2 Royal Villas with private pool, 23 luxury villas—16 of them with private pool—and 48 luxury pavilions. 2 restaurants, 3 bars. 2 swimming pools, spa, 2 tennis courts. Water sports. 55 minutes drive from Sir Sewoosagar Ramgoolam International Airport.

Seychelles

Mahé Island

Banyan Tree Seychelles
Anse Intendance, Mahé, Seychelles
T +248 383 500, F +248 383 600
www.banyantree.com/seychelles

36 pool villas with verandas, jacuzzi and swimming pools. Presidential Villa with infinity pool, outdoor Jacuzzi and large sundeck and living pavilion. 5 restaurants, pool bar. Banyan Tree Spa. Infinity pool, Island hopping excursions and water sport facilities. Located 30 minutes by car from Mahé International Airport.

North Island

North Island
North Island, Indian Ocean, Seychelles
T +248 293 100, F +248 293 150
www.north-island.com

11 villas with lounge, plunge pool. Each villa is equipped with an electro-buggy and 2 bicycles. Cuisine—each menu is created individually. Sunset beach bar. Spa with outdoor area. PADI dive center, gym. 4 beaches including a private honeymoon beach. 15 minutes from Mahé by helicopter.

Botswana

Okavango Delta

Vumbura Plains
Okavango Delta, Vumbura Plains, Botswana
T +27 11 807 1800
www.wilderness-safaris.com

2 camps linked by raised boardwalks, canvas tents under thatch with en suite facilities. Dining, lounge and bar area in each camp. Fan, indoor and outdoor showers. Located in the north of Mombo, access only by aircraft into Vumbura airstrip and then by vehicle to camp, 40 minutes flight from Maun.

South Africa

Cape Town

Mount Nelson Hotel
76 Orange Street, Cape Town, 8001, South Africa
T +27 21 483 1000, F +27 21 483 1782
www.mountnelson.co.za

144 bedrooms and 57 suites including a 2 bedroom penthouse suite. 2 restaurants, afternoon tea in the tea lounge, on the terrace or in the garden. Planet Champagne Bar. 2 floodlit tennis courts. 2 heated swimming pools, bodycare center. 34 km from Cape Town International Airport.

Hermanus

Birkenhead House
7th Avenue, Hermanus, Voelklip, 7200, South Africa
T +27 28 314 8000, F +27 28 314 1208
www.birkenheadhouse.com

11 suites—most of them with sea views. Dining room. 3 pools—one of them on dual levels. Spa, gym and treatment room. The whole hotel can be reserved for a maximum of 22 persons. Situated in Hermanus, 90 minutes drive from Cape Town.

Sabi Sabi Private
Game Reserve

Earth Lodge
Sabi Sabi Private Game Reserve, South Africa
T +27 13 735 5261, F +27 13 735 5260
www.sabisabi.com

13 suites with plunge pool, in- and outdoor shower, air condition and telephone. Dining veranda and boma. Swimming pool. Wellness center, spa, treatments. Conference facilities with TV. 500 km east of Johannesburg. Private airstrip.

Kruger
National Park

Singita Sweni Lodge
Kruger National Park, Sweni River, South Africa
T +27 21 683 3424, F +27 21 683 3502
www.singita.co.za

6 shaded suites with verandas, in- and outside shower. Dining room, wine cellar. Swimming pool, boma, gym and spa. 90 minutes flight from Johannesburg to Satara airstrip and from there a 40 minutes drive to the lodge.

Hoedspruit

Royal Malewane
P.O. Box 1542, Hoedspruit, 1380, South Africa
T +27 15 793 0150, F +27 15 793 2879
www.royalmalewane.com

6 Luxury suites with deck and private plunge pools, air conditioning and fireplace. Royal and Malewane Suites (210 m²) for 4 guests in 2 en-suite rooms with private lounge, dining facilities, pool, private butler, chef and private game drives. Dining area. Library, gym and bush spa. 50 km from Hoedspruit.

Johannesburg

Saxon
36 Saxon Road, Sandhurst, Johannesburg, 2196, South Africa
T +27 11 292 6000, F +27 11 292 6001
www.thesaxon.com

24 suites including 3 Presidential suites with separate lounge and dining. Restaurant, dining library, cocktail bar and Cigar Lounge. Outdoor heated pool, Spa including 2 glass gazebos for sun tanning, 8 treatment rooms, beauty treatments, gym, yoga.

Johannesburg

The Westcliff
67 Jan Smuts Avenue, Westcliff, Johannesburg, 2193, South Africa
T +27 11 646 2400, F +27 11 646 3500
www.westcliff.co.za

80 rooms and 35 suites, most have private balconies. 2 restaurants, afternoon tea in the Polo Lounge, terrace and bar. Function rooms and conference center for up to 150 people. Located in the select northern suburbs of Johannesburg.

Maledives

North Malé Atoll

One&Only Maledives at Reethi Rah
Reethi Rah, North Malé Atoll, Maledives
T +960 664 88 00, F +960 664 88 22
www.oneandonlyresorts.com

130 villas, each occupying its own secluded piece of sandy shore or private deck. Restaurants and in-villa dining. View over the ocean. ESPA: Steam rooms, stone saunas, hot pools with shoulder massages and Chi Pavilion for yoga and pilates. 35 km from Malé International Airport.

India

New Delhi

The Imperial
Hotel Imperial, 1 Janpath, New Delhi, India
T +91 11 2334 1234, F +91 11 2334 2555
www.theimperialindia.com

3 wings with 231 rooms and 43 suites. 5 restaurants. Outside swimming pool and 3 acres of lush green gardens. Located in the heart of New Delhi.

Mumbai

The Taj Mahal Palace & Tower
Apollo Bunder, Mumbai, 400 001, India
T +91 22 5665 0300, F +91 22 5665 0345
www.tajhotels.com

565 rooms including 46 suites. 12 restaurants including rooftop restaurant, grill, bars, nightclub, pool lounge and coffee bar. Meeting facilities. Jiva Spa and fitness. Situated on the waterfront. 30 km from the airport.

Jaipur

The Oberoi Rajvilas
Goner Road, Jaipur, Rajasthan 303 012, India
T +91 141 268 0101, F +91 141 268 0202
www.oberoihotels.com

54 rooms, 14 luxury tents, two one-bedroom pool villas, one two-bedroom Royal Villa. Conference facilities. Oberoi Spa by Banyan Tree offers personalized ayurvedic treatments, steam room, sauna, jacuzzi, heated outside pool and yoga. 40 minutes from Jaipur airport.

China

Hong Kong

The Peninsula Hong Kong
Salisbury Road, Kowloon, Hong Kong, China
T +852 2920 2888, F +852 2722 4170
www.peninsula.com

246 rooms, 54 suites. 7 restaurants including Felix restaurant, bar. Meeting facilities. New Peninsula Spa by ESPA, indoor swimming pool and fitness center. Helicopter transfers. Located at the heart of Kowloon, 40 minutes to the airport.

Hong Kong

The Landmark Mandarin Oriental Hong Kong
15 Queens Road Central, Hong Kong, China
T +852 2132 0188, F +852 2132 0199
www.mandarinoriental.com/landmark

113 rooms and suites, Amber, MO Bar and Spa Café. The Oriental Spa: 15 private deluxe treatment rooms, VIP spa suites. Rainforest showers, vitality pool, amethyst crystal steam room, rhassoul, laconium, hamam, sauna and Zen relaxation room. 40 minutes by car to Hong Kong International Airport.

Shanghai

Grand Hyatt Shanghai
Jin Mao Tower, 88 Century Boulevard, Pudong, Shanghai 200121, China
T +86 21 5049 1234, F +86 21 5049 1111
www.shanghai.grand.hyatt.com

555 rooms and suites. A range of restaurants and bars. Indoor pool, spa. 2 ballrooms, a Concert Hall/Auditorium, and 11 function rooms. 30 minutes to the Hongqiao Domestic Airport, 50 minutes to Pudong International Airport.

Beijing

The Peninsula Beijing
8 Goldfish Lane, Wangfujing, Beijing 100006, China
T +86 10 8516 2888, F +86 10 6510 6311
www.peninsula.com

468 rooms and 57 suites. 2 restaurants including Jing restaurant, bar, lobby lounge. Meeting facilities. Spa, swimming pool, beauty treatments. 30 km to Beijing International Airport.

Indonesia

Jakarta

The Dharmawangsa
Jalan Brawijaya Raya, No 26, Jakarta 12160, Indonesia
T +62 21 725 8181, F +62 21 725 8383
www.the-dharmawangsa.com

100 rooms and suites. 4 restaurants, 4 lounges, bar. Spa, outdoor and indoor pool, tennis. Meeting facilities. Set in residential area, 15 minutes to the business district, 45 minutes to Jakarta International Airport.

Bali

The Ritz-Carlton, Bali Resort & Spa
Jalun Karang Mas Sejahtera, Jimbar 80364, Bali, Indonesia
T +62 361 702 222, F +62 361 701 555
www.ritzcarlton.com/resorts/bali

375 guest rooms, suites and villas, 15 minutes from Ngurah Rai International Airport. Thalasso & Spa overlooking the Indian Ocean, with the world's largest Aquatonic seawater therapy, Marins and Guinot products.

Singapore

Singapore

Raffles Hotel Singapore
1 Beach Road, Singapore 189673, Singapore
T +65 6337 1886, F +65 6339 7650
www.singapore-raffles.raffles.com

103 suites. 18 restaurants and bars. 8 function areas. Business center. Raffles Amrita Spa and swimming pool. Located in the business and historic district, 20 minutes to Changi International Airport.

Singapore

The Fullerton Hotel Singapore
1 Fullerton Square, Singapore 049178, Singapore
T +65 6733 8388, F +65 6735 8388
www.fullertonhotel.com

400 rooms and suites. 4 restaurants, bar. Conference facilities. Outdoor swimming pool. Spa. Riverside location. 25 minutes to Singapore Changi Airport.

Thailand

Bangkok

The Oriental
48 Oriental Avenue, Bangkok 10500, Thailand
T +66 2 659 9000, F +66 2 659 0000
www.mandarinoriental.com

358 rooms, 35 suites. 7 restaurants, lounge, bar. Meeting facilities. Thai cooking school. 2 pools, spa. All rooms have a personal butler. Located on the banks of the Chao Phya River close to the city center.

Chiang Mai

Mandarin Oriental Dhara Dhevi
51/4 Chiang Mai, Sankampaeng Road Moo 1 T. Tasala A. Muang
Chiang Mai 50000, Thailand
T +66 53 888 888, F +66 53 888 928
www.mandarinoriental.com/chiangmai

144 suites, pavilions and villas. Open terraces, some of which feature private pool. 3,100 m² Dheva Spa, 25 treatment rooms and suites, spa menu, treatments that are inherent to the Lanna culture. 15 minutes to Chiang Mai International Airport.

Phuket

Aleenta Resort and Spa Phuket - Phangnga
Khao Pilai Beach, Phangnga, Thailand
T +66 2 519 2044, F +66 2 519 2045
www.aleenta.com/phuket

4 Beachfront Pool Suites with private plunge pools, 3 Pool Villas with luxurious living room and large private pools, 8 Ocean View Lofts with double height ceilings, private deck and direct access to 35 m long infinity pool, 10 Ocean View Residences with 2 bedrooms, living, dining and kitchen and private pools, and 5 Beachfront Villas with 3 bedrooms, living, dining, kitchen and infinity pool. Restaurant, bar and pool lounge. Private dining available. Spa with outdoor Spa. 20 minutes drive from Phuket International Airport.

Phuket

Amanpuri
Pansea Beach, Phuket 83000, Thailand
T +66 76 324 333, F +66 76 324 100
www.amanresorts.com

40 pavilions and 30 Thai villa homes with private outdoor terrace. Two restaurants serving Thai and European cuisine, bar. Meeting facilities. Spa, Beach Club, pool, gym, diving, tennis, cruises. Located on Phuket Island in the Andaman Sea, 25 minutes to Phuket Airport.

Phuket

Trisara
60/1 Moo 6, Srisoonthorn Road, Cherngtalay, Talang, Phuket 83110, Thailand
T +66 7631 0100, F +66 7631 0300
www.trisara.com

42 Pool Villas and Pool Suites with sea view featuring teak sundecks and private infinity pools. 12 Residential Villas managed by the resort. Restaurant, bar, private dining. Spa, gymnasium. Complimentary limousine transfer to and from Airport. 20 minutes by car south of Phuket International Airport.

Koh Samui

Sala Samui Resort and Spa
10/9 Moo 5, Baan Plai Lam, Bophut, Koh Samui Suratthani 84320, Thailand
T +66 77 245 888, F +66 77 245 889
www.salasamui.com

69 villas. Library, Internet & business center, boardroom. 53 private swimming pools, 2 beachfront swimming pools. Mandara Spa: 2 double spa suites and 2 double deluxe rooms. Traditional Thai massages, body scrubs, indoor or outside treatment. 10 minutes from Koh Samui Airport.

Cambodia

Phnom Penh

Raffles Hotel Le Royal
92 Rukhak Vithei Daun Penh, Sangkat Wat Phnom, Phnom Penh, Cambodia
T +855 23 981 888, F +855 23 981 168
www.phnompenh.raffles.com

170 rooms and suites. 5 restaurants and bars. Meeting facilities and 2 ballrooms. Spa. Located in the city center, walk distance to historic sites. 20 minutes to the airport.

Japan

Tokyo

Park Hyatt Tokyo
3-7-1-2 Nishi-Shinjuku, Shinjuku-ku, Tokyo, Japan 163-1055
T +81 3 5322 1234, F +81 3 5322 1288
www.tokyo.park.hyatt.com

154 rooms and 23 suites. 3 restaurants, 2 bars and a lounge. Library. Business center, conference facilities. Health and fitness sanctuary. Adjacent to the Tokyo Metropolitan Government buildings in West Shinjuku, 12 minutes from Shinjuku Station, the busiest rail and subway hub in all of Japan.

Australia

Sydney

The Westin Sydney
1 Martin Place, Sydney, New South Wales 2000, Australia
T +61 2 8223 1111, F +61 2 8223 1222
www.westin.com

The hotel combines Sydney's original General Post Office with a modern 31-story tower, providing 416 luxurious rooms and suites. Restaurant, bar, lobby lounge, health club. Conference facilities for up to 1,200 guests. Located in the heart of Sydney's central business district and on the doorstep of the best shopping, restaurants and attractions of the city.

Photo Credits

Editors	Martin Nicholas Kunz
	Patricia Massó
Editorial Coordination	Patricia Massó, Hanna Martin
Hotel Texts by	Patrice Farameh, Bärbel Holzberg,
	Heinfried Tacke, Riva Medien Frank
	Bantle (Frank Deppe, Jaennette Drauwe,
	Marei Drassdo, Erika Ranft, Tanja Schuler)
Imaging	Jan Hausberg
Translations by	C.E.T. Central European Translations
English	Michael Dobbins
German & Spanish	Stefanie Guim
French	Ricarda Hausen
Italian	Fjona Stühler

Editorial project by fusion publishing gmbh, stuttgart . los angeles
www.fusion-publishing.com

Published by teNeues Publishing Group

teNeues Verlag GmbH + Co. KG
Am Selder 37, 47906 Kempen, Germany
Tel.: 0049-(0)2152-916-0, Fax: 0049-(0)2152-916-111
Press department: arehn@teneues.de

teNeues Publishing Company
16 West 22nd Street, New York, NY 10010, USA
Tel.: 001-212-627-9090, Fax: 001-212-627-9511

teNeues Publishing UK Ltd.
P.O. Box 402, West Byfleet, KT14 7ZF, Great Britain
Tel.: 0044-1932-403509, Fax: 0044-1932-403514

teNeues France S.A.R.L.
93, rue Bannier, 45000 Orléans, France
Tel.: 0033-2-38541071, Fax: 0033-2-38625340

www.teneues.com

© 2007 teNeues Verlag GmbH + Co. KG, Kempen

Second Edition

ISBN: 978-3-8327-9143-8

Printed in Italy

Bibliographic information published by Die Deutsche Bibliothek. Die Deutsche Bibliothek lists this publication in the Deutsche Nationalbibliografie; detailed bibliographic data is available in the Internet at http://dnb.ddb.de.